PRAISE FO...

"This is an important book."
DR. JOHN R. KAUFMAN-MCKIVIGAN
Professor of History and Editor of the Frederick Douglass Papers
IUPUI (Indiana University Purdue University Indianapolis)

"James McCune Smith, the first Black doctor in America, was a remarkable man. Christopher L. Webber's 'Black Doctor' is a remarkable biography of Smith. Long overdue, it is a welcome addition to the literature of the African American freedom struggle. Thoroughly researched and engagingly written, this definitive biography of Smith offers important historical insights on African American leadership, the abolitionist movement and antebellum era politics in America."
PROFESSOR ROBERT C. SMITH, Ph.D. (retired)
San Francisco State University, Recipient of Howard University's
Distinguished Ph.D. Alumni Award

"Christopher L. Webber's Black Doctor: A Biography of James McCune Smith (1813 - 1865) is a vital work informing so many of us about the first fully trained and credentialed Black doctor in the United States. I was delighted to learn about Smith's incredible achievements in light of the structure of racism surrounding his context. I highly recommend Webber's thorough work and inspiring story into the challenge of being black in America."
THE REV. MICHAEL BATTLE, Ph.D.
Herbert Thompson Chair of Church and Society & Director
of the Desmond Tutu Center General Theological Seminary

"A thoroughly gripping life story of rising from ashes and becoming a true trailblazer. This is the important unsung history of Dr. James McCune Smith—READ IT."
E. LISA FORTE-MASON, ESQ.
Senior Warden, St. Philip's Episcopal Church

BLACK DOCTOR

BLACK DOCTOR

A BIOGRAPHY *of*

James McCune Smith, MD

the FIRST FULLY TRAINED *and* CREDENTIALED
BLACK DOCTOR *in* AMERICA

CHRISTOPHER L. WEBBER

MIMBRES PRESS
of Western New Mexico University

of Western New Mexico University

Mimbres Press of Western New Mexico University
www.mimbrespress.wnmu.edu

Copyright 2024 by Christopher L. Webber
All rights reserved. Printed in the United States of America. No part of this book may be used or reproduced in any manner whatsoever without written permission except in the case of brief quotations embodied in critical articles and reviews.

Media and Publisher Inquiries:
Mimbres Press of WNMU
1000 West College Ave.
Silver City, NE 88062

Cover and interior design GKS CREATIVE
Editing by Shelley Chung and Cindy Doty

The cover image is the only known portrait of Dr. James McCune Smith.

978-1-958870-24-2 (hardcover)
978-1-958870-23-5 (paperback)

FIRST EDITION

First printed in the United States

Library of Congress Case #1-14409248991

TABLE OF CONTENTS

Chapter One: Growing Up Black in New York: 1813–1832 1
Chapter Two: The Journey to Scotland: 1832 23
Chapter Three: Glasgow: 1832–1837 35
Chapter Four: Home Again: 1837–1838 53
Chapter Five: A Larger Stage: 1838–1840 71
Chapter Six: A Prophecy, an Appeal, and a Lesson from Haiti: 1841 93
Chapter Seven: *Amistad*, Maryland, and Albany: 1841 111
Chapter Eight: A Varied Life: 1842–1845 121
Chapter Nine: Timbucto: 1846 and Afterward 145
Chapter Ten: St. Philip's Church: 1847–1853 159
Chapter Eleven: The Colored Orphan Asylum: 1834–1860 177
Chapter Twelve: The Elective Franchise and Some Family Matters 197
Chapter Thirteen: Priorities, Family, and Purified Politics: 1845–1850 207
Chapter Fourteen: Dealing with Douglass and Other Matters: 1848–1852 215
Chapter Fifteen: Smith as a Writer: Communipaw, Ethiop, and Others 237
Chapter Sixteen: The Convention of 1853 and the Industrial School 251
Chapter Seventeen: A Rising Tide of Anger: 1854–1855 265
Chapter Eighteen: The Approaching Crisis: 1856–1860 289
Chapter Nineteen: The Last Chapter: 1861–1865 309
Appendix A: The Family of James McCune Smith 327
Bibliography 329
Notes 337
Acknowledgments 363
About the Author 365

CHAPTER ONE

Growing Up Black in New York 1813–1832

Born in Slavery in New York

Lavinia realized she was pregnant in mid-October 1812. She was only surprised that it hadn't happened sooner. Her owner had brought her and her three older sisters north as his slaves eight years earlier, but one by one the three older women had left, fleeing south to be with family. North or south made little difference in those days since slavery was still as legal in New York as it was in South Carolina. So Lavinia, at age eighteen, was left alone with her owner, Samuel Smith, who had come to New York to make money buying and selling cotton. Unfortunately, he wasn't very good at his trade. After eight years, he was living in a battered apartment in the worst part of the city and coming home drunk to beat Lavinia. She could put up with it for herself, but she had made up her mind not to raise a child in that environment.

He came home drunk the day she knew she was pregnant and went upstairs to get his whip. "Come up here," he yelled. She faced him from the bottom of the stairs. "If you dare touch me with that lash, I will tear you to pieces," she said. He stopped, stunned, but he could see she meant it. He was a good deal bigger than she and could whip her easily, but he wouldn't fight her. He slunk down the stairs and out the door, dropping the whip on the doorstep. She found out later that he had rented another apartment a few blocks away, but she never saw him again.[1]

James McCune Smith was born six months later on April 18, 1813. Technically, he was a slave and so was his mother, but his father knew better than to assert any claim to ownership. He may never have known that he had a son. But James knew who his father was and entered the name "Samuel Smith, merchant," when he arrived at the University of Glasgow and had to provide his father's name on an official form.[2]

So Smith's father was white and so was his mother's father and, of course, his father's father. Years later, when Horace Greely, a well-known New York publisher, wrote that Black Americans should go back to the land of their "forefathers," Smith corrected him. Referring to "the hundred thousand whites who will pass this night in the embrace of Black women," Smith asked, "Did you mean 'foremothers?'" Smith's mother and grandmothers were Black, but his forefathers were white and of European ancestry.[3]

James McCune Smith described his mother as "self-emancipated." Some slaves managed to buy their freedom. Lavinia simply asserted hers. But if she was to be free, Lavinia Smith had to find a way to make a living. Samuel Smith had not been a great breadwinner, but he had kept a roof over their heads and food on the table. Lavinia, at age eighteen, had never had to support herself; she did the laundry and the cooking, but she was a slave and she worked for her owner without being paid. What could she do now with a child on the way?

Lavinia talked to her friends about it. The Five Points neighborhood had a reputation as the worst in New York, but friends in such a neighborhood support each other, and Lavinia had friends who told her she could make some money by taking in other people's laundry. She also knew how to mend clothes, and she could do that for pay as well. New York City was growing fast and some people were getting rich. They could afford to pay someone else to do their laundry and mending. It wasn't easy work, especially in the months just before and after James was born, but Lavinia could do it and she could eke out a living for herself and for the baby.

It was never easy. Years later, James would write an essay about a washerwoman that would give readers a glimpse of his life in those days. He didn't identify his mother as the washerwoman, but it seems to be her life that he was exactly describing. He wrote like an eyewitness about a woman whose apartment was filled with wash tubs and drying clothes. He wrote about the sound of the iron being dunked: "*Dunk! Dunk!* Goes the iron, sadly, wearily, but steadily, as if the very heart of toil were throbbing its penultimate beats! *Dunk! Dunk!* And that small and delicately formed hand and wrist swell up with knotted muscles and bursting veins!"

Smith also described a "good-for-nothing looking, quarter grown bushy headed boy" in the apartment, "a shade or two lighter than his mother," who had to be called several times before he sprang into action to put more wood on the fire, light another candle, or bring a pail of water. It is not hard to imagine that the boy's name was James and that the scene witnessed by that boy was the scene remembered and described in an essay some forty years later.[4]

The Neighborhood

Hester Street, where James and Lavinia lived, was in the Five Points neighborhood of Manhattan, named for the way several streets came together and made five corners instead of the more usual four. There had once been a small pond there that was a source of water for the city. Tanneries and similar businesses that needed water had been built on its shore, but gradually the pond was filled in and houses were built there. As time went by, the houses built on the soft soil of the former pond shifted and sank and were abandoned by people able to afford something better. That left the sagging remnants to the poorest residents of the city: the free Black population and a growing Irish population. Contemporary observers commented on "the crowded and filthy state" of the area and "the intemperate, dissolute, and abandoned, habits of the inhabitants ... the proverbial filth of the streets, as well as the houses" or, in summary, the "appalling environment."[5]

Charles Dickens visited the Five Points on his American tour in 1842. He climbed up dark staircases, opened doors into dismal apartments, and he wrote that "all that is loathsome, drooping, and decayed is here."[6] Lydia Maria Child, who served as editor of the *National Anti-Slavery Standard* from 1840 to 1843, visited the Five Points at about the same time, not long after James and Lavinia had moved elsewhere, and compared it to an "open tomb." "How souls or bodies could live there I could not imagine.... There you will see nearly every form of human misery, every sign of human degradation ... oh, it made my heart ache for many a day.... What a place to ask oneself, 'Will the millennium ever come?'"[7]

None of that, of course, tells us anything about the residents themselves who would certainly have preferred to live elsewhere had it been possible. But it was not possible, and the inevitable frustration was expressed in a variety of ways. For James McCune Smith and his friends, one way was to form alliances with friends and clash with rival groups. Children growing up in the Five Points had to fight to survive. Parents often accompanied their children to school to protect them, but the children also learned to defend themselves and some of those who survived the challenge of such a childhood went on to make a difference in the world outside the Five Points.

The Five Points was a dreadful neighborhood, but years later what Smith remembered about it was the thrill of competing to survive. Smith was never a big man, but he had friends who were older and bigger and stronger, and he was happy to go into battle with them on his side. Philip Bell was five years older and would be a lifelong friend. He would grow up to be a newspaper publisher and editor. George Downing, who later built up one of the best-known restaurants in the city "fought his way through gangs of insulting white children, and leading other colored boys he sometimes drove the white fellows from the street."[8] Ira Aldridge, who would become a famous Shakespearean actor, was six years older than James and apparently a leader in those neighborhood clashes.

Smith recalled a knock-down, drag-out fight on a corner of Hester Street between Aldridge and a boy called Joe Prince in which one—probably Prince, but he doesn't say—was badly beaten. There also seem to have been clashes between neighborhood gangs, sometimes Black versus Irish, "sprinkling our young, hot blood along the streets of New York."[9] Smith recalled how he and Aldridge had been involved in "many a heady fight amid the memorable marshes of the classical Collect [Street]. Little did I think when his fine eye flashed and his trumpet voice cheered us on to the conflict of stones and clubs, that the same eye and voice would one day raise a shrill of admiration in an enlightened and polished audience."[10] To use a well-worn phrase, it was "a rough neighborhood" and one not likely to produce polished actors, successful restaurant owners, and skillful doctors. But environment can work to shape character in a variety of unexpected ways. Smith and his friends learned early on to enjoy the challenge of a fight and not to worry about the odds.

Early Education: The African School

Perhaps, then, it is not surprising that it was another boy from the neighborhood, an older companion and lifelong friend, Philip Bell, who took the most important step in drawing James McCune Smith away from the street battles of the Five Points neighborhood. It was Philip Bell, Smith tells us, who "guided my childish footsteps to Charley Andrew's School."[11] Charley Andrew's school was more formally known as the New York African Free School No. 2 and it was a special place, offering great opportunity to its students, but requiring them to conform to a rigid pattern. The African Free School was the first significant project of the New York Manumission Society, which was established two years earlier to promote the freeing of slaves and the protection of those who were free. The society brought together such leading New Yorkers as John Jay and Alexander Hamilton and leading merchants, especially some wealthy Quakers.[12]

Their efforts were centered first of all on defending the Black residents of the city from kidnappers intent on selling them to plantation owners in the South. Slavery was still legal in New York state and 20 percent of the city's households owned at least one slave. Two-thirds of the city's 3,500 Black residents in 1790 were slaves.[13] Free or slave made little difference, however, to the kidnappers. Smith estimated that between the time when the New York emancipation act was passed in 1799 and the time when it went into effect in 1827, some 20 percent of the Black population of New York was sold into slavery.[14] Recognizing this, the Manumission Society understood that while they could work to end slavery in the long term, they could make an immediate difference by intercepting kidnappers and bringing charges against them. A cynic might note that the society's campaign against kidnapping was, at least for some of the members, a campaign to preserve their own property.

Security against kidnapping was important, but so was gaining access to good jobs and that, in turn, depended on education. Most New York schools turned Black children away; the African Free School, founded by the Manumission Society in 1787, welcomed them and set out to demonstrate that Black children "were not inferior to those of fairer complexions ... in acquiring a knowledge of Letters."[15]

But the Manumission Society had even larger ambitions: the society hoped to create a model community by selecting and guiding not only the children but their families. The trustees of the society would visit families to determine their moral fitness and no student would be admitted to their school without the approval of two trustees and the headmaster. The approved families, in turn, would maintain "good characters" for "Sobriety and Honesty—and peaceable and orderly living." Should a student or family fail to meet expectations, the teachers would post the name of the individual and the details of their failure as a warning and example to others.

The Manumission Society had a vision of the orderly world they hoped to shape in which they would instruct parents and parents would instruct children. Parents would give commands "with prudence and moderation and enforce them with a becoming resolution," but never in anger. Children would avoid profane language and be kind to animals. Parents would also find "suitable employment" for their children at an appropriate age and not allow them to "waste their time in idleness, mingle in bad company . . . [or] contract those bad habits, which are calculated to render the subjects of them pests to society . . . or [subject to] close confinement at a maturer age in a state prison or house of correction." The society itself would find employment for students if parents were unable to do so, placing them with "persons of kindness and humanity." Parents would be consulted about such placements if they wished.[16] In a word, the society's vision was "paternalism."

The African Free School did, however, offer a possible way toward better economic opportunity for its graduates and there were not many alternatives. Even so, the number of students declined during the last decade of the eighteenth century until the trustees acted to hire a Black teacher, John Teasman, in 1797 and make him headmaster two years later. Shortly, attendance went up by 30 percent.

Teasman's vision of a peaceful and orderly community, however, was not exactly the same as that of the society. When parades were organized to celebrate the end of the slave trade or the first anniversary of the founding of the African Society for Mutual Relief, the Manumission Society and some Black leaders as well thought that such demonstrations were inappropriate and likely to provoke white anger. John Teasman thought otherwise and was involved in spite of requests from the Manumission Society that he cease and desist. In 1809, Teasman's continued failure to support the Manumission Society's opposition to "undignified" parades and celebrations led to his dismissal. The society then hired Charles C. Andrews, an Englishman, to take Teasman's place at double Teasman's salary.[17]

Charles C. Andrews was a good choice in many ways. He made it his mission in life to give his students an education equal to or better than what any white child could obtain. Many Black students and their parents were willing to tolerate the rigidities of the African Free School program for the sake of the benefits available. By 1820, the school had outgrown its original building, so a larger building with a capacity of 500 students was erected and designated the African Free School No. 2.[18] The building had one large room on each of its two floors, each one providing space for up to 250 children seated at desks in groups of twenty-five. The floor sloped up toward the back to give Charles Andrews or any teacher seated in the front a better view of the students. They were assisted by monitors, chosen from the students, who had slightly elevated positions at the end of a row.[19]

Andrews was an Englishman by birth. What brought him to America is unknown, but he had a variety of talents, and he found his calling at the African Free School. James McCune Smith said of his former teacher that he was "not deeply learned, but thorough" and "a good disciplinarian." More importantly, he cared deeply about his students and would pay attention to their individual gifts. Sometimes, he would pay for additional teachers himself to develop particular talents and interests. He liked to boast that his boys were equal or even superior to any other students in the city, and he would challenge them to compete at his annual examinations. When he saw that Black sailors, away from the prejudices of life on land, often found better opportunities, he added classes in navigation.[20] Andrews was not an abolitionist, but he believed that his pupils had as much capacity to acquire knowledge as any other children, and some thought "he even regarded his black boys as a little smarter than whites."[21]

Andrews constructed a program that kept everyone on the same track in a school day that ran from 9:00 a.m. to noon and from 2:00 p.m. to 5:00 p.m. five days a week and from 9:00 a.m. to noon on Saturday. Each morning and afternoon session had assigned subjects, usually for the whole school, though monitors worked on other subjects with smaller groups. Using the Lancastrian or Monitorial system, popular in the first third of the nineteenth century, the more advanced students taught less advanced ones so that a few adult masters were able to educate large numbers of students in basic and even advanced skills at relatively low cost. So in the African Free School on Monday afternoon, for example, "the Monitor General of Arithmetic" was directed to "arrange all the ciphering classes, and set them in operation, at their seats, under suitable monitors appointed for that purpose." Ciphering went on until 4:00 p.m. and then work on grammar continued until dismissal.

Whatever the disadvantages of such a system, it had the important advantage of giving the monitors experience in leadership. It was they, not the teachers, who had to maintain order. When Andrews was absent because of illness, the trustees placed Smith in charge of the whole school and pronounced themselves well satisfied with his management. They called him a "lad of promise."[22]

Among the records of the school that have survived are a poem and a dialog which are among the earliest known writings of James McCune Smith. The poem is entitled "Night:"

> Night is a time of sweet repose,
> When wearied men may rest;
> Forgetting all his cares and woes,
> He dreams that he is blest.
> The feather'd tribes to roost are gone;
> Beasts of the forests roam.
> And, until morning's early dawn,
> The night'ngale sings alone.
> Then, while his master soundly sleeps,
> Behold his watchful tray
> Guards well the house, and safely keeps
> The robbers far away.

Smith was fourteen years old when he wrote that poem and he shows a working knowledge of meter and rhyme, but there is nothing at all original about the ideas expressed. Smith would become an eloquent essayist, but never a poet, although he would continue to read poetry and to quote it.[23]

At age fourteen, in the first half of the nineteenth century, most students, Black or white, would consider their education completed. They could read and write, add and subtract, and therefore function perfectly well in most of the better jobs available. A few would go on to college at that age. The graduates of the African Free School were as well prepared to play an important part in the life of their city as any young white people, but what opportunities were available for them? One skeptic asked, "What possible good can a classical education yield them? Will we feel any better because the man who waits on our table can read Virgil and Horace?"[24] A new graduate asked essentially the same question from his own perspective in 1819:

> I am happy in having been one of the favored number who have enjoyed the blessed advantages of this institution.... [But] what signifies it? Why should I strive hard and acquire all the constituents of a man, if the prevailing genius of the land admit me not as such, or but in an inferior degree? Pardon me if I feel insignificant and weak. Pardon me if I feel discouragement to oppress me to the very earth.... What are my prospects? To what shall I turn my hand? Shall I be a mechanic? No one will employ me; white boys won't work with me. Shall I be a merchant? No one will have me in his office; white clerks won't associate with me. Drudgery and servitude then, are my prospective portion. Can you be surprised at my discouragement? Child as I am, of the same Almighty Being, and equally accountable both here and hereafter, as much so as any of the great human family.[25]

There was an emerging cohort of strong voices among African Americans—Peter Williams Jr., Samuel Cornish, Theodore Wright, and others who were clergy and editors—asserting the importance of providing the best education available and confident that over time the presence of educated Black citizens would make a difference in their world.

Graduates of the school like James McCune Smith, Ira Aldridge, Philip Bell, and others had only praise for the school and what it had done for them, but the fact that it was called "the African School" should be noticed. The Manumission Society undoubtedly deserves much credit for organizing schools for children not otherwise provided for, but the designation "African" was not calculated to reduce divisions in society. The children were not, after all, immigrants; probably fewer of them had non-native parents than did the white children of New York. Placing the label "African" on them and their school marked them off as different in a way that would not easily be overcome. A history of the school speaks with "commiseration" of "this injured and long degraded race." But children thought of in those terms were not likely to be welcomed as equals no matter how well they could read, write, and calculate. Indeed, the children were taught to think of themselves as a separate race, as "Africans," and the commencement address by one of the students in 1824 reflects that identification with another continent than their actual birthplace: "O Africa! The land of my fathers, ancestrial of the sable exiles of America! My heart bleeds for thy children, while the clanking of their chains and the voice of their groaning ascend to heaven like the voice of Abel."[26]

But if the children learned to think of themselves as "sable exiles," how could they also think of themselves as fully American? Thus, while Andrews trained his charges to aspire, there was a deep ambivalence as to the role the school might play in American life.

Andrews himself seems to have embodied that ambivalence. He was, for example, a member of the American Colonization Society, founded in 1816 by Robert Finley of New Jersey, and involving an unlikely coalition of northerners opposed to slavery and southerners dedicated to removing free Black people from the slave states. Northern members believed that free Blacks would be better off elsewhere and southern members believed their slaves would be more content without the witness of free Black people in their midst. It seemed logical to both groups to send as many free Black people as possible to Africa. The great majority of free Black Americans, however, believed that colonization had nothing to offer them. They saw themselves as native-born Americans who knew nothing of Africa and had no desire to be uprooted and carried there.

The first Negro National Convention, held in Philadelphia in two sessions, 1829 and 1830, was called to provide free Black Americans with an opportunity to come together and make their opposition to colonization plans clear. In January 1831, a convention of African Americans in New York also denounced the Colonization Society. "This is our home," they stated in an address to the citizens of New York, "and this is our country. Beneath its sod lie the bones of our fathers: for it some of them fought, bled, and died. Here we were born and here we will die."

It was this hostility to the Colonization Society that led the National Negro Convention in 1835 to adopt unanimously a resolution "to remove the title of African from their institutions."[27] That Charles Andrews was a member of the Colonization Society angered many of them. When he took two Black teachers into his school to prepare them to serve as teachers in Liberia and when he advised Charles Russwurm, a prominent writer, on his plans to go to Liberia as a school principal, that also angered many. They saw references to Africa in school programs and speeches as contrary to their vision for themselves and their children as Americans.

The last straw of Black patience was carried away when a story began to make the rounds. A visitor, it was reported, had knocked on the school door one day and Andrews had sent a student to see who was there. The student returned to report that "a colored gentleman" wished to see him. Andrews received the visitor cordially, but when the visitor had left, he angrily caned the student for using the phrase "a colored gentleman." Parents responded angrily and demanded that Andrews be replaced by a Black principal. Andrews still had his supporters who valued the thoroughness of his program, but they were outnumbered by those he had angered. The Manumission Society let Andrews go, but it was already becoming evident that the original goals of the Manumission Society were being replaced by those of the Colonization Society[28] and that neither organization understood the deepest concerns of those they thought to serve.

Smith and La Fayette

James McCune Smith had his first taste of fame on September 10, 1824, when he was eleven years old and still a slave. As one of the leading students in the African Free School No. 2, he had been called on to make a short speech of welcome to Gilbert du Motier, Marquis de La Fayette, one of the last surviving heroes of the American Revolution. La Fayette had shown a special interest in America's racial problems and had accepted a position as an honorary member of the board of the African Free School. Smith's speech, which may have been written for him by a trustee, was brief and very humble:

> General La Fayette: In behalf of myself and my fellow school mates, may I be permitted to express our sincere and respectful gratitude to you for the condescension you have manifested this day, in visiting this Institution, which is one of the noblest specimens of New-York philanthropy. Here, Sir, you behold hundreds of the poor children of Africa, sharing with those of a lighter hue, in the blessings of education; and while it will be our pleasure to remember the great deeds you have done for America, it will be our delight also to cherish the memory of General La Fayette as a friend to African Emancipation, and as a member of this Institution.

Bowing politely to the little boy, La Fayette said, "I thank you, my dear child."[29]

The incident attracted attention in Philadelphia and drew an invitation for Smith to repeat the performance on the deck of a steamer floating down the Delaware. His reward was a pocketful of small change; he wrapped twenty-five cents in a piece of cloth to send to his mother as his first earnings.[30]

Emancipation

Back in New York, Smith was living in a state where slavery was still legal and James McCune Smith was technically a slave. The state had, however, set in place in 1799 a gradual transition to freedom. Children born after July 4, 1799, were to be free, but they were required to serve their owner until age twenty-nine for males and age twenty-five for females. After July 4, 1827, all slaves, male or female, were to be set free. Even so, what the state gave with one hand, it took away or diminished with the other. Until New York State adopted a new constitution in 1821, all citizens were required to own $250 worth of property (roughly $6,000 in 2020) in order to vote. After that, the property requirement was removed for white citizens but left in place for those who were Black.[31] Slavery was ended, but equality was not given.

James McCune Smith was fourteen years old in 1827 when slavery in New York ended. He had never known what it meant to be a slave in the cotton fields of the South, and his technical status as a slave seems not to have limited him, but the change of legal status had enormous meaning nevertheless. He would never forget the celebration that marked the event. Black New Yorkers had, of course, been looking forward to the day for twenty-eight years—and disagreeing vehemently over the form the celebration should take.

Ever since the Revolution, there had been differences between the attitudes of Black Americans and white Americans as to what should be celebrated and when. For white Americans, it was natural to celebrate the Fourth of July as the date when Americans declared themselves to be free and independent. For Black Americans, the case was not so clear. The vast majority of them were not free and the ringing phrases of the Declaration of Independence—"that all men are created equal, that they are endowed by their Creator with certain unalienable rights, that among these are Life, Liberty, and the Pursuit of Happiness"—described what was at best a distant hope, not a present reality.

Reluctant to celebrate the Fourth of July under those circumstances, Black Americans seized on the abolition of the slave trade in 1808 as a more significant day to mark, and celebrations were held on January 1 of that year in Philadelphia and New York. White and Black friends of abolition alike feared inciting whites to riot by asserting Black rights, but as many or more were unwilling to let their natural desire to celebrate be displaced by fear of intolerant white rowdies. So parades and celebrations were held, and they were largely unopposed.

Annual celebrations of the end of the slave trade continued for a number of years but were gradually abandoned when the promise of fuller freedom was unrealized. The abolition of slavery in the West Indies, effective on August 1, 1834, provided a new and better occasion to celebrate, and Black Americans celebrated that date in several places for many years. But, meanwhile, for New Yorkers, the date of July 4, 1827, had taken precedence, and it was a date they had been anticipating since it was set by the legislature in 1799.

Given twenty-eight years to prepare for the celebration, there was ample time for differences of opinion to be developed—but not to be resolved. Black New Yorkers did generally agree that they should celebrate the occasion on July 5th so that it would have its own special meaning and not be subordinated to the national festival. Choosing the 5th would also eliminate possible conflict with drunken whites who might be celebrating the 4th too well. Beyond that, there was less agreement.

The small leadership group of educated and relatively affluent leaders feared more than anything else that Black celebrants might give white citizens opportunity to mock them. They thought the day should be celebrated quietly with church services and prayers of thanksgiving. Most middle-class Black leaders, like most middle-class white leaders, deplored the tumultuous orgies unleashed in particular by Andrew Jackson's election in 1828. The Quaker dislike of outward show also played an important part in shaping attitudes because the Quakers were, of all religious groups, the one most dedicated to assisting the Black population. But ordinary Black people, like ordinary white people, worked hard for a living and were happy to have an occasional excuse to do something for the fun of it: to hold a parade, to sing and dance and enjoy the moment. It might not be respectable, but it was fun, and they thought it was appropriate sometimes to have fun.

It was a difference of opinion that finally could not be resolved. When the day came, dignified church services were held, but so, too, were parades. Some three to four thousand Black celebrants marched in a procession with banners that ended at the African Methodist Episcopal Zion Church where speeches were made.[32] White rowdies did not disrupt the event. Smith's pastor, Peter Williams, had been one of those opposed to the parade, but despite his influence on his young protégé, Smith was on hand for the festivities. He saw it not from the viewpoint of his mentor, but from the perspective of a fourteen-year-old who had been a slave and was now free. Years later, Smith vividly recalled the celebration of that day:

> That was a celebration! A real, full-souled, full-voiced shouting for joy, and marching through the crowded streets, with feet jubilant to songs of freedom.
> First of all, Grand Marshal of the day was Samuel Hardenburgh, a splendid-looking black man, in cocked

hat and drawn sword, mounted on a milk-white steed; then his aids on horseback, dashing up and down the line; then the orator of the day, also mounted, with a handsome scroll, appearing like a baton in his right hand; then in due order, splendidly dressed in scarfs of silk with gold-edgings, and with colored bands of music, and their banners appropriately lettered and painted, followed, "The New York African Society for Mutual Relief," "The WILBERFORCE BENEVOLENT SOCIETY," and "THE CLARKSON BENEVOLENT SOCIETY"; then the people five or six abreast, from grown men to small boys. The side-walks were crowded with the wives, daughters, sisters, and mothers of the celebrants, representing every State in the Union, and not a few with gay bandanna handkerchiefs, betraying their West Indian birth: neither was Africa itself unrepresented, hundreds who had survived the middle passage and a youth in slavery joined in the joyful procession. . . . It was a proud day in the City of New York for our people, that 5th day of July, 1827 . . . it was a proud day, never to be forgotten by young lads, who . . . first felt themselves impelled along that grand procession of liberty, which through perils oft, and dangers oft, through the gloom of midnight, dark and seemingly hopeless, dark and seemingly rayless, but now, through God's blessing, opening up to the joyful light of day, is still "marching on."[33]

Understandably, the fourteen-year-old Smith took no notice—even in writing about it almost forty years later—of the dignified services that had been held in various churches on the previous day. If he had been in church that day, he would have heard his pastor, Peter Williams, point out that "the freedom to which we have attained is defective." In New York City, he said, "the rights of men are decided by the colour of their skin." Black citizens were not allowed in the cabins of steamers on the Hudson River, nor were they allowed to board the horse-drawn carriages that made their way up and down Broadway and other avenues. When a Black man attempted to board one of the new omnibuses, the driver warded him off with a whip to the amusement of bystanders. Even barbershops were segregated and Black barbers refused to serve Black customers lest they lose their white patrons.[34] So slavery as an institution no longer existed in New York State, but restrictions remained on every side.

When the celebration was over, Theodore Wright, pastor of the Shiloh Presbyterian Church, spoke to the New York State Anti-Slavery Society and summarized the situation:

> The colored man, at every progressive step, literally runs the gauntlet. He is scarred from head to foot in all the walks of life. The evils of prejudice are widespread and wicked . . . and rob the people of color of their political rights. He who addresses you might be arrested to-night, and . . . if arrested as a slave, would not be allowed a trial by jury . . .
>
> Why is all this? Sir, it is to be traced to the spirit of slavery existing in the breasts of men, even in those who think they have sympathy for the oppressed. This is the great support of the system of slavery. Oh! there is enough in this feeling to cause tears of blood to flow from the eyes of those who possess it. It is this that deprives him of his manhood, brings him down from that elevated position which God designed he should enjoy to a place with chatels and things. Oh! If we had time to delineate the effects of this

spirit, we should keep you here till midnight, stating facts, and telling tales of woe, the thoughts of which makes our spirits to sink within us.[35]

Between School and College

The celebration was over, but the real world was very little changed. Smith had still one more year at the African Free School before graduating at the top of his class in May of 1828 and going out at the age of thirteen into a world that was not at all prepared to give him the opportunity either to use his obvious abilities or to develop them further.[36] Smith did, however, continue to study with Peter Williams in the evening and on Sundays.[37]

Smith wanted to study medicine and become a doctor, but there was no pathway to that goal that a Black candidate could follow. Many white doctors in those days gained recognition as doctors by serving as apprentices with an established physician, but no white doctor would take a Black apprentice. A growing number of medical schools provided better training, but that also was a pathway closed to Black candidates. Smith applied to the Schools of Medicine at Columbia College in the city and Geneva College in upstate New York but was rejected. Both schools had been founded by Episcopalians and still had close denominational ties. James McCune Smith was an Episcopalian, but Smith was also Black and that, in those days, counted for more than his faith.[38] Wealthy men and community leaders worked on his behalf but to no avail.[39]

With most doors closed to him, Smith became a blacksmith's assistant, apprenticed to Thomas & Son, stove and grate makers, at No. 61 Nassau Street; his sometime colleague, Philip Bell, said that Smith pumped the bellows with one hand while holding a Latin grammar in the other. But he was fired in 1831, although he was said to be the best workman in the establishment. So Smith, for all his scholastic accomplishments, found himself unemployed at the age of eighteen and, like most other graduates of the African Free School, unable to find a career ladder to climb. Smith did, however, have the support of his pastor, and that opened a unique opportunity.[40]

Support from His Church
As Philip Bell guided Smith's steps to the African Free School, it seems likely that he also guided his steps to St. Philip's Church, on Centre Street, a block and a half from the Five Points, and that guidance stood him in good stead when he found opportunities closed to him. Bell was an Episcopalian, and Black Episcopalians had come together in the early years of the century to form a congregation meeting first at Trinity Church Wall Street, and then in a building of their own in the Five Points neighborhood. The pastor of the congregation was Peter Williams Jr., whose father had purchased his freedom and become a leader in the New York Methodist community. Peter Williams Jr., however, seems to have been much influenced as a teenager by a white Methodist pastor who had become an Episcopalian. Following his mentor into the Episcopal Church, Williams found the Black congregation meeting at Trinity and before long was a lay leader and eventually an ordained priest, the first Black priest in the Diocese of New York and only the second in the Episcopal Church.

An early graduate of the African Free School, Peter Williams Jr. had, according to James McCune Smith, "mastered Logic and Algebra, read Latin with some facility, was extravagantly fond of Metaphysics, and, what is remarkable with the slender advantages he enjoyed, he had formed a style in composition so clear, concise, and elegant, that few men of twice his years and with every advantage have excelled it."[41] Williams continued his studies under the private guidance of Episcopal clergy as he prepared for ordination. His natural ability was evident when he delivered an oration on the abolition of the slave trade in 1808 that was so polished and eloquent that some white listeners claimed it must have been written for him by a white man. It was later published with certificates of authenticity signed by, among others, the Episcopal bishop.[42]

As a leading alumnus, Williams took a continuing interest in the African School and showed a special interest in the young James McCune Smith, meeting frequently with him after his graduation to guide him in his reading. Many years later, Smith still remembered how Saturday night was not only "wash night" when "the grime and honest sweat of anvil and bellows gave place to a glorious ablution," but also "Latin or Greek-Grammar night with one whole day in prospect for hard study, (except intervals at church service,) when Caesar, or Virgil . . . steadied with their rugged and knotty hardships, the wild dreams of my boy ambition."[43]

As Smith continued his studies, Williams would have been increasingly aware of the young man's potential, and when it was clear that he could not get the education he wanted and needed in New York, it was Williams who took the lead in raising the funds needed to send him abroad.[44] It took four years, but by the summer of 1832, the necessary funds were in place to send the young man to Scotland.[45] There, in five more years, he would get a better education than any available in New York.

CHAPTER TWO

The Journey to Scotland 1832

The Voyage Begins

As the *Caledonia* left the New York Harbor on August 16, 1832, James McCune Smith was thrilled with the adventure. Everything was new and exciting. For someone who had not previously been farther afield than Philadelphia, it was a journey to another world. Smith's first journal entry reflects his conflicting emotions as he watched the lighthouses on Sandy Hook sink in the distance.[46] "Whoever bound on a long voyage for the first time beholds those tall prim, white-washed light-houses gradually lessen in the distance, will never forget... the blank that fell upon his heart when the last little specks were obliterated by the remorseless weaves."[47]

From the first page of his journal, Smith seems to have had future readers in mind. The prose is ornate and filled with literary allusions, especially to Lord Byron, who had died dramatically less than ten years earlier fighting for Greek freedom. The fact that Smith misquotes Byron in his first journal entry would suggest that he had not brought along his copy of Byron's poems but had memorized many of them. "It is impossible," Smith wrote (though he would make the attempt!) "to describe the new class of emotions that rush upon the mind, when sea and sky become the sole and sublime objects that meet one's ardent gaze. The best attempts of the ablest writers fail when they essay [*sic*] to describe 'the magnificent mirror where / The Almighty glasses himself in storm.'"[48]

The lines are from Byron who had actually written of the "glorious mirror, where the Almighty's form / Glasses itself in tempests." Just a few lines earlier in the same poem, Byron had written lines that would also have appealed to the young advocate of Black freedom: "Yet, Freedom! yet thy banner, torn, but flying, / Streams like the thunderstorm *against* the wind!"[49] Smith, like Byron, was off to a new land in pursuit of freedom.

The *Caledonia*, Smith's ship, was a sailing ship in regular service between England and America. Earlier in the year, an ad for the *Caledonia* in an English newspaper offered emigrants room in the "lofty and spacious" steerage for £5 (about $4) and half price for children fourteen and under. The ship was advertised as "coppered and copper-fastened" with a "burthen of 450 tons."[50] In its day, it was a typical, average-size sailing ship. For comparison, the *Mayflower*, two centuries earlier, was a ship less than half the size with 102 passengers and a crew of twenty-five to thirty. The *Caledonia* had ninety-one "souls on board," presumably including crew and passengers. Steerage, even in the early twentieth century, "offered only the most basic amenities, typically with limited toilet use, no privacy, and poor food,"[51] but Smith made no reference in his journal to living conditions on board. He wrote in his journal of his "state room," so apparently, he was more comfortably provided for than would have been the case in steerage. He had, after all, been earning his living for four years and presumably had saved something. More important, he had the support of some substantial Black citizens.

Two days at sea and a hundred miles from land, one of the sailors showed symptoms of what was first thought to be Asiatic cholera, an epidemic that had spread across Asia and Europe in those years leaving numerous deaths in its wake. Only that same summer, an epidemic had swept across Europe and caused a catastrophe in New York. There were forty-five deaths in the city on July 10 and thirty-eight on July 30.[52] The worst of the epidemic was over by the time the *Caledonia* sailed, but the memory of its impact would have been all too vivid. The terrified passengers huddled at the opposite end of the ship while the sailors chafed the man's limbs and administered huge doses of pepper and brandy. Smith's interest in medicine was forgotten as he fled to his cabin and resorted to prayer. Whether it was that or the brandy and pepper that was effective is unknowable, but the seaman recovered quickly and was back on duty in a matter of hours.[53]

The next day was Sunday and Smith's thoughts turned naturally to the Creator with thanksgiving especially for the safety of the voyage. Again, Smith painted a word picture of the "fine breeze" that "curled the tops of the dark blue waves with beautiful foam-crests." The ocean became the floor of a great church to Smith's imagination and the cloudless sky the dome, while the "glorious sun" became "the ministering high-priest of Nature's temple and of Nature's Sabbath." When the time came for his own church service, Smith read the Office of Morning Prayer from his Episcopal Book of Common Prayer as he had learned to do from Peter Williams, but the novel setting gave him a new appreciation of the liturgy and his dependence on his Creator.

> Literally feeling each succeeding moment of existence dependent on His mercy, and buoyed upon that element which represents to moral man the noblest idea of his attributes, who would not feel a new zest, a loftier devotion in the sublimity and pattern in which the rubrics of the church abound?[54]

The next published entry from Smith's journal was undated but spoke of a week having passed while "we wended our lonely way cross the deep" until the "stirring cry of 'a sail! a sail!' brought every one on deck." The ship in question was a merchant ship heavily laden with sugar from the West Indies. Smith called it the *Druid*, which is odd because there was a succession of ships by that name in the Royal Navy, but not in merchant service. However that may be, Smith proceeded to deride the "clumsy . . .

snail-paced" *Druid* and to extol the beauty of the American ship. Once again, he found the perfect phrase in Byron: "She walks the waters like a thing of life,"—though this time the line is from *The Corsair*.[55] Smith took the opportunity to praise American ships as the "epitome of the great and rising country, whose star-spangled banner proudly floats o'er her deck" and represents the effort of workers "from many nations." The patriotic language was balanced, however, by the wish that the beautiful American ship could represent the spirit of liberty in foreign ports instead of "the malignant prejudice which is a canker and curse to the soil, whence she sprung."[56]

On the tenth and eleventh days of the voyage, Smith made two brief journal entries. On August 25, sailing across the Grand Banks of Newfoundland, he noted the pea-green color of the water and the thick fog that kept several members of the crew and the captain peering anxiously ahead to avoid "falling into the chill embraces of an iceberg; a storm that night swept away the main topgallant mast." To his regret, Smith managed to sleep through the storm and miss the excitement. A week later, the Irish coast came into view as "a dim, blue, hazy line" in the distance. As the ship moved slowly along the Irish coast, the Irish steerage passengers thronged the side, straining to see a familiar landmark. "Happy they!" Smith noted. "Their exile is at an end. Mine has scarcely begun."

The day's end, however, brought out Smith's poetic side again as he noted that the sun "gradually shorn of his brighter beams . . . assumed at first a golden, and then a crimson hue" until it "seemed like a half extinguished ball of fire poised on the plane of ocean . . . Flinging o'er the clouds such gorgeous tints of purple and gold, as made them a fit canopy for the God of day, and they reflecting upon the water a tinge, which made it appear like a sea of blood." When "Night came on with its bright array of stars," Smith relaxed by sitting on the bulwarks and indulging himself in some homesick reminiscing, "talking of home, sweet home, the dear friends and the dear parent whom I had left behind." Those thoughts were interrupted by the sound of dancing from the bow where several of the sailors were scraping out "something between a screech and a grunt" from a battered fiddle and capering "in steps and time that were evidently 'variations' from the original tune."

Wind and tide now ran in their favor and the *Caledonia* moved swiftly northward in the Irish Sea, around Holyhead, the northwest point of Wales, and then eastward again into the port of Liverpool. Arriving at 10:00 p.m., they saw the city's lights sparkling in the darkness in a way that the weary traveler found "exceedingly splendid."

But when Smith came on deck the next morning, the view was very different. The rising sun revealed Liverpool in all its industrial squalor: "A multitude of mill shafts, black and smoky, whirling round and round, seem the scorched remains of the previous night's superb exhibition. The long wall enclosing the docks, the dingy color of the tall brick houses, and the narrowness of the streets beyond, remind you of the enclosure and varied windings of an immense prison house."[57]

Smith had grown up in a bustling port city of similar size, so this reaction to a first glimpse of Liverpool is surprising at first. But Liverpool was also, far more than New York, a manufacturing city. Cotton, imported especially from the southern states, flowed into the harbor of Liverpool to be bought and traded and fed into factories powered by the coal mines of Wales and northern England. It was the smoke of those factories that darkened Smith's morning view of the city. Less obvious was the fact that the cotton on which Liverpool depended was grown and harvested by slaves in the American South. Also less obvious at first glance was the dependence of those mills on a labor system almost as dehumanizing as slavery. In 1833, a year after Smith's arrival in England, the first limitations on child labor were instituted: children under the age of thirteen could no longer work more than nine hours a day and those under eighteen could work only twelve hours a day. At least the slaves in the cotton fields had to stop work after sundown! The short winter days in England provided no rest for the workers in factories lit with recently developed gas and oil lamps.

Smith was not unaware of all that, but it counted for less to him than the fact that such labor was at least nominally "free."

> 'I am free' was the thought which flashed through my mind, as I trod the strong wharf with a foot which coveted every inch of the space. . . . I could embrace the soil on which I now live, since it yields not only to all who dwell, but to all who come to it, a greater amount of rational liberty than is secured to man in any other portion of the globe.

Apologists for slavery had often made unfavorable comparisons between the conditions of the slave and those of the northern factory worker. For Smith, there was no comparison:

> True it is, that the poor toil—and toil harder and longer perhaps than many of the slaves in the western world; but they toil not under the lash. And if they labor long and arduously, it is for themselves and theirs ... He knows that when evening comes and his toil is at an end, he may return to his humble but happy abode, and find it not robbed of the wife of his bosom, or of the children of his love."[58]

In reality, of course, the "wife of his bosom" might be walking home with her husband from their common employment and the children might not have been back from the mill very long themselves. Yet some of those same workers, thirty years later, dependent though they were on cotton from the South for their livelihood, assembled in Manchester to send a letter to Lincoln expressing their support for the war to end slavery. However different or similar their circumstances might have been, their sympathies were with the slaves. Many factory owners felt differently, of course, and Liverpool was said to have been the center of English support for the Confederacy. The Confederate navy was largely built in Liverpool for lack of southern shipyards, and the last active Confederate force, the CSS *Shenandoah*, did not finally surrender in Liverpool until seven months after Lee surrendered at Appomattox.

All that, of course, was still to come. Immediately on Smith's mind was making contact with English friends and acquaintances. That a nineteen-year-old Black American had contacts in England may be surprising, but Smith seems to have gone straight from the ship to the home of "my old Friend, Mrs. W____" who, on what must have been very short notice, not only provided him with "an excellent dinner," but brought at least one other old friend, identified only as "N____" to share the occasion.

September 9, 1832, was a Sunday, so after dinner, traditionally served in the middle of the day, Smith and "N" "sallied forth to church." Evensong, a service of hymns, prayers, Bible readings, and (on Sunday) a sermon, remains today a popular form of worship in the Church of England, and Smith, as a member of the Episcopal Church, would have been very familiar with the service. What was unfamiliar to Smith—and a pleasant experience—was the welcome they were given. He describes how, when they entered the church:

> [O]ur swarthy skins did not exclude those civilities which are due to man from man, in the temple of his Maker.–Several pew-doors were flung open, and books courteously offered to us. There were no cold looks, no supercilious or sanctimonious frowns; none appeared to have reached that pitch of devotion in which creatures frown upon the works of their Creator—upon their fellow creatures, not for the hue of the soul, but of the skin.
>
> What a contrast when compared with the reception that would have been given us in an American church!

> Alas for my country! Alas for its religion and the promulgators of it! On these last I cannot but look with feelings of disgust and horror—disgust at their clinging to public opinion—horror at the awful fate that must inevitably be theirs when there shall rise up against them, the thousands of lost souls that have been driven from the threshold of the sanctuary, because of the prejudices of the church.[59]

Smith was almost equally surprised and pleased by the size of the congregation and the "tone of deep devotion" that united the congregation in its participation in "our matchless liturgy."

Eager to experience and absorb as much as possible, Smith was up early the next day and, again, seeking out contacts provided by his American supporters. His first stop was the office of "C—, B—, & Co." where Mr. Crawford was not in.[60] Smith was able, however, to present introductory letters to Mr. Crawford's son and be given an invitation to breakfast the next morning. Lacking any further agenda, he spent the rest of the day rambling and feeling homesick, "dreaming of dear home, and wishing for the companionship of that dear friend who has hitherto trod with me the uphill path of learning.[61] Cruel is the fate that has separated us at the very moment when we began to appreciate the beauties of ancient lore!"[62]

The next day, Smith "chartered a coach" and had himself driven out of the city to the "princely mansion" of John Crawford, Esq., on the banks of the River Mersey where he was introduced to and welcomed by a number of members of the London Anti-Slavery Society. Smith would only have learned after arriving in Liverpool that the House of Commons had passed a final reading of a bill abolishing slavery in most of the British Empire on July 26, and that its great advocate, William Wilberforce, had died just three days later.

Smith was particularly impressed with the fact that all those in the gathering were completely familiar with the names of leading American abolitionists and wanted detailed information from him about the conditions under which the slaves lived and his opinion of the progress of the abolition movement. He was even more impressed by the fact that several pieces of breakfast China were enhanced with a picture of a kneeling slave and the inscription of a verse from the Bible: "Remember them that are in bonds, as being bound with them." What a commitment it must imply, Smith thought.[63] But Smith was hard-pressed to help the English abolitionists understand the minds of those who were prejudiced against Black people. Smith wrote in his journal that they seemed at a loss to understand the slave owner's point of view and, indeed, seemed as skeptical of its existence as was "the African king of the existence of solid water."[64]

That evening, Smith was back in the city to attend a lecture at the amphitheater.[65] Some three thousand people filled the auditorium for a lecture by a representative of West Indian planters, George Borthwick, whose goal was to persuade his audience of the merits of a gradual emancipation process and reimbursement of the planters for the "property" that would be taken from them if slavery were abolished. Smith was impressed by Borthwick's resonant voice and debating skills, trained at the University of Glasgow and refined by study at Oxford, but Smith thought the orator was "more subtle than comprehensive" and reveled in "darling mares of sophistry rather than gaze on the sunlight of truth." Smith enjoyed the way an English audience would "notify him of his error" with hisses and groans when he "presumed too far on their acumen, or credulity."

Borthwick's greatest "error" of the evening, Smith believed, was to suggest that slave owners were entitled to compensation because it would be "as unfair to deprive the planter of his slaves as to take from an English gentleman his coach and horses." That brought down on the speaker "one simultaneous groan of indignation, the most awful sound to which I have ever listened; and a hundred stentorian lungs cried out 'Do you compare a man to a horse?'"

The next morning, Smith was introduced to Margaret Gill, the wife of Ira Aldridge, one of his schoolmates from the African Free School and a colleague in the street battles of the Five Points. In the short time that Smith had been pumping a blacksmith's bellows, Aldridge, six years older than Smith,[66] had already made a name for himself in the theater world. Gaining experience at the African Grove Theater in New York, a pioneering African American project established in 1821, Aldridge traveled to England in 1824 as valet to a white actor and a year later made his debut at London's Royal Coburg Theatre.

Aldridge was performing in London when Smith arrived in Liverpool, so that afternoon his wife entertained Smith by taking him for a walk through a unique cemetery constructed in the valley left behind when the stone was quarried for Liverpool's docks. Flowers and trees now grew from the floor of the valley while tombs had been carved out of the living rock at the sides. In the center of the valley, where a small spring gushed from the living rock, Smith took special notice of the grave of William Huskisson, former member of Parliament for Liverpool and an early casualty of the industrial revolution. Having gone three years earlier to see George Stephenson's pioneering steam locomotive, the Rocket, Huskisson was unfortunately run over by the machine and became the first widely noticed railroad casualty. Pondering Huskisson's "melancholy fate" did nothing to lighten Smith's mood.

The next day, Smith wandered through the city on his own and found it again a generally depressing place. He admired the gigantic draft horses hauling their loads through the streets and thought them capable of hauling loads four times as great as could be pulled by the cart horses in New York, but the residences seemed "horridly dull and gloomy" and the great Merchants Exchange was "a somber building." The great monument to Nelson at the center of the square did nothing to lift Smith's spirits. It depicted Victory placing her wreath on the brow of the fallen Nelson while "from beneath the drapery of conquered flags, the grisly arm of death is

The Journey to Scotland 1832

stretched and the skeleton fingers clutch the victim's heart. Death amid Victory! Genius perishing in the funeral pyre itself had kindled."[67] Smith found none of the city's scenes inspiring. It was interesting, perhaps, to be a tourist for his first few days in a new world, but he needed to get to Glasgow and be able to focus his energy on his purpose in coming.

On Smith's next to last day in Liverpool, he dined at noon with John Crawford again. Crawford's daughter was there and a small group of men active in the abolition movement. That evening there was a pleasant change from business-centered gatherings and tours of the dark city and depressing cemetery. Smith found himself "whirling down the mazy dance" among the guests of a "Mr. W——." The next night, Smith packed his bags and at 2:00 p.m. the following day, he was on board the steamer *Aliza Craig*. On the day after that, September 16, 1832, he arrived in Glasgow.[68]

When *The Colored American* announced that it would print excerpts from Smith's journal "written during his five years residence in Europe," it noted that during that time, he had visited London and Paris. The implication is that the journal covered that entire period, but *The Colored American* printed only the entries that were made from his departure from New York until he boarded a ship in Liverpool for the last leg of his journey to Glasgow. Unfortunately, nothing more remains of the journal, and our knowledge of the Glasgow years comes only from university records, newspaper accounts, and the reports of the Glasgow Emancipation Society.

CHAPTER THREE

Glasgow
1832–1837

Glasgow, like Liverpool, owes its existence to its harbor. Like Liverpool and unlike London, Glasgow had the advantage of easy access to the Atlantic Ocean and the Western world. Inevitably, both cities traded in cotton, but Liverpool specialized in cotton while Glasgow became wealthy by importing American tobacco. Scottish merchants had also begun to explore trade opportunities in the East and to export Glasgow manufactured goods to India. Business leaders generally were unsympathetic to abolitionists, but Glasgow had less stake in the American South than cotton-centered Liverpool and, therefore, a greater sympathy with the abolition movement.

The University of Glasgow
As Glasgow grew wealthy, its ancient university thrived as well.[69] The University of Glasgow was founded in 1451, before Europeans had discovered America, and prides itself today on being the fourth oldest university in the English-speaking world. Famous names have been associated with the university. Joseph Lister was a professor of surgery there and made the important discovery that wounds healed more quickly when sterilized. James Watt, the inventor of the modern steam engine, made the industrial revolution possible with its steam transport and steam-powered factories. The

economist Adam Smith was a student and then a professor there at about the same time and wrote his groundbreaking economic study, *The Wealth of Nations*, in Glasgow.

The university in Smith's day was changing fast, growing in size and diversity as changing times required better-educated leaders in business and government. Professorships of surgery and midwifery, chemistry, botany, and materia medica (substances used for healing) were established in the twenty years before Smith's arrival, and the student body grew to over a thousand.[70] The facilities for surgery were increased in 1824 and a new building for the Chemistry Department was constructed in 1830.[71] To study medicine involved a knowledge of anatomy and a knowledge of anatomy required dissection and the practice of dissection required bodies. Cadavers for dissection were scarce, however, and medical schools were not always careful about where the bodies came from. Some medical faculty and students did what they felt was necessary to pursue their studies. Criminals were routinely condemned not only to be hanged but also to be dissected because only the bodies of condemned criminals could be legally dissected, and the need for cadavers was growing. Some of the suppliers of cadavers, known as "resurrectionists," went beyond exhuming corpses and occasionally produced fresh corpses by murdering people who happened to fall into their clutches.[72] In 1814, a raid on the students' quarters found a number of bodies partially dissected and concealed in a "mash-tub."[73]

In 1832, the year that James McCune Smith arrived in Glasgow, new legislation was enacted providing that unclaimed bodies in prisons and asylums could be acquired by authorized medical students. The legislation provided that anyone intending to study anatomy had to obtain a license from the home secretary. Usually, one or two teachers in each institution took out this license, and hence were known as licensed teachers. With these new provisions, there would be corpses enough for the students, and those corpses would be legally acquired and properly supervised. Since Smith arrived in Glasgow just as the new rules were going into effect, he would have been able to study anatomy without worrying about the sources of the cadavers he would dissect.

But he would not be dissecting cadavers immediately. Smith had gotten the best education available for young Black people in New York City, and he had supplemented that education with a program of study with Peter Williams at St. Philip's Church, but he did not have the college degree required for admission to the medical school. His first challenge in Glasgow would be to acquire a bachelor's degree.

Undergraduate Life

The undergraduate program of study at the University of Glasgow when Smith arrived was divided between "Juniors" and "Seniors" with no expectation that students would spend a specific number of years at either level. They would read and they would attend lectures and, when they were ready, they would be examined and granted a degree if they satisfied the examiners. Modern universities typically list hundreds of courses that students may elect and a few that are required. Glasgow University in 1833 offered courses in nine subjects: humanity, Greek, logic, moral philosophy, natural philosophy, mathematics, astronomy, natural history, and civil history. All students would take most of them.

Fundamental to a good education at the University of Glasgow was a working knowledge of Latin, which was listed in the Table of Subjects as "Humanity." Lectures were no longer given in Latin, but a working knowledge of ancient languages was still indispensable. The minimum requirement was familiarity with Livy, Virgil, and Horace, but honors students were expected to be familiar also with Cicero, Tacitus, and Juvenal. In the same way in Greek, a minimum requirement was knowledge of the New Testament and Homer. Honors students were expected to be familiar also with Thucydides and Herodotus or Aristophanes, while earning the highest honors required knowledge as well of Sophocles, Euripides, Aeschylus, and Aristotle. Similar standards were set in the various branches of philosophy and mathematics while the standard for highest honors in logic seems to sum up what was required in all departments: "Perfect accuracy in all branches of Examination, with proof of eminent talents and acquirements." At a minimum, students were expected to show an adequate knowledge of logic, moral and natural philosophy, and mathematics, as well as "an adequate knowledge of the principles of the Greek and Latin tongues, and of Latin composition."[74]

First-year students began their day at 7:30 a.m. by being examined on their ability in Latin. The professor would give them a text for the day from Horace, Virgil, or Ovid and then a text from Sallust or Cicero and proceed to question them "with the most minute accuracy" about everything from the structure of the sentences to the historical and geographical references. Students were then given a subject for essays in English and Latin, prose and poetry, which they were to hand in on Saturday. These would be marked by the professor and commented on in class.

Other classes met on the hour from 10:00 a.m. until 3:00 p.m. Most classes met daily from Monday through Saturday. No student, however, would be sitting in classrooms hearing lectures eight hours a day, six days a week. They would select the courses they needed and leave themselves time for reading and, undoubtedly, for conversations in the nearby pubs and other locations. There was also no single tuition charge, but rather a fee for each series of lectures, typically £3.3.[75] Students would go to the home of the professor to sign up for the course and pay the required fee. There were scholarships, known as "bursaries," available for students who needed them.[76]

James McCune Smith's teachers at the African Free School and his pastor, Peter Williams, could take credit for the fact that Smith, in his first year, won a prize in Latin[77] and, in his second year, a prize in logic.[78]

The Glasgow Emancipation Society

Smith arrived in Scotland at a radical transition point for Scottish abolitionists. Until weeks before his arrival, Scottish and English abolitionists alike had focused their attention on the Parliament where laws were made for the British Empire. Slavery in England had been declared impossible in 1772 when Lord Mansfield ruled: "The state of slavery is of such a nature that it is incapable of being introduced on any reasons, moral or political, but only by positive law. . . . It is so odious, that nothing can be suffered to support it, but positive law." Since slavery had never been established by law in England or Scotland, slavery could not exist in those places. But the empire was different because there slavery existed by law and needed to be abolished by law. For fifty years, English abolitionists had worked to persuade Parliament to outlaw slavery in the British Empire.

William Wilberforce had become known to the world as the leader in the abolition movement, working tirelessly to bring about an end to the traffic in human lives. When that goal was accomplished in the summer of 1833, the need for abolition societies seemed to many to be at an end, and the great anti-slavery societies voted themselves out of existence.

Slavery, however, did still exist in the United States, and those who had fought for abolition in the empire were well aware of it and felt some responsibility for it. Slavery had existed in the American colonies, after all, for almost two centuries and for most of that time the colonies were under British rule. Forty-some years of American independence could not absolve the British of their responsibility. Some thought it likely that Americans would not respond well to being criticized by their former English rulers, and the British were sensitive to that, but it was also argued that they could not simply walk away from the evil they had left behind. Gradually, new societies were created and in 1840, a World Anti-Slavery Convention was called to meet in London and focus attention on slavery where it still existed and debate what might be done to bring it to an end.

Though Smith's journal is lost, it can be assumed that the same pattern evident in Liverpool would have appeared in Glasgow with Smith's arrival.

Leading abolitionists would have been waiting for him, would have welcomed him, and would have assembled with others to hear from him. Smith would have told them what was going on in America from the viewpoint of an emancipated slave. He could tell them firsthand of the continuing need to fight against slavery. So the need was clear. They had firsthand testimony. In December, the new Glasgow Emancipation Society was created.[79]

Young as he was and new to Scotland as he was, Smith nevertheless played a prominent role in the society from the beginning. The society organized itself with a president, three vice presidents, a treasurer, three secretaries, and a Committee of Management. Members of the committee were to include all "ministers of the gospel and pastors of churches" and all who contributed five shillings or more. The list of contributors showed James McCune Smith as one of twenty-four who contributed fifteen shillings or more and would, therefore, have been members of the committee. The first resolution adopted at the first meeting made its purpose clear: "Convinced that Slavery is inconsistent with the spirit and precepts of Christianity, and subversive of the best interests of mankind,—Resolved that a Society be now formed to promote its universal extinction."[80]

Life in Scotland

But however important the abolition of slavery was to James McCune Smith, he had not come to Scotland to give his time to that. Lacking Smith's journal, we have only an occasional hint of how James McCune Smith did spend his time in Scotland. Many hours, of course, must have been spent in reading and study, but there were also long vacation periods. There is evidence that he sometimes traveled away from Glasgow. When the time came to book a cabin for the return voyage, Smith told the captain of the ship he hoped to board that, "I have repeatedly traveled in the best cabins of the first steamers in Britain." That would seem to indicate journeys to Liverpool and other coastal cities, possibly to London, probably to speak to abolition societies.

The New York City Riots of 1834

What Smith had missed by his journey to Scotland and years abroad was a breakdown in New York society that showed itself in two riots, the second of which developed into an extended period of lawlessness that left houses and churches in ruins. One study of New York riots between 1712 and 1873, published in 1873, blames it all on the abolitionists and tells us that "a peaceable solution of the question was rendered impossible, by the action of the Abolitionists ... who governed by the short logic, that slavery being wrong, it could not exist a moment without sin, and therefore must be abandoned at once without regard to consequences.... The Abolitionists were considered by all as enemies to the Union whom the lower classes felt should be put down, if necessary, by violence."[81]

So simplistic a view overlooks a number of factors, not least the dreadful conditions under which immigrants and the poorest working people lived in those days and their justified feeling that they had a grievance against someone which they were ready to express violently if given any excuse. Wealthy New Yorkers, benefiting from their investments in southern cotton and shipping lines, were happy to turn that anger away from themselves by letting the Irish immigrants rage against their Black neighbors instead. The abolition movement provided the opportunity.

It was the newborn American Anti-Slavery Society that unintentionally provided the spark that set off the worst rioting New York had ever seen. In July 1834, the society was still getting organized and looking only to recruit members and make itself better known. As July 4, 1834, approached, church leaders like Peter Williams sought to head off the possibility of trouble by working with Lewis Tappan and leaders of the Anti-Slavery Society to provide an alternative to the annual parade. As they planned it, a dignified service would be held in the Chatham Street Chapel with Black and white choirs and participants.

There were other New Yorkers, however, who saw it as an opportunity to further a different agenda. One newspaper, the *Courier and Enquirer*, announced the meeting this way: "At eleven, the *Fanatics* meet at Chatham-street Chapel, to have their zeal inflamed by the doctrines of abolition and amalgamation."[82] Responding to the implied invitation, a hooting, stamping, white mob invaded the galleries and rained down epithets and prayer books on those below. A squad of "watchmen" from the mayor's office arrived in time to prevent more serious trouble.

The event was rescheduled for Monday, July 7, but further trouble developed when it turned out that a music society thought they had permission to use the meeting space. With both groups claiming a right to the building, a fight broke out and there were serious injuries. When the police arrived, they broke up the fight and locked the building, but a part of the crowd recognized Lewis Tappan and followed him home with hoots and yells and threw rocks at his house.

The next evening, a crowd assembled again. When they found the chapel empty, they decided to express their rage at the English for their criticisms of American hypocrisy on the subject of slavery by surging into the nearby Bowery Theater, whose stage manager was English. Forcing their way into the theater, the mob brought the play to a halt until, again, the police arrived and took control of the situation.

Undeterred by this, the crowd then turned toward the house of Arthur Tappan, who like his brother was a leading abolitionist. Arriving at his house, the mob broke into the abandoned building, smashing windows and doors and throwing furniture out into the street where they soon had a bonfire going. This drew firemen to the scene and more police, and the crowd dispersed long after midnight. Each successive night, however, the anger and size of the mob seemed to increase. The next night, they attacked the church of a leading abolitionist preacher and, when the police intervened, they turned to the preacher's house, which he and his family had abandoned, and did what they could to trash the building before, again, the police arrived and drove them off.

The Episcopal bishop, Benjamin Onderdonk, saw what was happening and begged the authorities to take steps to protect St. Philip's Church, citing his knowledge of "the respectable and uniformly decent and orderly character" of the congregation of that church.[83] Nonetheless, momentum continued to build and the following night, an attack was made on Arthur Tappan's store, then on another church with an abolitionist pastor, and at last on St. Philip's Church, which they effectively destroyed along with the home of Peter Williams, the rector, and a number of adjoining houses.

Finally, the authorities organized willing citizens into volunteer companies under the police, mobilized the volunteer military companies of the city, and brought out most of the fire departments. Although the rioters created barricades in the street, the military units advanced with axes and bayonets in a show of force that persuaded the rioters they could do no more damage.[84] Eventually, after more than a week of violence, a semblance of order was restored.[85] *The New York Times* wrote that the events were "disgraceful" and had originated "in the hatred of whites for the blacks."[86]

What led to such violence? One underlying issue certainly was the insecurity of the Irish immigrants who seem to have provided most of the manpower involved. Newly arrived in a strange country and unable to find decent jobs and housing, they were easily led to focus their fears and insecurity on a racial group with whom they had no experience. The abolitionist goal of freeing the slaves also frightened them with the prospect of millions of new workers competing for their jobs. William Lloyd Garrison was portrayed as a "traitor" whose "maniacal ravings" would lead to the dissolution of the Union. The role of wealthy New Yorkers, heavily invested in the cotton industry, in stirring up the mob has already been mentioned. The role of Irish newspapers and even their church in providing a rationale should also be noticed. "Why," wrote the editor of a church newspaper, "should the sable race of Africa, to whom the inscrutable wisdom of providence has denied the power of intellect, the amenity of the moral affections, and the grace and whiteness of form, presume to enter the lists of human perfection with . . . superior grades of society . . . which they can never attain?"[87]

The New York Times blamed it all on the abolitionists:

> In this city the public excitement against the abolitionists has now arrived at an almost incredible pitch. They have but themselves to blame for the consequences of their rash violations of law and decorum, their wrathful denunciations of their fellow-citizens.... The community have taught them a lesson which it is to be hoped they will profit by in after days upon other occasions.[88]

The Bishop and the Pastor

The Episcopal bishop also apparently saw abolitionists behind the trouble. With his church destroyed and his home badly damaged, Peter Williams received a letter from his bishop assuring him of "the sincere sympathy I feel for you and for your people" and calling on him to resign at once from the Anti-Slavery Society and to announce publicly that he had done so. Williams did resign at once from the board of the society but not the society itself, citing his ordination vow of obedience to the bishop and noting that while he wished the members of the society "all success ... in their endeavors, by all means sanctioned by law, humanity, and religion, to obtain freedom for my brethren, and to elevate them to the enjoyment of equal rights with other citizens of the community ... it was exclusively our duty to labor to qualify our people for the enjoyment of those rights." Williams went on to cite specifically his support for James McCune Smith, "a superior scholar for his opportunities," as an example of his efforts to work toward the enjoyment of equal rights.

Unfortunately, the bishop published an edited version of Williams's letter and Williams thought it best not to carry on a public argument with his bishop. He did, however, in a letter to Gerrit Smith later that summer, point out that "the letter was not published as I wrote it. My strongest anti-slavery sentiments were omitted." He told Smith that he still believed the principles of the Anti-Slavery Society were, "those of the Gospel of Christ, and of the declaration of American independence, and [I] can never renounce them."[89]

Becoming a Doctor

Distracted or not by reports of events in New York, Smith completed the work he had gone to Scotland to do. The program leading to the MD degree was still only one year long, but a three-year residence in Glasgow was required and chemistry was part of the curriculum for the MA.[90] For the MD, Smith would take courses in surgery, midwifery, anatomy, botany, and materia medica, the various substances—animal, vegetable, and mineral—thought to have healing properties. Actual experience had also become a requirement for the medical degree and Smith seems to have spent time that year at the Royal Infirmary, a hospital chartered in 1791 and holding 208 beds when Smith was there. We know that he also spent time at the Lock Hospital, established in 1805 for women working as prostitutes and requiring treatment for venereal disease. His experience there led to an article published in *The New York Journal of Medicine* in 1844.

In the spring of 1837, less than five years after arriving in Scotland and only one year after becoming a candidate for the degree, James McCune Smith presented himself to the medical faculty of the university and convinced his examiners that he was well qualified to go forth to practice medicine. Degrees were awarded in April and James McCune Smith, after one year of specialized study, was awarded the degree for which he had come: Doctor of Medicine.[91]

Going Home

On the fourth of May 1837, James McCune Smith, MD, went down to the Glasgow harbor to make arrangements for his return journey to America. Finding an American ship preparing to sail for New York, he sought out the captain and found himself once again facing the realities of American life even before leaving Scottish soil. *The Glasgow New Liberator* provided a full account of the exchange:

Gentleman [Smith].	What is the price of the passage to New York in your vessel, Sir?
Captain.	How do you wish to go?
Gentleman.	In the cabin.
Captain.	I have very good accommodation in my.............
Gentleman.	But I wish to go in the best.
Captain.	I cannot take you in my best cabin.
Gentleman.	Why not, Sir?
Captain.	[Staring the young gentleman in the face for some minutes.] Are you not a COLORED MAN?
Gentleman.	Certainly I am, Sir.
Captain.	Then I cannot take you in my cabin—I have not been accustomed to live with *colored people*.

Here, a third person, who was in the captain's company, chipped in to say: "If he took you in his cabin, it would prevent other passengers from going."

Smith then asked whether there were any American passengers, and being told "that there were none," replied, "No British subject would refuse to go in the same cabin with me because of my complexion. Since I have repeatedly traveled in the best cabins of the first steamers in Britain without meeting with any such objection."

That led the captain to say, "Although all my passengers were perfectly willing, yet I would not suffer you to go in my cabin, for I have not been accustomed to live with *colored people.*" The captain added that as such was the custom in the United States, and as this was an American vessel, he would follow the same rule here.

Captain Bigby did not change his stand nor did Smith change his with the result that James McCune Smith did not return to America in the brig *Canonicus*.[92] The exchange between Smith and the captain, however, was splashed on the pages of the Glasgow newspapers and many others, including eventually such American papers as *The Liberator* and *The Colored American*.

John Murray of the Glasgow Emancipation Society wrote a long open letter to the captain of the *Canonicus*:

> This, sir, is a public offense . . . because you publicly advertised your vessel for passengers, without stipulation as to color or any other exception. . . . You admit men of all religious denomination—Baptist, Presbyterian, Methodist, Episcopalian, Roman Catholic, Jew, Turk, Mohammedan or infidel, and you would give a passage to or associate with any of these or with any white man, although he may be flying from his creditors, whom he may have defrauded, or from the gallows to which the laws of his country have sentenced him. But to a *"colored man"* who has sustained an unblemished character, who has pursued his studies with credit and distinction, surrounded daily with white students.

Murray went on for five more paragraphs and ended his denunciation of the captain with the prayer "that you and your countrymen, who are verily guilty concerning your brother in this matter may be made free from this sin."[93]

A second, shorter statement came from the Glasgow Emancipation Society and said,

> [W]e happen to know the excellent young man who has been thus treated—thus insulted because of the color of his skin—his Almighty Maker's work! We believe no one in the Glasgow College was more esteemed for his amiable qualities and literary acquirements, and by none more than the Professors of our University who showed their esteem by marked attention to him.

In mid-June, the same newspapers published a third statement in an open letter from the Emancipation Society to James McCune Smith dated June 15: "When you are about to leave our shores," the letter said, "we cannot deny ourselves the gratification of tendering you a formal testimony of our esteem." It continued:

> When you first appeared among us, the circumstance was in a high degree calculated to excite our sympathy on your behalf, that a young man should be found seeking, in the institutions of Scotland, those intellectual accomplishments which he was denied an opportunity of acquiring in those of his native land, on account of his complexion not suiting the prevailing taste of a prevailing party of his countrymen. Our first feelings toward you, dear Sir, we acknowledge, were chiefly feelings of compassion. But after a brief acquaintance, you became the object of senti-

ments much more honorable to yourself. We felt ourselves called upon to esteem you for your virtues, and to admire you for your intellectual powers and attainments.... We did not, indeed, require to be convinced for the first time, that the man of color is possessed of all moral and intellectual capabilities, in equal measure with the white; but you made the doctrine less a matter of abstraction to us, and impressed us with the sight and the consciousness of the present living reality.

The society wrote of the contribution Smith had made to their work with the "scholar's taste ... an orator's eloquence ... [and] a gentleman's courtesy and bearing" that Smith had brought to their work together. The letter assured him of their prayers that God would prosper him in his work as a physician and in his efforts to deliver his brethren and theirs "from ignominy, sorrow, and oppression." They ended the letter by telling him that he had been enrolled as an honorary member of the Committee of the Glasgow Emancipation Society.[94]

Interlude

One missing piece in the story of Smith's medical education is the tradition that he went to Paris to gain experience as an intern in a French hospital.[95] *The Medical Register of the City of New York* tells us that Smith "availed himself of the medical and surgical advantages to be obtained in Paris—his sojourn extending over a period of a few months" and that this happened "before ... his final departure for New York"—but that was written more than thirty years later and after Smith's death. It is just possible that he could have done that after receiving his degree in April and before setting sail for New York in late July. It might also have been possible for him to have spent time in Paris during the long summer vacation, from April to October, of the previous year, but he would have gone at that point without any formal medical training and it seems unlikely for that reason.

On the other hand, there is an unexplained gap between the farewell party in Glasgow and Smith's arrival in New York. At his formal welcome home celebration in New York, Smith said "I have now been three weeks in the land of prejudice." That gives at least an approximate date for Smith's arrival in New York. The reception was on September 23, so Smith must have arrived in New York on or about the beginning of the month. The farewell party in Glasgow was held on June 15, so there are now approximately ten weeks spent neither in Glasgow nor New York and of which there is no record. Allowing a minimum of three weeks for the voyage to New York, there would have been almost two months that might have been used productively as a visiting intern in a Parisian hospital.

Philip Bell complicates the matter by saying that Smith went to France with Peter Williams before receiving his degree:

> [I]n 1837, after passing a very successful examination he received his diploma as M. D. His guardian, Rev. Peter Williams, being in Europe at the time, they visited London and Paris; in the latter city he attended a course of lectures delivered we believe by the celebrated Valpeau.[96] This was during the vacation at Glasgow, and on his return he received his degree.[97]

Bell was writing almost thirty years later and may well have the sequence wrong, but there is little reason to doubt that Smith did spend significant time in Paris, perhaps on two occasions, once early in the year with Williams and again after his farewell from Glasgow. Smith's later interest in the statistical analysis of problems as diverse as slavery in the South and German immigration in New York is an indication of a significant French influence on his work. French doctors were involved in an ongoing debate through the late eighteenth and nineteenth centuries over the value of statistical analysis in the practice of medicine. One school argued vigorously that the relationship between doctor and patient was too personal for statistics to be of use, but another faction argued strongly that statistical methods could help evaluate the usefulness of various therapies and the severity of epidemics.[98] Smith clearly sided with the statisticians.

CHAPTER FOUR

Home Again
1837–1838

Perspective

James McCune Smith was nineteen years old when he left for Scotland and twenty-four when he returned. He left quietly as a promising young student, but returned to an outpouring of tributes that reflected the hopes of a population that was just beginning to find its voice. Critical events had taken place in Smith's absence. Certainly, he would have read about them belatedly and at a distance, but that would not be the same as living through them. Newspapers would also fail to provide the perspective of those who did live through them. Smith would live into this history over the following days and weeks of his new life. Something has been said already about the destructive rioting that took place in Smith's absence, but it is important to fill in some background on the developing anti-slavery and Black rights movement.

For the framers of the United States Constitution, slavery was the sin whose name could not be spoken. "Persons held to servitude" was their obfuscation: a phrase behind which to hide. They knew slavery was wrong but had no will to name it, much less to deal with it. Washington, Jefferson, and Patrick Henry all knew slavery was wrong, but it was familiar and comfortable and they could not bring themselves to act in a way that would have brought to living reality the truth they had proclaimed to the world: "That all men are created equal." They did outlaw the slave trade in 1807. Those who outlawed it thought slavery would wither away as a result. They had not reckoned with the invention of the cotton gin and steam engine and the insatiable appetite of the world for cotton cloth. It so happened that the same states where slavery remained legal were the very states best suited to the growing of cotton. Northern states could outlaw slavery and still profit from it by importing slave-grown cotton and processing it in New England mills. Even so, they acted slowly and reluctantly. New York State finally outlawed slavery in 1827. Connecticut, last of the New England states to outlaw slavery, failed to do so until 1848.

James McCune Smith would have known this history, of course. He would certainly have been aware of the emergence of competing responses to the evil of slavery. First, in 1816, when Smith was only three years old, the American Colonization Society was founded. It brought together an unlikely coalition of northern merchants and southern aristocrats who, for different reasons, had come to believe that American society would be better off without Black members. The northerners, including such leaders as the presidents of Princeton, Columbia, Harvard, and Yale, believed that Black Americans could never find an equal place in American society and that they would have more opportunity to live in freedom in Africa. The southern members were slave owners who believed their slaves would be less rebellious if they no longer saw free Black people in their communities.

Beginning in 1821, hundreds of free Black people emigrated to Liberia, under the auspices of the ACS, but far more rejected that option. The Black response to the colonization movement was slow in coming, but the first National Negro Convention, held in Philadelphia in the fall of 1829 and spring of 1830, gave Black Americans a voice and said clearly that they had no wish to emigrate to an unfamiliar continent. Richard Allen, the founder of the African Methodist Episcopal Church and convener of the first convention, spoke for most of his colleagues when he said, "This land which we have watered with our tears and our blood, is now our mother country and we are well satisfied to stay where wisdom abounds and the gospel is free."[99]

Home Again 1837–1838

A series of National Negro Conventions were held in the years when Smith was in Scotland. They produced a sense of common purpose in rejecting colonization and creating a growing network of leaders, but slavery would not be ended unless whites and Blacks worked together. At the end of 1833, white abolitionists Lewis Tappan and William Lloyd Garrison brought together a coalition of Black and white leaders to form the American Anti-Slavery Society. Smith's friend Philip Bell and his pastor, Peter Williams, were among the signers of the society's constitution.[100] Garrison and Tappan, however, could not work together and eventually created a division in the abolition movement that forced Black leaders to choose between them. The Colonization Society also, though rejected by most Black leaders, continued to exercise a certain attraction and to draw away some leading Black figures. All of this was involved in the reshaping of the world to which Smith returned.

At almost exactly the same time that James McCune Smith was reentering American life, *The Colored American* printed a letter from an upstate New Yorker named Gerrit Smith. Gerrit Smith and James McCune Smith would meet before the next year was over and would become close partners in several major efforts to change the direction of American life. Gerrit Smith wrote to ask:

> What can we at the North do towards abolishing slavery in the South? One thing we can do; we can throw down its greatest prop by purging our hearts of this monster, prejudice. The great justifying doctrine of the slaveholder is that the colored man is not a man; not worthy to be numbered amongst men; not fit to take care of himself—fit only to be a slave. And he proves his doctrine by appealing to the ignorance and degradation to which we reduce the colored man at the North. What can we do? I repeat it, we can purge our hearts of this prejudice. [101]

Gerrit Smith would learn that it was not that simple to change human hearts, but he was prepared to learn and grow and become deeply involved in the abolition movement. James McCune Smith, who may have known of Gerrit Smith's contribution to his own education, wrote to him to express his pleasure that Gerrit Smith also was a member of the Anti-Slavery Society.[102] Gerrit Smith would become a close and trusted partner of James McCune Smith, and he would contribute substantially from his considerable wealth in the effort. He would take one important step before the end of the year by joining the American Anti-Slavery Society.[103] The society had survived its rocky beginning in the riots of 1834 and become the strongest voice in the country for the abolition of slavery. Anchored in New York by the wealth of the Tappan brothers and in Boston by the voice of William Lloyd Garrison and his paper, *The Liberator*, it would force the nation to pay attention. Smith's membership would give them another increasingly powerful voice.

Arrival

Although the exact date of Smith's arrival in New York is uncertain, it must, by his own testimony, have been in the first week of September. By a remarkable coincidence, we do know the exact date of another arrival in New York that same week: Frederick Douglass, escaping from slavery in Maryland, arrived in New York on September 4, 1837. Smith, of course, had never heard of Frederick Douglass, who was still using his birth name of Frederick Bailey. They might have walked past each other in the harbor, but Smith had friends who would have welcomed him into their homes and helped him find office space and a place to live; Douglass had no such support. Years later, he wrote that he had found himself "without home and without friends, in the midst of thousands of my own brethren, (and yet) I was afraid to speak to anyone for fear of speaking to the wrong one."[104] Eventually, James McCune Smith would write the preface to Douglass's

Home Again 1837–1838

second narrative of his life, *My Bondage and My Freedom*, and they would work closely together. Smith would write a regular column for a newspaper that Douglass would produce. But that was much later; they did not meet each other when their paths might have crossed in September of 1837.

Return to New York: The Changed Scene

James McCune Smith came back to a New York City that had gone through radical, even traumatic, change in his absence. Undoubtedly, Smith had kept in touch as best he could, but when letters took three or four weeks in each direction, "news" would always be out of date and even in a world accustomed to writing and reading long and carefully composed letters, nothing could quite convey the impact of such traumatic events as the riots of 1834. Smith would need time to live into the new relationship between the Black and white residents of New York.

The rioting had made an impact on the human and physical fabric of the city. So did the "Great Fire of 1835" in the following year, a blaze that had been visible from Philadelphia and destroyed almost seven hundred buildings in a nineteen-block area.[105] Former New York mayor, Philip Hone, described it as "the most awful calamity that has ever visited these United States."[106] The physical scars left by the fire and the riots had largely been healed, however, by 1837. Lewis Tappan had left his mansion unrepaired all summer as a silent witness to the violence that had coursed through the streets of the city three years earlier, but now his mansion had been repaired. St. Philip's Church also had been repaired and refurnished, and some semblance of normal life had been reestablished. But the fabric of community life was, of course, changing in other ways. Immigrants were flooding into the city, patterns of industry and commerce were changing, and the Black residents of the city and state, though they were a smaller and shrinking percentage of the population as immigrants flooded in and Black people moved away, were organizing and speaking up in new ways.

Smith Returns and Lectures

Though there was no mention of Smith's name in the July and August weekly issues of *The Colored American* or *The Liberator*, the September issues reported on Smith's return to his old community in a number of ways. First, appropriately but perhaps surprisingly, was a notice of his arrival on the New York scene not as a doctor but as a lecturer. *The Colored American* of September 17 announced a lecture on "ANTI-PHRENOLOGY" to be given by "Jas. M'Cune Smith, M.S., M.A.," (but, oddly, not "M.D."). Smith, the advertisement said, "respectfully informs his friends and fellow citizens that he will deliver a lecture, shewing [*sic*] the fallacy of the pretensions upon which Phrenology is founded." The lecture was to be given on September 18 in the Philomathean Hall at a charge of twenty-five cents.

Phrenology was a pseudoscience that could trace its origins to the ancient Greeks but had enjoyed a new burst of popularity in the first half of the nineteenth century. The idea was that different areas of the brain were more or less developed in particular individuals, and that experts could analyze these strengths and weaknesses by feeling the contours of the individual head with their hands or even with calipers. The phrenologists were, of course, ahead of their time in believing that specialized functions of the brain are located in particular areas of the skull, but how intricate those specialized areas are or how to locate them—our knowledge is still rudimentary—of that the phrenologists had no idea. Nevertheless, phrenology had become a popular pseudoscience in Europe and America. It was especially popular in Edinburgh, but not as popular in Glasgow. A French scientist, Jean Pierre Flourens, had conducted experiments long before Smith arrived in Glasgow demonstrating that removal of parts of the brains of pigeons and rabbits had very different results from those the phrenologists expected and had helped undercut their theories. If Smith had indeed spent some time in Paris, he would have had some of the latest information on the subject.

The pseudoscience of phrenology was not unrelated to the suggestion that the shape of the skull reflected the superiority of the white race. Even

Home Again 1837–1838

a committed abolitionist like the author Lydia Maria Child could report as fact an analysis of the "facial angle" in Caucasian, Asiatic, American Indian, Ethiopian, and "Ourang Outang" ranging from 85 degrees for the Caucasian to 70 for the Ethiopian and 67 for the Ourang Outang. Child believed that this only "proves that the Caucasian race, through a succession of ages, has been exposed to influences eminently calculated to develop the moral and intellectual faculties." Expose other races to those same influences, she seemed to suggest, and their skulls would shape up in due time. Perhaps Ourang Outangs, properly educated, would also become philosophers eventually. But Charles Darwin had only returned the year before from his voyage on the HMS *Beagle* and had not yet begun to write about evolution.

A report on Smith's lecture was provided immediately in the *New-York Commercial Advertiser* and reprinted in *The Colored American* two weeks later. "As a lecturer," said the reporter, "Dr. S. possesses many points of excellence ... modest demeanor ... absence of all pedantry, and the facility of his elocution." Smith had skulls to exhibit (as well as skills) and he drew on a blackboard to illustrate his points. He argued that there was no relationship between the external convexities of the skull and the internal concavities. Going more deeply into the subject, he demonstrated that there was no relationship between the folds of the cerebellum and the "artificial and imaginary separations into distinct organs which phrenology supposes." The newspaper reporter thought it was all very well done: "There was nothing in the lecture, either in matter or manner, to which the most fastidious critic could take exception."[107]

The Colored American thought that phrenology bordered on witchcraft, but also thought there were a good many in Smith's audience who accepted its principles, so he had set himself a difficult task to persuade them. *The Colored American*, like the *Commercial Advertiser*, thought that phrenology tended toward "infidelity and ruin." "If God has given a man the Bumpification of Destructiveness," said the reporter, then he will be destructive and if not, "he must of necessity be the contrary." *The Colored American*'s reporter thought Smith had the unpopular side of the argument but had "sustained himself with honor to his talent and acquirements." More immediately important to Smith, *The Colored American* concluded with the hope that "our friends and our brethren will give their patronage to Dr. Smith." "Give him a chance," the paper urged, "and with good health, under God, he will make the Moral, Literary, and Physiological world ALL his own."

This lecture, Smith's professional debut, served several purposes. First, Smith had given himself the opportunity to demonstrate his intellectual and professional abilities to a representative audience of New Yorkers. The newspaper reported that there had been "a number of gentlemen belonging to the several learned professions, all of whom appeared to be interested, and indeed highly gratified." Second, he had provided evidence that prejudices based on race were false. The reporter suggested that "all good men must rejoice in the improvement and elevation of individuals among our colored fellow citizens, of which Dr. Smith is an illustrious example." Any doubters could have "ocular and auricular demonstration that there is one at least who has just claim to the character of a scholar and a gentleman."[108]

And finally, and perhaps most immediately important to himself, Smith had taken a first step toward establishing himself as a medical professional to whom other citizens could turn in their times of need. To get attention for his new practice, Smith had a tool not previously available to the Black community: in his absence, his old friend Philip Bell had become the publisher of a brand-new weekly newspaper called *The Colored American*, so Smith would have no difficulty in gaining publicity.[109] In fact, *The Colored American* was publishing portions of Smith's journal of his trip to Scotland with almost every issue and in February 1838, would reprint the whole story of his encounter with the captain of the brig *Canonicus*. Newspaper readers in New York would become well aware of Smith's name and accomplishments. His fame spread abroad as well; he went to Philadelphia in December to give a lecture on "the importance of classical and mathematical studies." *The United States Gazette* called the address "a highly creditable production."[110]

But the lectures were a means to an end. A young doctor needs to make himself known, and a little advertising could help as well. In the November 11, 1837, issue of *The Colored American* a small ad appear toward the bottom of an inside page:

> DRUGS AND MEDICINES for sale at 93
> West Broadway: also fancy articles of every
> description.

This address, 93 West Broadway, would become an important center not only for African Americans and others in poor health, but also for those who were active politically. The office and drugstore had a back room that provided a convenient meeting place for Smith and his friends as they talked over current events and made plans for their own involvement. One contemporary New York historian records a family tradition handed down from her great-grandaunt who remembered a back room in Smith's pharmacy with a library and comfortable chairs that provided a "popular meeting place for politically active black citizens."[111] This address, it should also be noted, was across town from the Five Points and in a much better neighborhood than the one where Smith had grown up and where St. Philip's Church still stood.

That first ad might easily have been overlooked, especially since Smith's name was not mentioned. But Smith would continue to advertise regularly. The next week there were four ads, one was the same as the ad placed the previous week, but three new ads spelled out the larger scope of Smith's medical practice:

> MEDICAL CONSULTATIONS — Dr. James
> McCune Smith continues to be consulted in medical
> cases of every description at his office,
> No. 93 West Broadway.
>
> SHAKER'S HERBS — A large assortment of Shaker's
> Herbs for sale, wholesale and retail, at the lowest prices,
> at Dr. Smith's Medicine Store, No. 93 West Broadway.
>
> Bleeding, Tooth-drawing, Cupping and Leeching
> performed by Dr. Smith at his office, 93 West Broadway.

The last ad gets down to specifics. Medical practice in the early nineteenth century was far from the computerized, specialized medical care provided in the twenty-first century. The theory that germs cause disease had been proposed in the last half of the sixteenth century, but not until the latter half of the nineteenth century did Louis Pasteur and Robert Koch provide persuasive evidence of the existence of microorganisms and demonstrate their relationship to disease. Even so, it was not until the twentieth century that sulfa drugs were developed so that germs could be attacked with effective remedies.

Smith, with the best medical education available in his day, had been trained in the techniques of an earlier time. Cupping, leeching, and bleeding are ancient medical practices still in use in some societies and in various systems of alternative medicine. Cupping is used to draw blood to an area of the body and promote healing. Leeches and lancets are used to draw blood and reduce a fever. In later ads, Smith offered leeches for sale by the hundred for those who preferred to treat themselves. Tooth-drawing is self-explanatory and is, of course, sometimes still necessary. Dentists now have anesthetics to deal with pain, and Dr. Smith would not have had that tool available. But however limited the tools available to him, James McCune

Smith had been trained in the latest techniques, and he would provide what help he could to citizens of the city who turned to him for healing.[112]

Two further developments in Smith's advertising campaign came in July 1839 when specific hours were listed and a third address. Dr. Smith could now be consulted at 93 West Broadway between 7:00 a.m. and 10:00 a.m., 2:00 p.m. and 3:00 p.m., and 8:00 p.m. to 10:00 p.m. The ad also says, "House 151 Reade street, two doors from Greenwich street."[113] Where Smith himself had been living until this time is uncertain, perhaps in a back room of his office. Now, apparently, after almost two years of practice, he had a home of his own a short distance away and could be found there in an emergency.[114]

The morning and evening hours seem designed for people who were unable to take time off from work to see their doctor, but apparently clients might also find the doctor at home if they needed him outside office hours. It should be remembered, however, that doctors until at least the middle of the twentieth century still made house calls and when the doctor was out of the office, he was most likely to be visiting patients at home. In the nineteenth century, hospitals were rare and created primarily to serve the poor. Those with a large enough home to have private bedrooms where a sick person could be cared for would expect the doctor to come to them.

Welcome Home (At Last!)

A logical sequence of events for the return of a long absent, newly credentialed member of the community might seem to begin with a welcome party, continue with an inaugural lecture, and conclude with the opening of the office. But that was not what happened. It is not clear exactly when the office opened, but it is clear that the lecture came before the welcome back. *The Colored American* of September 23rd, five days after the lecture, announced that there would be a public meeting of "the Friends and Admirers of Dr. James M'Cune Smith" on Tuesday, the 26th of September, at the Broadway Tabernacle. The announcement oddly omitted reference to his medical degree and said that he was returning "crowned rich in LITERARY HONORS" as if the medical accomplishments were unimportant or as if the writer remembered what he had done in the African Free School rather than what he had set out to do afterward. They would "manifest the high regard and esteem that they entertain for him," the announcement continued, for "the honorable manner in which he has triumphantly represented the intellect and natural capacities, of the outraged and oppressed of America." This welcome home, apparently, would be a celebration with a focus on what Smith's accomplishments represented. They brought honor and recognition to Black New Yorkers and they would be thanking him for what he had done for them.

The scope of the plan made for the event is evident in the choice of a location. The meeting would be held in the newly opened Broadway Tabernacle, the most impressive church of its day in Manhattan. Built to replace the Chatham Street Chapel that had been at the center of the riots of 1834, the Broadway Tabernacle, like its predecessor, had been created specifically to hold audiences for Charles Grandison Finney, the best-known evangelist of his day. Lewis Tappan, a prominent New York businessman, was an evangelical Christian and an abolitionist and he had brought Finney to New York to shape the faith of New Yorkers as he hoped also to shape their views on slavery and abolition. There is no evidence that Tappan was present at the welcome for Smith, but it would not have been held in his building without his consent—and it would not have had his consent unless he and the leading Black abolitionists of the city saw Smith's return as an opportunity to make a statement, to demonstrate to the city what Black people could accomplish, and how false were the arguments for slavery that claimed Black people were not capable of any higher attainments.

Ransom P. Wake, who had been one of James McCune Smith's teachers at the African Free School, was the spokesman of the evening. He had only the year before become head of the boys department of the newly opened Colored School No. 2. It was a small sign of progress that this new school was a "Colored School" rather than an "African School."[115] In the next year, Wake would give one of the Philomathean Society's lectures on the subject of "Oratorical Delivery."[116] Smith's homecoming celebration would give Wake a chance to demonstrate his skills in welcoming his old pupil back to the city. More importantly, he would also use the occasion, as the organizers surely intended, to "send a message." Wake began:

> The occasion that assembles us here is calculated to raise us in our own estimation, in the estimation of the world, and in the estimation of everyone whose good opinion is worth having—to raise us above the mean and sordid prejudice which has unjustly, tyrannically, and oppressively trampled on our rights as men—on our privileges as American citizens and on our feelings as individuals. We have assembled to celebrate a proud and signal triumph over this foul and hideous slavery-begotten monster which the American people are cherishing in their bosoms, to enter our solemn protest (and hope) to root out this moral canker that is destroying the heart of the nation and which renders the name of America a hissing and byword among the nations of the world—but still a nation we are proud to call our home, oppressed as we are and have been in it—but we hope for better things.

It is hard to imagine a more forceful and succinct statement of the central and polarizing issue of American life through most, if not all, of its history. James McCune Smith was never mentioned. The gathering was called in his honor, but he was not the text but the pretext for the making of a statement.

Having made that central point, Wake moved on to say something about the announced subject of the gathering: "Dr. James McCune Smith, the subject of our gratulations this evening, having from early youth evinced powers of mind and indications of talent of a superior order . . . induced some influential friends to make an effort to give him the advantages of an education suitable to his natural capabilities" and that led him to "wend . . . his lonely way across the trackless ocean" to a land where "no matter what may be the complexion of the individual . . . they would still exclaim with their own poet, 'A man's a man for a' that.'"

In that exile, Wake continued, Smith had spent five years "in a vigorous and successful course of study" and now returns "to his native land, clothed with 'honors bravely won' . . . [and] with abundant testimonials of literary and professional ability from those whose known wisdom and worth in the literary world place their assertions beyond the reach of the gainsayer, the scorner, or the prejudiced." At this point in the proceedings, Smith himself finally appeared "and was introduced amidst unbounded applause from all parts of the house."

When the applause died down, Wake heaped praise on Smith for his accomplishments and future prospects:

> I congratulate you in your close connection and familiar intimacy with the genius of Literature, while partaking of Scotia's boundless hospitality . . . I congratulate you for the able manner in which you have represented the character and intellectual capabilities of those with whom you are proud to be identified. . . . I congratulate you on the cheering prospects held out to you since your return. . . . In the name of this assemblage of your admiring friends and countrymen, I greet you with a cordial and hearty welcome to your native land. Long may endure the golden opinions for which you have so nobly contended and so

> bravely won. Ever green be the laurels with which fame has encircled your brow. May Heaven's choicest blessings, and the affections of a grateful people cheer your heart in the pilgrimage of life. May the hand of time press lightly on your brow, and long may you live to be an ornament to your country—an advocate for the oppressed—a scourge to the oppressor, and a benefactor to mankind.

After all that, Smith was at last given the opportunity to speak for himself. He made no attempt to compete with Wake's oratory, but simply told his audience how their gathering "gives rise to emotions in my mind which it is less difficult for you to imagine than for me to express." This gathering, he told them, "far exceeds anything which I deserve or can thank you for." He expressed his appreciation at some length but his speech was less than half as long as Wake's introduction and said nothing except "thank you." He then turned over the podium to Thomas S. Sydney, a member of the planning committee, who brought the program to an end by presenting a series of resolutions. It was necessary, he said, to

> bespeak from and on the part of this audience a loud unanimous emphatic affirmative response: a response so loud that going forth it may convince the privileged order of this land that we perceive and duly appreciate every triumph which our interest makes over slavery, prejudice and colonization. So unanimous that it may inspire Dr. Smith manfully to triumph over all these unhappy circumstances and obstacles which identify him with the oppressed of America. . . . So emphatic that it may reach the South and whisper in the ear of the despairing captive the sweet tones of hope and forthcoming deliverance.

The three resolutions presented expressed joy in Smith's return, full confidence in his professional ability and "unexceptionable moral character," and appreciation for the "noble-hearted, the philanthropic of Glasgow" for their "kind and courteous treatment toward our cherished fellow-citizen." These resolutions were unanimously adopted and the meeting was adjourned.[117]

Even after all of that, however, Smith had not yet been sufficiently welcomed. Exactly one week later, on October 3, a second welcome celebration was held, this time in Troy, New York, in the upstate area near Albany. The organizer of that event was Daniel Payne who was only two years older than Smith. Born free in Charleston, South Carolina, Payne had created a school for Black children but moved north when the state passed a new law against teaching Black children that forced him to close it.[118] Eventually, he would become a bishop in the African Methodist Episcopal Church and finally president of Wilberforce College, but in 1837, after a year in a Lutheran seminary in Pennsylvania, he was serving as pastor of a Presbyterian church in East Troy, New York, and chair of a committee that wanted to include upstate New York in Smith's welcome home.

As chair of the Mental and Moral Improvement Society of Troy, Payne convened a gathering of "all the respectable colored inhabitants of Troy" to make "a public expression of their unqualified esteem and hearty welcome of our fellow countryman, Dr. James McCune Smith to his native land." Payne opened the meeting with prayer and then made a "suitable and lucid speech" welcoming Smith as Ransom P. Wake had done in New York. This time, the emphasis was clearly on honoring Smith, but here also Smith's achievements were set in the larger context of America's racial divide.

"You have returned in triumph to your native land," Payne told Smith, with "blooming, deathless laurels encircling your brows, demanding the respect and admiration of the enlightened world. We open our arms to receive you, oppressed, persecuted, afflicted as we are, trusting that you will employ your exalted talents and profound erudition, in advocating our rights

Home Again 1837–1838

and pleading our righteous cause."[119] If Smith himself spoke, the report said nothing of it. So the Troy event was relatively brief and low-key, but just for that reason seems to have been designed to "send a message." Smith was to be honored, but his achievement was to be used for the benefit of the larger community. Both in New York and in Troy, the "welcome home" party had a very visible subtext: "We're glad you are here. There's a fight going on. We look forward to your help."

Organizing for Justice

Help was needed, especially in the struggle for equal justice under the law. More important than the physical changes in the city that had taken place in Smith's absence was the founding of the American Anti-Slavery Society by William Lloyd Garrison and others in 1833. A year later, a New York State Anti-Slavery Society had been formed in Utica. Loud voices of opposition were being heard as well. When the New York State Anti-Slavery Society went back to Utica for their first annual meeting, protesters drove them out of the church where they were meeting and forced them to reconvene nineteen miles away in Peterboro to complete their agenda.

More Lectures

One piece of his former life that Smith could pick up easily was his involvement in the Philomathean Society that he and Philip Bell had helped to found before Smith left for Scotland. At the end of December, the Philomathean Society announced its list of upcoming lectures, a series of eight speakers giving two to four lectures each on subjects ranging from chemistry to "Evidences of Christianity." Among the speakers would be Philip Bell (history) and Ransom F. Wake (oratory). Smith would be giving a series of four lectures on "Organs of Sense." Tickets for the series of twenty-eight lectures would cost $2.50. Separate lectures could be attended for twelve-and-a-half cents. But the society's reach exceeded its grasp. *The Colored American* provided an editorial bemoaning the poor response to the opportunity being provided: "We attended the last lecture . . . and our heart was GRIEVED at the *thinness of the audience*. . . . It is shameful, brethren, that in a city like this, where we have eighteen thousand colored citizens, such men as Dr. Brown should be suffered to lecture to empty seats and empty walls . . . the subjects are important ones, are practically treated, and made so plain that all may understand them. . . . Will our young people *please to attend?*"[120]

Smith seems to have made it his priority to establish his intellectual credentials—but what else can a doctor do to make himself known to the community? Smith's first event, after all, had been a lecture on phrenology. His next several events—apart from the two "welcome home" celebrations—were additional lectures. One of those lectures was given in Philadelphia at the Adelphi School, which was built between 1831 and 1834 by an association of Quakers "for the Instruction of Poor Children" and with a special focus on the education of the city's "colored population." The lecturer, the newspaper reported, "is a young man of color, who . . . besides his scholastic attainments, which are said to be of a high order, is spoken of as possessing an excellent address, a good voice, pleasing manners, and good delivery."

This burst of intellectual activity was impressive, but neither that nor Smith's quickly established medical practice could long prevent him from dealing with that central issue of American life which both welcome parties had highlighted. Smith had been quick to join and work with the Glasgow Emancipation Society; he would also need to join the New York Anti-Slavery Society and get "up to speed" on the state of the anti-slavery struggle in America. He had left as a teenager last employed as an assistant blacksmith. He returned as a doctor with training and credentials unknown before that time not only in the Black population but the white population as well. Perhaps his lectures on medical and scientific subjects would give him further credentials with the white population, and he would be able to speak to white Americans in a way Black people had not done before.

CHAPTER FIVE

*A Larger Stage
1838–1840*

Division in the Ranks

An established custom in New York City in the first half of the nineteenth century was the gathering in early May of all the major charitable organizations in the country. Sometimes so many came that there was no meeting space for them in Manhattan, and some had to meet in Brooklyn. In 1838, the American Anti-Slavery Society came to New York and invited James McCune Smith to be one of five principal speakers—and the only Black speaker—on the program. It was an opportunity to make his mark on the largest stage available in the abolition movement, a movement which, *The Colored American* told its readers, brings together "the first talent and piety of the land, and its business embraces and blends the highest interests of our country—the interests of time and eternity are alike involved."[121]

Smith's assigned topic was a logical one: "[T]hat we contemplate with heartfelt satisfaction" the efforts made by similar societies in England and France to abolish slavery. Smith, after all, had been in Britain and probably France less than a year earlier and involved in the work of the Glasgow Emancipation Society, but the topic inevitably was more of a report on events elsewhere than an opportunity to confront the issues of American society directly. Smith brought it back to that at the end. He surveyed the work done to end slavery in the British Empire and by the French grant of independence to Haiti (recognition of a *fait accompli*) and the promise of freedom soon for the quarter of a million slaves remaining in the French Empire. All that was good, Smith told his audience, but how, he asked,

> can we co-operate with Great Britain, how can we emulate her example, unless we abolish the last vestiges of slavery in our own states. . . . Or how can we call upon the South for immediate and entire emancipation, whilst we permit gradual emancipation in the North? . . . Let us begin at home. Let us first purify our own soil and then may we call upon the South to follow the example. An eloquent gentleman who addressed you this morning observed, that if the whole moral and intellectual power of the North be brought to bear upon the South it must accomplish the abolition of slavery. . . . It is my firm belief, a belief which springs from the deepest and strongest conviction, that that which will tell most, and do most toward the abolition of southern slavery will be the sight of freed colored men, elevated in these northern white communities to the dignity and privileges of citizens of the republic.[122]

Unfortunately, that was not the focal concern of the American Anti-Slavery Society. That society was formed to attack slavery in the South, and it would never enlist the wholehearted cooperation and support of Black leaders like Smith while it remained, as it always did, not deeply aware of or concerned by the disadvantages faced daily by nominally free Black citizens in the North. Smith took the opportunity to make that point, but the society never really responded to his challenge.

The Colored American, however, took note of Smith's speech. The other speeches, it reported, were "eloquent and effective," but it was Smith's speech that the paper reported most fully:

Our friend, Dr. Smith, on the occasion stood forth for us, a proud instance of talents and acquirements—an irrefutable evidence of the perfect equality, morally and mentally, of the colored man with his pale-faced brethren. It is our wisdom, as a people, to bring forward such men as the Dr., on such occasions—by so doing, our cause will be greatly benefitted, and our interests promoted. The hands of our friends could not otherwise than be strengthened, and the ranks of our enemies confused. Where is the necessity of colonizing such men as Dr. Smith? Much better make them senators of the land.[123]

One of the other speakers was Gerrit Smith, and this was presumably the first time the two Smiths had met. They would become good friends—a rare interracial friendship in those days— and work together on several important projects.

One month later, the Black citizens of the city of New York assembled to work on the agenda to which Smith had pointed. There had been a meeting the previous summer to deal with the new state requirement that Black voters be property owners, and to "deluge" the state assembly with petitions. Nothing had happened, so now, it seemed, a continuing effort needed to be organized. First the meeting adopted a resolution saying that the formation of a political association would be an important first step toward restoring the suffrage to all Black New Yorkers—"a right once exercised, now unfairly withheld."[124] Then they adopted a constitution and elected officers. It is noteworthy that although they chose a president, two secretaries, seven vice presidents, and an eight-member executive committee and heard speeches by five of those present, James McCune Smith was not selected to any office or called on to speak.[125] No doubt they were glad to have him back, but there was other talent and ability and they had sufficient talent to work on their concerns without him. It would also become clear that Smith was not in total sympathy with this particular movement.

But Smith would be involved in such issues. In December, a public meeting was called to rally opponents of the Colonization Society. The society had recently made a new attempt to draw Black citizens to its plans by offering to buy ships and put them in the hands of Black Americans. The signers of the statement calling for the meeting deemed it necessary "that we should again give our opinions publicity, that the world and all those connected with the Colonization Societies may know that all attempts to remove us from our native land, either by appeals to our passions or pecuniary interests, or by . . . increasing the already existing prejudice . . . will always meet with opposition." James McCune Smith was one of twenty sponsors of the gathering.[126]

The meeting was held in January and filled the Broadway Hall. James McCune Smith was the first of a long roster of speakers, and he noted that the sheer size of the audience was important:

> Mr. President it is with a feeling of proud satisfaction that I look over this vast hall filled to overflowing with a representation of all that is respectable, talented and pious in our community, assembled to denounce the principles and measures of the American Colonization Society. And although, sir, as an oppressed minority it is our most prudent course to refrain from attracting public notoriety by distinct public meetings, yet there are occasions when this general rule must be violated. When men whom we never solicited thrust their advice upon us; when men whom we never injured load us with malignant abuse; when cold, crafty, and designing men select us, the few and feeble, as the instruments by which they may strike a death blow at the vitals of the Republic, then we are called upon by our

duty to ourselves, to those very men, and to our country, by all that is holy in principle and noble in patriotism, to meet and lift our warning voice to our fellow citizens.

Smith was the first of a long list of speakers, but he made perhaps the most interesting argument of the night. The Colonization Society, Smith told his audience, could not accomplish its purpose. There was no way it could transport millions of Black Americans to Africa. But it could "craftily instill into the minds of the people the dogma that there is a natural inequality among the citizens of the republic. . . . The Society has further disseminated the idea of the natural inferiority of the colored people by creating and keeping alive a feeling of prejudice or pity in regard to us. That this prejudice assumes the inferiority of the colored people is sufficiently plain. Pity does the same; men do not pity their equals." This feeling of pity and inequality, Smith argued, has even penetrated the ranks of the abolitionists. "I repudiate this pity," Smith told his audience. "We ask for no man's pity; we ask for our rights."

Other speakers followed and Smith's old friend Philip Bell brought the meeting to an end by offering a resolution:

> [T]hat our sympathies for the slave, the love we bear our native land, our respect and veneration for the institutions and government of our country are so many cords which bind us to our home, the soil of our birth, which has been wet by the tears and fertilized by the blood of our ancestors . . . we will tell the white Americans that their country shall be our country—where they live we will live, where they die, there will we be buried, and our graves will remain as monuments of our suffering and triumph.[127]

In February 1839, the New York City Anti-Slavery Society met and Lewis Tappan, as chairman, dominated the event. The convention had met in the Broadway Hall on Tuesday evening but moved to the larger Chatham Street Chapel for the next three days. Snow was falling and drifting outside, but the chapel was full for the Friday evening session. Earlier sessions had been filled with reports from various churches of their activities and a condemnation of the gag rule that Congress had imposed on itself to prevent resolutions against slavery being considered. The final report was brought by Simeon Jocelyn, a staunch leader among white New York abolitionists. He began by suggesting that a Committee of Correspondence should be created to respond to the governor's annual report, especially as it related to the colored population. He also suggested that the committee should "obtain statistics comparing their [colored] numbers in the almshouses and prisons as compared with the number of *Irish* in the same." That might have set off another riot had it been carried out. But moving on to the substance of the report, Jocelyn, a white man, read off a long list of recommendations for "elevating the colored people." His "to do" list for such elevation included Sabbath school instruction, temperance societies, moral reform societies, anti-slavery societies, education, "encouragement of the businessmen among them," and "to print a book for them on domestic economy." Twelfth was a recommendation "to send lecturers on these subjects among them." The thirteenth and final recommendation was that they should "patronize their organ, the *Colored American*." Black members of the audience must have felt that they had already been patronized themselves.

Lewis Tappan, presiding, recommended committees to deal with these matters and then added one more: "[T]hat the want of the elective franchise is the source of all the evils under which the colored people in this State labor, and that the obtainment of it by them will be the great lever for their elevation." McCune Smith must have been gratified by that turn in the direction of the meeting, but two other speakers rose to speak favorably of the report before Smith could bring the evening to an end by suggesting the report "did not strike at the root of the evil" because "all the oppressions under which the colored people in this State labor" were a result of their inability to vote. "The only means of elevating them is to give them equal rights in voting."[128]

A first meeting to deal with the right to vote had been held in the summer of 1837 and another in 1838, but other organizational issues must have taken priority. And surely Smith was also tending to business: dealing with patients who came to consult him or to be treated and making house calls on those too sick to come to his office. In his spare time, Smith was also assisting his old friend Philip Bell as a co-editor of *The Colored American*. If he was not making headlines, he was writing headlines.

More Divisions in the Ranks

The American Anti-Slavery Society had been founded in December of 1833 with the deliberate intention of creating an inclusive association of all those opposed to the institution of slavery. With thousands of members and a significant budget, the society was in position to make itself heard in the growing debate over the future of slavery. It was also a tinderbox waiting for a spark to set it off.

The American Anti-Slavery Society was an organization dominated by its white members, in particular the Tappan brothers in New York and William Lloyd Garrison in Boston. They believed passionately that slavery was wrong, but they seemed unaware of any larger issue of racism in the society as a whole. When the annual meeting was over, in May of 1839, Philip Bell used his role as editor of *The Colored American* to point out that Black slavery was not the only issue of concern to Black members and that, in effect, the Black and white members lived in different worlds and had radically different issues. The founders had true principles, he wrote, and deep convictions:

> [They] organized themselves into an association with martyrdom staring them in the face. But these strong men with sound principles ... made secondary and collateral what ought to have been the primary object of all their efforts ... in their zeal and fiery indignation against slavery in the South. They half overlooked slavery in the North. At this moment more is known among abolitionists of slavery in the Carolinas than of the deep and daunting thralldom which grinds to the dust the colored inhabitants of New York. And more efforts are made by them to rend the physical chains of Southern slaves than to burst the soul crushing bondage of the Northern states ... it was and is the duty of every abolitionist first to abolitionize his own heart.[129]

Bell cited the familiar Biblical injunction to deal with the beam in your own eye before attempting to deal with the mote in your brother's eye.

One year later, however, the unlikely coalition self-destructed. When delegates poured into New York for the annual meeting in May of 1840, Philip Bell of *The Colored American* saw what was coming. It would be, he wrote, a meeting "more largely attended ... more excitable in its proceedings ... than any former one. In fine, we know not but the reputation of anti-slavery hereafter hangs upon the proceedings of the approaching meeting. Many will be present to introduce amendments to the constitution and many to oppose them. Many will be present to agitate other matters, and many also to oppose them."

Bell was expecting anger and conflict. "If the meeting should not break up with more of alienated feeling than when it commences," he said, "we shall be most happily disappointed."[130]

But he was not happily disappointed. The issue that finally could not be resolved was not slavery but the role of women in the organization. Women had been active supporters of the AAS from the beginning and Garrison, leading the New England delegates, had encouraged their participation. Now he had come to believe that they should be included in the leadership and was prepared to nominate Abby Foster Kelly for a place on the board.

Kelly was a capable leader, but her gender was all that mattered to New York's evangelical contingent. Lewis and Arthur Tappan, leaders of the New York delegation, were conservative evangelicals whose Biblical faith allowed no room for women in leadership roles. Except for opposition to slavery, they and Garrison had nothing at all in common. But while Garrison was eager for a battle and had brought extra troops from Boston to support him, the Tappan brothers preferred to avoid open conflict.

In the event, however, Arthur Tappan was there to preside at the opening meeting. The afternoon session brought an address by Henry Highland Garnet, a treasurer's report showing greatly increased income, and a report from Lewis Tappan on the *Amistad* captives. The afternoon session then adjourned with the members "having been greatly interested and refreshed by the exercises."

The evening session, however, was less successful. This time, Tappan was absent and Gerrit Smith, who had come to believe that women should have an expanded role in the society, served as presiding officer.[131] The issue was joined when the nominating committee brought in a report that recommended Abby Kelly for membership on the business committee. This brought objections and a vote was taken that showed 557 in favor and 451 opposed. Lewis Tappan and two others thereupon resigned from the business committee and were replaced.

The next day, it was announced that those who were uncomfortable with the course of the society could meet in the basement of the church that afternoon to form a new organization, the American and Foreign Anti-Slavery Society. Some three hundred individuals withdrew at the appointed hour and went downstairs. Another hundred delegates, preferring to avoid commitment at that point, simply went home. The remaining delegates finished out their order of business adopting, among others, a controversial resolution claiming that societies not in alliance with the American Anti-Slavery Society were "opposed to the principles of Liberty." In spite of objections, the resolution was passed and the meeting adjourned *sine die*.[132]

There would be no healing of the breach in the forces of abolition. Garrison and his allies adopted a course increasingly critical of the churches for their failure to form a unanimous front against slavery while the Tappan brothers and their allies insisted that they were acting against slavery on the basis of their faith. Philip Bell and *The Colored American* found much to criticize in both societies but decided to stay with the old society for the time being, though recognizing that most of their friends and associates, colored and white, had chosen the new organization.

New York State Meetings

Still hanging unresolved was the issue of Black voting rights in New York State. A meeting had been called in the summer of 1837 as Smith was returning from Scotland. Those attending had been called on to "deluge the Legislature with petitions." If they had done so, the legislature had been unmoved. Now it was time to try again. Even before the May conventions had gathered, *The Colored American* raised the issue but raised it in an oddly halfhearted way. In a city where public transportation was segregated and individual names in the street directory were identified as "col'd," the newspaper—whose name itself indicated a divided society—seemed reluctant to deal straightforwardly with racial issues:

> While we believe that, being of the *American nation*, we ought to identify ourselves with the American people, and with American interests, yet there are and will be, special interests for us to attend to, so long as American caste exists, and we have not equal rights, in common

with the American people. When such shall be our condition, there will then be no longer special interests to be attended to.

Having expressed that hope for a different world, the paper recognized the facts of life in the real world around them and endorsed the idea of a state convention of Black citizens to press their case with the legislature. "There exists," the paper said, "with the colored population of this state, almost every reason why we should have a convention." Unfortunately, the general population had more interesting things holding its attention.

With the conclusion of the anti-slavery convention in May, the attention of *The Colored American* and many ordinary citizens, Black and white, shifted to the fate of the *Amistad* captives being worked out in Connecticut courts. The dramatic story of how slaves had taken over a Spanish ship and managed to reach waters off the Connecticut coast was being covered by newspapers everywhere, but the headline story, typically, was not the one that mattered most in the long term. What happened to the *Amistad* captives would make little lasting difference in American society. What would make a difference was the much more substantive issue of the right to vote. *The Colored American* was receiving letters suggesting the need for a New York state convention. In fact, in spite of national conventions and the divisions in the anti-slavery movement, the organizing of a convention to focus on the right to vote had been moving forward and a date was set for a meeting in Albany. A New York City meeting was convened on July 27, 1840, to select delegates to a convention to be held late in August.

Unfortunately, the first thing the New York City meeting demonstrated was that there was no agreement even as to the usefulness of a convention. No sooner was a resolution brought forward approving the idea of a convention than an amendment was offered suggesting that a convention representing one-fiftieth of the population was unlikely to accomplish anything useful. The chair ruled the amendment out of order, but he was overruled by the meeting. Further amendments were offered to support a convention, and more resolutions were presented to oppose them. James McCune Smith weighed in on the negative side "at great length—and in his usual forcible manner." The debate went on to "a late hour" when it was agreed "that this meeting do adjourn to some other time and place to hear the subject further discussed."

When the convention reassembled eight days later, it received a report that a committee had been formed to nominate five delegates, but the committee reported first of all that they recommended increasing the number of delegates from five to twenty-five, or "as many of them to go as can bear their own expenses." The committee put forward twenty-five names but four promptly declined and were replaced by four others, one of whom was James McCune Smith. Smith had declined nomination originally because, as he had explained at great length at the first meeting, he was opposed to the idea of a Black convention. After that, the meeting became even more confused. Smith explained again that he was opposed to the convention because he was opposed to any "distinct complexional organization." He was, however, nominated anyway and elected and agreed to serve and to work for the objectives of the convention.

In the same issue of *The Colored American* that reported both these meetings, Smith wrote an expanded explanation of his difficulty with the convention idea. First, he said, it seemed to him that it was a bad use of limited resources; second, he feared that drawing attention to complexion would have negative consequences; a similar recent action in Pennsylvania had resulted in the complete loss of the franchise for the colored population. Smith's third objection was less clear but seemed to suggest that some wider movement would be better: "a movement based on principle and carried on by all the influences irrespective of complexion that can be brought to bear." His fourth and final objection was that "a colored Convention of the kind in question 'does evil that good may come.'" Smith cited three names and alluded to others who were anxious to join in the convention but unwilling to do so because its terms, "a colored convention," shut them out. Presumably, the names were those of white citizens who hoped to join in protesting the racial limitation clause. Smith's own problem remained a fundamental objection to action based on color rather than principle and a fear that such an approach "will end in riveting more firmly the chains that bind us."[133]

The well-known author Lydia Maria Child was now editing the *National Anti-Slavery Standard*, the organ of the American Anti-Slavery Society in New York and a paper that seldom mentioned Smith or those involved with the rival American and Foreign Anti-Slavery Society. In this situation, however, an unsigned editorial expressed approval of Smith's position, but did so in a way that seemed to carry Smith's position to an extreme and imagine a world that was still far in the future when Black people could live like white people without any consciousness of color. "Those supporting the Convention were doubtless eloquent and said they were men, but the world will believe," the paper told the world,

> that they think somewhat of letting the community see that the "colored man" is a "colored man" instead of proving that they have the same rights as other men, for the reason that they are like other men. . . . We are glad to see Doct. J. M'Cune Smith using the same ground. . . . The right of suffrage is a human right—not a "colored" human Right, and he who pleads that he should enjoy it or be deprived of it because of his color, pleads to a falsehood, and dishonors himself. We talk plainly. Our soul is sick at seeing the great family of man that should be a "vast brotherhood," thrown onto clans that germinate an exterminating hostility against each other. No class of community have been *compelled* to be clannish more than the colored people, and now that the spirit of Freedom is

just ready to bring the barrier of caste with a level to the dust, none seem more bent on keeping it up than some of the colored people in this State.[134]

Child's position seems parallel to the twenty-first century argument against signs saying "Black Lives Matter" on the grounds that "All Lives Matter." The latter statement is true, of course, but it is specifically Black lives that are disproportionately at risk and it was specifically Black voters who had been disenfranchised. Smith made his point, but he was willing to go to the convention rather than create a further division in the ranks. The first priority was that everyone be allowed to vote. It would be preferable that Black and white voters together work for such a change, but Smith seemed to feel it was better to work with those who were working on issues that mattered than not to work at all.

So the proposed convention was held and although Smith had agreed to go, there is no evidence that he actually did so. His name does not appear on the list of delegates nor—though he always took a leading role in debates—was he listed among the speakers. It is entirely possible that some medical emergency prevented his attendance. It seems more likely, however, that he decided to stay with his original objection to the convention. Months later, in a letter to James G. Birney of the Liberty Party, Smith restated his objection to the convention as "a caste convention in order to abolish caste."[135]

With or without Smith, however, upward of 140 delegates from Long Island to Buffalo gathered in Albany and spent three days considering how they should act. The convention, inevitably, passed a number of resolutions. One "[r]esolved, that the gathering together of so large an assembly of the worth and talent of our people . . . cannot but be regarded as auspicious in the extreme." It was still a new experience for Black people to come together and find themselves part of a large number of committed and capable individuals with a common experience and agenda. The last resolution was the one that mattered, because it stated the specific reason they had come:

> That we esteem it our duty as beings, divine in our nature, and human in our relations and sympathies, to put forth strong and earnest efforts, each and all of us, in our several callings, for the political enfranchisement of our people upon which so much of our religious, literary and local happiness virtually depends . . . and will leave no peaceful and rational means untried to accomplish these ends.

Lydia Maria Child and James McCune Smith should both have been pleased to see that the resolution staked no claim to the franchise on the basis of being colored but "as beings, divine in our nature, and human in our relations and sympathies." The formal petition, however, did refer specifically to "complexional difference"; it was, after all, the revised Constitution of the State of New York that had made such difference a matter of concern to Black citizens by denying them the right to vote unless they owned $250 worth of property.

When the convention was over, its actions were published in a booklet of fifty-six pages, but a summary needs only a paragraph. First, the convention put in place a continuing structure with a central committee located in Albany and county committees throughout the state. These committees would be responsible for drawing up petitions as needed to assert the rights of the colored population. Second, the convention drew up an address to the colored population defining their duties and their rights. A second address was sent to the general population of the state setting out the connection between the rights of the colored population and the duties and interests of the people of the state in general. Above all, the address insisted that those asking for the right to vote were Americans with a deep investment in their country:

> We are the descendants of some of the earliest settlers of the State. We can trace our ancestry back to those who first pierced the almost impenetrable forests that then lifted their high and stately heads in silent grandeur to the skies. *We are Americans.* We were born in no foreign clime. Here, where we behold the noble rivers, and the rich fields, and the healthful skies, that may be called American; here, amid the institutions that now surround us, we first beheld the light of the impartial sun. We have not been brought up under the influence of other strange, aristocratic, and uncongenial political relations. In this respect, we profess to be American and republican. With the nature, features, and operations of our government, we have been familiarized from youth; and its democratic character is accordant with the flow of feelings, and the current of our thoughts.

The third and final action of the convention was to draw up a petition to the legislature for a revision of the constitution to enable all citizens to vote without regard to color.[136] That petition was circulated to committees around the state and eventually returned to the state legislature in Albany.

In November, Black residents of New York City were advised that there would be a meeting at the Philomathean Hall to follow up on the Albany meeting, and there would be a petition to the legislature for them to sign. The petition noted that the original constitution of the state had made no distinction of color but allowed all citizens equally who paid taxes and "hired a tenement worth forty shillings a year . . . to vote for members of Assembly and town officers." The new constitution, on the other hand, which was established after slavery was abolished, established color as a qualification of voting and thereby established an "odious disparity between the two castes." The petition "most respectfully and humbly" asked that measures be taken "so to amend the Constitution, as that color may no longer be one of the qualifications of voters."

On December 24 (Christmas Eve was a less demanding occasion in those days!) a large meeting was held in Buffalo and resolutions were passed endorsing the actions taken in Albany and noting: "Our fathers fought, bled and died for the Liberties of this country that we might enjoy equal rights with all citizens." The petition was submitted, and many others as well from around the state, and a legislative committee held hearings during the winter. Those who went to the hearings came away encouraged. They felt they had been listened to sympathetically. No doubt, it was encouraging to find that they were listened to at all.

One other convention of abolitionists was held in New York State that year. On August 5, a gathering in Syracuse nominated Gerrit Smith for governor of the state on a Liberty Party ticket. The Liberty Party had come into existence only the year before to provide abolitionists a voice in the world of electoral politics. Neither of the two major parties, the Whigs or the Democrats, was willing to take a stand against slavery since it would cost them any chance to win electoral votes in the South. A national gathering in 1839 had nominated James G. Birney, a former slave owner from Kentucky, for president on a Liberty Party ticket. Now Gerrit Smith would head a state ticket in New York. The party gained fewer than seven thousand votes nationally in 1840, but it can be seen as the very small first step toward the victory twenty years later of Abraham Lincoln and the new Republican Party. Four years later, in 1844, the Liberty Party would attract 62,000 votes and eight years later it would merge with other factions to form the Free Soil Party and draw almost 300,000 ballots. That party in turn merged with others to form the Republican Party in 1854, fight a national campaign in 1856, and win the White House four years after that. The New York State Convention of Colored Voters in 1840 would seem to have been simply one more element in a rising tide of sentiment that began with the National Negro Convention in 1830 and found an additional voice in the American Anti-Slavery Society and such newspapers as *The Liberator*, *The Colored American*, and *Frederick Douglass' Paper*. But for the present, *The Colored American* summed it up well in saying: "Abolitionists in this State, who have become sick at heart of the two political parties . . . have now before them a ticket for which they can vote in good conscience, without scattering their votes to the winds, or disenfranchising themselves by staying at home." Of course, they would need to own property to cast those votes.

A Medical Study
After the summer meetings leading to the Albany convention, Smith was free for a short while at last to concentrate on his medical practice. On September 3 he began making notes on an unusual case in which he and another doctor, John Watson, attempted unsuccessfully to deal with an array of problems that ultimately led to the death of the patient. Smith headed his report: "Case of Ptyalism. Fatal Termination." Ptyalism is the production of excess saliva and is common during pregnancy, especially early in pregnancy. Usually, it is not a serious problem and doctors will recommend such simple remedies as sucking on hard candies or munching on crackers or eating small meals frequently. The case Smith and Watson dealt with seems to have been more complex. The patient, a young woman who had been married for nine years and had one child, had not only a badly swollen tongue but also recurrent severe pain in the ileocecal region between the large and small intestine. The patient thought that the swelling of her tongue was a result of calomel pills given to her by a doctor she had consulted before turning to Smith and Watson.

Calomel is a mercury compound once commonly used in medicine. It does kill bacteria (though the existence of bacteria was still unknown), but it can also do irreversible damage to the patient. It was given to George Washington in his final hours; it was also given sometimes to babies who were teething. It can cause gastrointestinal distress, so a modern doctor writes that the woman's problems may have been "iatrogenic"—which is a doctor's way of saying that the trouble may have been caused by the doctor or by the medical treatment. Watson reported that the patient's breath had an odor of mercury, but the obvious problem was a swollen tongue and they thought they could deal with that. Smith blistered the nape of her neck and applied leeches to the salivary glands. This did reduce the swelling of her lips and helped her to swallow. He also gave her another powder containing mercury. When Watson was called in for further consultation, he made deep cuts in the upper surface of the tongue which caused the patient to bleed for several hours—but did reduce the swelling.

Smith's notes for October 9, the final day of the patient's life, are as follows: "Scarification: bled freely for an hour yesterday. Tongue reduced one half since yesterday . . . does not interfere with deglutition [swallowing] which she readily performed. P. is exceedingly weak . . . [s]ome delirium during the night. Stimulants. Patient died at 10 P.M." Smith, however, was not satisfied with the outcome and wrote a report for the New York Medical and Surgical Society. He had applied for membership in the society, but was asked to withdraw his application since the organization was newly formed and his membership "might interfere with the 'harmony' of the young institution." Under the circumstances, it was John Watson who read the report to the society, but Smith's handwritten four-page report is evidence of his willingness to learn from an unsuccessful case.[137]

Death of Peter Williams

Nine days after the death of the unnamed patient, a routine event in a doctor's life, Smith was shocked by the sudden death of Peter Williams, his pastor and the nearest person to a father that he had ever known. Williams had not only guided him and tutored him but also provided the funding to enable him to travel to Scotland and spend five years abroad while gaining the education and credentials he needed to fulfill the ambitions that would otherwise have been far beyond his reach.

Peter Williams was a father figure in the larger community as well. He was only fifty-four years old but he had been a prominent leader among Black New Yorkers for over thirty years. He had been the only pastor the congregation at St. Philip's Church had ever known, and he had not only made it a large and influential congregation but laid the foundation for continued growth and greater influence. Philip Bell, who had led Smith to St. Philip's when they were children and who also had known no other pastor, wrote:

> Mr. Williams was not only devoted to the interests of the Church over which he was placed as Rector, but he had deeply at heart the interests of our whole people. Had he not been devoted to their interests, naturally inclined as he was to retirement, he would not have been found associated, as we find him, with so many operations for the improvement and welfare of our people.

Bell cited a sermon preached by Williams nine years earlier on the subject of colonization. "The sentiment," Bell wrote, "is cutting, but the spirit, peculiar to him is kind. In full faith in them, in spirit and letter, he subsequently lived, and unchanged in his views, he died." The paragraph Bell cited is remarkable not only for the clarity of its refutation of the colonizationist rhetoric, but for its sympathy for the fate of Native Americans and a sense of commonality with them:

> The colonies planted by white men on the shores of America, so far from benefitting the aborigines, corrupted their morals, and caused their ruin; and yet those who say we are the most vile people in the world would send us to Africa to improve the character and condition of the natives. Such arguments would not be listened to for a

moment were not the minds of the community strangely warped by prejudice.

Bell went on to cite the words with which Williams had directly refuted the colonizationist approach:

> Much has also been said by Colonizationists about improving the character and condition of the people of colour of this country by sending them to Africa. This is more inconsistent still. We are to be improved by being sent far from civilized society. This is a novel mode of improvement. What is there in the burning sun, the arid plains, and barbarous customs of Africa, that is so peculiarly favorable to our improvement? What hinders our improving here, where schools and colleges abound, where the gospel is preached at every corner, and where all the arts and sciences are verging fast to perfection? Nothing, nothing but prejudice. It requires no large expenditures, no hazardous enterprises to raise the people of colour in the United States to as highly improved a state as any class of the community. All that is necessary is that those who profess to be anxious for it should lay aside their prejudices and act towards them as they do by others.[138]

Ironically, Williams in death was given the recognition he had asked for in life and been denied. Almost exactly twenty years from the time when he had been ordained to the ministry of the Episcopal Church, Williams's body was carried into the church for burial.[139] The leading clergy of the diocese that had never recognized Williams or his parish were there for his funeral. The bishop came and the rectors of Trinity Church Wall Street and all the largest congregations. Black candidates for ordination had been kept from entering the seminary, but the seminarians were there also. The Book of Common Prayer makes no provision for a eulogy at a funeral; the liturgy is designed to praise God for the promise of resurrection life, not to honor the deceased, but Bishop Onderdonk, ordinarily a stickler for rules and tradition, eulogized Peter Williams while denying that he was doing so:

> Let me not be charged with adulation. That were to use the pulpit most unworthily. But I have often said, and would now say, in conscious sincerity and integrity of heart, that in all the wide range of my observation, I never knew a pastor whose whole soul seemed more engaged in the great work to which he had been set apart. I have seen this in the happy results of his ministry, and felt it in the many occasions on which he had taken counsel with me, in matters pertaining to his high and holy trust. But wherefore say this here? O, not to eulogize the dead; but that we, dear brethren of the clergy, may lay these things to heart, and ask if we could thus appear before our great Lord and Master, if now our summons should come.[140]

CHAPTER SIX

A Prophecy, an Appeal, and a Lesson from Haiti
1841

In January 1841, James McCune Smith had been back in New York for three and a half years.

He had established himself in a medical practice. He was playing a significant part in the life of the community. He was helping to edit a newspaper and being called on to speak on major occasions. On the other hand, his pastor, his mentor and sponsor, the man who had been there to guide and support him on his way was suddenly gone and there was no one to take his place.

Doctors are not often civic leaders, nor, in fact, are priests, but Smith as a doctor was probably freer to take that role than Williams. He had already begun to play that part, now he set out the vision that would guide him.

Smith's next lecture may have been the most remarkable document he ever produced. It was not so much a lecture as a prophecy, a statement of breathtaking scope, in which James McCune Smith defined the role of Black Americans in American society far into the future. In January of 1841 he traveled to Boston and gave a speech, which he titled "The Destiny of the People of Color." What was the future, Smith asked, of the Black population of the United States?

Reading his answer, names spring to mind—Martin Luther King Jr., of course—but many others as well: James Weldon Johnson, Richard Wright,

Langston Hughes, Booker T. Washington, Duke Ellington, Ralph Ellison, Lorraine Hansberry, Barack Obama, Louis Armstrong, Maya Angelou, George Washington Carver. The list is endless, but none of them were names known to James McCune Smith. Smith knew only a few names such as Phillis Wheatley, a poet, and Benjamin Banneker, an astronomer and scientist. He could not have known the other names, but he knew that such people would live and he prophesied, he foresaw, their existence.

Smith himself would go on to produce great literature himself, but at the age of twenty-seven he prophesied a future for Black Americans that ranged far beyond what sensible people could have imagined. The vast majority of the Black population was still enslaved, deprived of all opportunity for education and advancement. The free population was also largely deprived of the means to change their condition. One leading liberal clergyman at about the same time prophesied that the Black population of America was destined to die out "as all lesser races do."[141] Smith had a different vision. He saw a future that no one else had imagined. He saw the Black population of America contributing to the national life out of all proportion to their numbers, not because of disproportionate talent but because their natural abilities would have been increased and amplified by the trials they had endured.

"What has been is what will be," was Smith's opening gambit, "like circumstances will produce like effects." He would first search history for times and places with some resemblance to those of the United States in the nineteenth century and find guidance there for the future of America and the people of color. Three circumstances, he suggested, were central to the position of "the colored people" in America, and the conjunction of those three was unique in human history: 1) they are held in bondage, 2) the government is Republican, and 3) those held in bondage are of a different complexion. Never before had this set of conditions come together. It would be the destiny, therefore, of the people of color in America to act in a new way.

First, Smith contended, the colored people of America, unlike the Jews in Egypt, would be set free from bondage without leaving the enslaving society. The Jews had reasoned that *ubi libertas, ibi patria*—where liberty is, there is my country—so they would leave Egypt to be free. The colored people of America, Smith argued, had rejected that option. For them, *ubi patria, ibi libertas*. Living in a republic, they would find their freedom within its borders. Over a hundred years later, Martin Luther King Jr. would give an audience in Washington the same dream. Freedom, he said, would be found within this republic, indeed in the same places where they had been most oppressed: "Go back to Mississippi, go back to Alabama, go back to South Carolina, go back to Georgia, go back to Louisiana, go back to the slums and ghettos of our northern cities, knowing that somehow this situation can and will be changed."

And although they named different features of the country they inhabited, surely Smith and King had a shared vision. Smith put it this way:

> The time must come when from the Aroostock to the Gulf of Mexico, from the Atlantic to where the Pacific calmly laves the shores of Oregon, there shall go forth a blast from the trump of freedom, at which our chains shall be broken, our fetters fall, and the American people swelling beyond the links in which Pride and Prejudice have bound them shall become the free and equal participants of one government, one destiny.

King said it this way:

> Let freedom ring from the prodigious hilltops of New Hampshire.
> Let freedom ring from the mighty mountains of New York.
> Let freedom ring from the heightening Alleghenies of Pennsylvania.

> Let freedom ring from the snowcapped Rockies of Colorado.
> Let freedom ring from the curvaceous slopes of California.
>
> But not only that:
>
> Let freedom ring from Stone Mountain of Georgia.
> Let freedom ring from Lookout Mountain of Tennessee.
> Let freedom ring from every hill and molehill of Mississippi.
> From every mountainside, let freedom ring.

Try reading Smith's phrases to any random group of Americans and ask, "Who said it?" The answer will almost certainly be, "Martin Luther King Jr." One wonders whether King had been reading Smith. But perhaps Lincoln had been reading Smith as well since Smith went on to point out that the "Institution of Slavery" is based on the doctrine that might makes right. He said, "We are not in position of physical superiority: yet we must overturn the doctrine 'might makes right.'" Seventeen years later, an almost unknown railroad lawyer from Illinois named Abraham Lincoln came to the Great Hall at Cooper Union in New York to make his case for the Republican nomination in 1860 and told his audience that they must "have faith that right makes might, and in that faith, let us, to the end, dare to do our duty, as we understand it."

So Smith argued first that the colored people must remain where they were and "await liberty on the soil of their birth" and so "prove the common equality of the human family and common brotherhood of man."

Second, Smith suggested that republics in history had, unlike tyrannies, not lasted long, but this was because they had been built on slavery. Sparta, Athens, and Rome were not really democracies but "polyarchies" in which a smaller "republican" elite ruled a more numerous class of slaves who eventually rose up and destroyed the synthetic republic. America's situation, however, was different because the slaves were fewer in number than their masters and powerless to rebel. Therefore, Smith contended, the slaves in this instance "must resort to moral weapons" that will triumph over slavery and save the republic. "What will be the result? Slavery must cease and over its grave there will grow up a pure republic." This, he pointed out, is an eminently conservative approach. "We will save the form of government and convert it into a substance."

Martin Luther King Jr. had the same dream but used a different analogy. He suggested that the signers of the Declaration of Independence had signed "a promissory note to which every American was to fall heir. This note was a promise that all men, yes, Black men as well as white men, would be guaranteed the 'unalienable Rights' of 'Life, Liberty and the pursuit of Happiness.'" That promissory note, King told Americans, had come due and America must become what it was always meant to be: what Smith had called "a pure Republic" in which former slaves and former masters would work out a common destiny.

But it was Smith's final paragraphs that seem at this point the most prophetic. How, he asked, had oppressed minorities gained power in other times and places? He pointed to the Jews who had gained power by amassing such an amount of money as made them able to rule their former oppressors. He pointed to the Irish and the achievements of Daniel O'Connell who, "without a sword in his hand, wields more potent sway over Britain . . . than did Oliver Cromwell." O'Connell would die without obtaining Irish freedom, but he had gained a number of victories for an oppressed people through the use of politics.

Smith saw no way for the colored people to obtain financial or political power, but he maintained nevertheless: "It is the law . . . that an oppressed minority shall ultimately obtain a ruling influence over their oppressors." Turning to statistics as he loved to do, Smith showed that the standard of living in the Black population had increased significantly in the last decade and used mortality rates as evidence. The deaths per thousand had fallen from one in every twenty-one to one in thirty-four just in the past ten years. More comfortable circumstances, however, would make people more aware of the *privation of rights* under which we labor. This will lead us to an effort to obtain those rights, and since physical force is out of the question, the effort must be purely intellectual. . . . [W]e must reason down the prejudices that bar us from rights. We will then be in a state of transition, the passing from slavery to freedom by our inborn efforts. And this transition state has ever proved the most purely intellectual in the history of any people.

Then, in a stunning paragraph and a half, Smith came to the essence of his vision:

> For we are destined to write the literature of this republic which is still, in letters, a mere province of Great Britain. We have already, even from the depths of slavery, furnished the only music which the country has yet produced. We are also destined to write the poetry of the nation; for as real poetry gushes forth from minds imbued with a lofty perception of the truth, so our faculties, enlarged in the intellectual struggle for liberty, will necessarily become fired with glimpses at the glorious and the true and will weave their inspiration into song.
>
> We are destined to produce the oratory of this republic; for since true oratory can only spring from honest efforts in behalf of the RIGHT, such will of necessity arise amid our struggle—no holiday speeches in which shall be uttered eloquent falsehoods, garnished untruths and hollow boasting of a state of things which exist only in the imagination, but on the contrary we shall utter the earnest pleadings of downtrodden humanity seeking security from wrongs too long inflicted, no longer to be endured. In fine,

we are destined to spread over our common country the holy influence of principles, the glorious light of truth.[142]

John Stauffer, who has edited and published much of Smith's writing, says of this speech that Smith, in effect, "envisioned a Zion in America, where blacks, 'raised up by God,' could create a new city upon a hill."[143] Perhaps we could go even further and say that Smith was suggesting that only when Black Americans were able to participate freely in the building of that city, could it become for all its inhabitants the shining beacon the founders had envisioned.

How few shared that vision might have been measured in the national election that same year. In spite of Smith's plea for unity, Garrison held to his doctrine of nonparticipation in the political process, and many of his followers did likewise. The result was that the national election of 1840 produced only 6,797 votes for the Liberty Party or 0.3 percent of the total. They did twice as well in New York State where Gerrit Smith earned 2,662 votes as the Liberty Party candidate for governor or 0.6 percent of the total. It was not, however, an impressive showing and could be seen as justification for William Lloyd Garrison's stand against voting at all.

Haiti and America

In January of 1841, the Philomathean Society published a schedule of thirteen lectures to be given, one each week, with an admission charge of "12 ½ cents." The subjects ranged from "The responsibility of Man to the development of his Intellectual Faculties" to "Music—Its practical influence on Society." Ninth on the list was a lecture to be given by James McCune Smith on "The Circulation of the Blood."

But Smith did not limit his lecturing to the Philomathean Society's schedule. The lecture in January on the destiny of the people of color was not part of that plan nor was a lecture Smith gave in February on Haiti. That lecture was published and offered for sale as it dealt with an issue of immediate importance not only to Black Americans but to white Americans as well. Slaveholders in the South trembled at the mention of Haiti, and the members of the Colonization Society were also concerned. If free Black Americans migrated to Haiti, as many were tempted to do and some did, what did it mean for the Colonization Society's work in Africa?

Haiti is a small country, slightly larger than Maryland, occupying only the western third of an island ninety miles southeast of Cuba and some seven hundred miles southeast of Miami. It is the poorest nation in the western hemisphere—one of the poorest in the whole world—and usually gets American attention only when it has a disastrous earthquake or a revolution. In the first half of the nineteenth century, it was revolution that put Haiti much on the minds of many Americans. For Black Americans it was a symbol of hope: Black slaves had rebelled against their masters and established a seemingly stable democratic government. Some Black Americans promoted it as a viable alternative to the Colonization Society's African emigration schemes. Africa was an unknown and distant continent, but Haiti was not that far away. Some Black Americans moved to Haiti and, though some returned in disappointment, others stayed.

But if Haiti was a symbol of hope to Black Americans, it was a threatening sword of Damocles hanging over white slave owners in the American South. The Haitian Revolution, playing out over the span of years from 1791 to 1804, sent waves of emigrants, both Black and white, fleeing the chaos of Haiti to find sanctuary in Baltimore, Norfolk, Charleston, New Orleans, New York, and other American port cities. These refugees brought with them tales of uncontrolled violence committed by slaves against their owners. Southern slave owners needed little imagination to transfer such scenes to their own region. When slave rebellions took place in the southern states, as they did sporadically in the first half of the nineteenth century, slave owners saw them against the background of Haiti—and trembled. Gabriel's Conspiracy that threatened Richmond, Virginia, in 1800 was inspired in part by events in Haiti.

A Prophecy, an Appeal, and a Lesson from Haiti 1841

The result of this double image of Haiti was that its government remained unrecognized by the United States until after the beginning of the Civil War. With administrations in Washington heavily influenced if not dominated by the slave states, the notion of a free Black nation nearby was unacceptable and not to be recognized. That made it, on the other hand, one more cause to be pressed by abolitionists and their allies. *The Colored American*, for example, editorialized in 1839 that

> our commerce with Hayti ... suffers ... for the want of an accredited American consul, whom we will not send—and why? Because
> "We find our fellows guilty of a skin
> Not colored like our own"
> We have recognized Texas, and the present government of France, and the South American republics and Mexico; but we refuse to recognize Hayti, because our negro breeders are unwilling that we should do so.[144]

That horrific events had taken place in Haiti is beyond doubt. A history of that country first published in 1971 is titled *Written in Blood* and includes the following account of actions of Toussaint Louverture, who was the leader of the rebellious Black slaves:

> Toussaint entered Les Cayes in triumph on 1 August. As bells pealed and gun salutes resounded, he went directly to the cathedral. There, after his customary Te Deum, he mounted the pulpit and with sacerdotal mien pronounced a sermon of forgiveness and proclaimed general amnesty. Then, designating Dessalines governor of the South, Toussaint returned first to Leogane, where, on his orders, 300 prisoners of war were shot and

bayoneted. Leaving their bodies unburied in the August sun, he proceeded to Port-au-Prince. Here he promoted Dessalines to *general de division* and Christophe to brigadier, and ordered the execution of 50 captured Rigaudin officers. The site where they met their death is known to this day as Croix-des-Martyrs. At St. Marc, 600 more rebels awaited Toussaint's vengeance; it took three days to kill them off in batches on the blood-drenched sandy beach. At Gonaives, 72 prisoners were shot, and 8 of their leaders blown from gun muzzles. As for the conquered South, Dessalines—in Lacroix's words, "one of the most ferocious beings ever born"—had Toussaint's mandate to purge it of Rigaudins. Surrounded by a corps of executioners and torturers, Dessalines complied. Burying victims alive; impaling them, upright, on bayonets (his own specialty, which came simply to be known as "La Baionnette"); sawing them between planks; or shooting or cutting the throats of the more fortunate; Dessalines is said to have slaughtered anywhere from 5,000 to 10,000—predominantly *gens de couleur*—persons over twelve years of age. When it was over and the South pacified, Toussaint reproached his bloodthirsty lieutenant with characteristic mildness: "I told him to prune the tree, not uproot it."[145]

In 1836, the short-lived *Quarterly Anti-Slavery Magazine* featured an article by the editor on "The Horrors of St. Domingo" that recognized the violence but effectively demonstrated that some of the worst violence took place not at the hands of the Black slaves, but in the initial conflict between the white governing class and the *petit blancs* who rebelled against the increasing restrictions placed on them by the white upper class.

Against this background, Smith set out to explore the history of the Haitian Revolution and its implications for both white and Black Americans. It is remarkable that he cited the article in the *Quarterly Anti-Slavery Magazine* only once and did so simply to show that the productiveness of the island had been restored under Toussaint's leadership. Much more often he quoted the unfriendly account in Jonathan Brown's *The History and Present Condition of St. Domingo*. But Smith used his sources primarily for statistics and quotations and worked them into his own analysis of Haiti's revolution.

As Smith told the story of Haiti, a focus on race would distort the picture. Not race but caste was what divided Haitians, and there were four distinct castes: the white planters, the *petit blancs* who were also white but not part of the aristocracy, the "people of color" who were the result of sexual relationships between the white planters and their slaves, and the slaves who were Black, indeed two-thirds of them born in Africa.[146]

That there was terror, Smith did not deny, but he argued that the worst bloodshed began in the war between the *petit blancs* and the plantation owners while the free colored people and Black slaves remained at peace. Not until two years after the revolution had begun did the Black slaves also rebel, and Smith made no attempt to deny that dreadful events took place also in that phase of the revolution, but what Smith wanted his audience to understand was that the very real "horrors of St. Domingo" did not result from Black rule, as many Americans believed, but as a consequence of centuries of white oppression. The "horrors" took place in the waves of revolution, not when the war was finally over and a peaceful Black government installed. Those killed by Toussaint or his agents, as in the description above, were not white, but divisive elements within the Black armies. Smith told his audience to remember "that this insurrection was the legitimate fruit of slavery, against which it was a spontaneous rebellion. It was not therefore the fruit of emancipation, but the consequence of withholding from men their liberty."[147]

What was distinctive about Smith's account of the Haitian revolution was the clear structure he provided. He acknowledged at the outset that the events in Haiti had produced "feelings of horror and detestation," but where others had provided graphic accounts of the violence and bloodshed, Smith set out first to analyze the causes of the violence that he traced to its "particular domestic institutions," the geography of the island, and the influence of the French Revolution. He then went on to provide his own account of the revolution itself and of Toussaint Louverture, the central figure in the revolution.

The "particular domestic institutions" that Smith described as "caste" have been often looked at simply as race. Smith wanted people to understand that it was much more complicated. The island of Santo Domingo was the first land discovered by Christopher Columbus in the western hemisphere and, in the three centuries before the revolution, it had developed, Smith pointed out, a distinctive caste system with four separate classes distinguished by law. The white slave owners, vastly outnumbered by the Black slaves, were at the top of this structure and the slaves at the bottom. In between were the *petit blancs*, whites who were shopkeepers and the like, and the free people of color. In 1789, official reports listed 31,000 whites, 28,000 free people of color, and some 465,000 slaves. Since owners were taxed on the basis of slaves they owned, the last number is probably low.[148]

The free people of color, who would have been classified as "Black" in the United States, were not enslaved but were increasingly restricted by law. They were forbidden, for example, to practice medicine or to be employed as clerks or to travel to France where they might get an education. It was not they, however, but the *petits blancs* who ignited the revolution. Learning that the revolution in France had produced a declaration of "the rights of man," but that the French National Assembly had established a system of government for Haiti based on the wealthy planters, the lower caste of white residents rebelled and took up arms against the plantation owners.

Smith traced the course of what he called "three revolutions": one that established equality among the white population, a second that established the emancipation of the slaves, and a third that freed Haiti from France. But the situation was even more complicated because it was the *petit blancs* who first demanded equality, then the free colored people who insisted on their rights, and finally the slaves who rose in rebellion in their turn.

All this Smith dealt with in the limited space of a single lecture before speaking more briefly about the former slave, Toussaint Louverture, who was depicted in some accounts as a ruthless tyrant and in others as a generous and forgiving leader. Smith looked at Toussaint rather differently and saw him first of all as a human being caught up in events he did not initiate. He described Toussaint first in more personal terms:

> [B]orn forty-seven years before the commencement of the revolt, he had reached the prime of manhood, a slave, with a soul uncontaminated by the degradation which surrounded him. Living in a state of society where worse than polygamy was actually urged we find him at this period faithful to one wife—the wife of his youth—and the father of an interesting family. Linked with such tender ties, and enlightened with some degree of education, which his indulgent master, M. Bayou, had given him, he fulfilled, up to the moment of revolt, the duties of a Christian man in slavery.[149]

Smith went on to tell how Toussaint enabled his master to escape from the island when war broke out and how he sent support to him in his exile.

All sides seem agreed that Toussaint was able to keep his troops under an iron discipline and stabilize the population so that plantations came back into production. Smith wrote of the "bright and happy state of things which the genius of Toussaint had almost created out of elements the most discordant" but noted that it was "of short duration." What Smith barely mentioned is the way Haiti had become a pawn in the European conflicts of the Napoleonic era, nor did he say much about the last French attempt to recapture the island and the terms under which they withdrew, terms which left Haiti with an enormous, crippling debt from which the hapless state has never recovered.

What he did do was to end his lecture with the suggestion that the United States was threatened not with a slave uprising but with the beginnings of a caste system since it provided public funds for the education of white children, but not for those of color. Since the lecture was given to raise funds for the Colored Orphan Asylum, Smith cited that institution as an example of what ought to be done to avoid the evils of a caste system and the dangers of insurrection. The fact that the lecture was published and offered for sale three months later and reprinted two years after that would indicate that there was a continuing interest in the subject.

It is, perhaps. not surprising that when the lecture on Haiti was offered for sale in June, it was in the context of a short essay in *The Colored American*, presumably by the editor, Smith's friend Philip Bell, since it speaks of "our distinguished and learned friend, Dt. [sic] James McCune Smith."

"The immolations and martyrdoms on the plains of St. Domingo," Bell wrote, are linked with Thermopylae and Bunker Hill as "evidence that as a race we cannot be crushed." He continued:

> The love of country, we believe, is a deep and lasting love. . . . We have cause always to love our country, but especially when that country is a great and growing one. It matters not what may have been its usage to us, we still find there are times when we feel as if we would yield up even life itself to have our names placed upon the list of its benefactors.[150]

That deeply felt patriotism was something the Colonization Society and its supporters would never understand about their opposition. Black Americans would take pride in the accomplishments of the Haitians who were also descendants of African slaves, but for most of them, Haiti was not their country; they were Americans and they wanted white Americans to understand that they, too, were patriots.

Report on the Franchise Petitions

One way of expressing that love of country was, of course, by voting for representatives in Albany and Washington, and it was a continuing frustration to Black citizens that they were restricted in doing that. They had met in convention in the summer of 1840 to organize and create a grassroots movement to petition the legislature for change. The result was a torrent of petitions arriving in Albany from citizens throughout the state. Day after day, the petitions arrived and were referred to the Committee on the Judiciary. Some leaders in the petition movement went to Albany themselves to speak to legislators. James G. Birney, the Liberal Party's candidate for president in 1840, went to Albany in support of the petitions and wrote to James McCune Smith urging him to come also. Smith responded that in view of his opposition to the convention that organized the petitions, he could not come.[151] Other petitioners, however, presumably including Birney, did go to Albany and reported themselves "encouraged" by their reception.

They had every reason to feel that way. In March, the New York State Assembly Committee on the Judiciary issued its response to the petitions that had been presented. The Committee Report, dated March 10, 1841, was, in effect, a complete endorsement of the petitions and ended with a resolution to be considered by the House at its next session. The resolution provided a proposed amendment to the Constitution of the State of New York to read:

> Every male citizen, of the age of twenty-one years, who shall have been an inhabitant of this State one year next preceding any election, and for the last six months a resident of the county where he may offer his vote, shall be entitled to vote in the town or ward where he actually resides, and not elsewhere, for all officers that now are or hereafter may be elected by the people.

The report itself, in less than four pages, recited the history of the New York State Constitution, which originally had made no distinction of color but had required all voters to be property owners on the theory that such ownership "provided some evidence of his capacity to exercise the elective franchise." The colored population, "dragged by force to this continent and made subject to a degrading servitude," had had little opportunity to improve their minds and "we may well be surprised that they have not sunk altogether into a state of hopeless and irretrievable ignorance and crime." It has been the "obligation" of the citizens of the state, the report continued, to remedy that situation and enough has been done to justify admitting them to an equal citizenship. "Every observing man perceives that the colored people of our State . . . have afforded a sufficient degree of intelligence . . . to justify the extension to them of the unrestricted right of suffrage." As for the property qualification, the report noted that ownership of property "is often the result of accident, fraud or crime!"

No wonder those who had worked so hard to assemble and present the petitions had felt "encouraged." The committee ordered "ten times the usual number" of copies of their report to be printed so that every legislator and staff member would be able to study their analysis. But when the legislative session came to an end, nothing had happened. Twice, once on April 16 and once on April 17, "Mr. Culver moved . . . that the preliminary steps be taken so to amend the Constitution as to provide for the extension of

A Prophecy, an Appeal, and a Lesson from Haiti 1841

the right to suffrage of colored persons" and "Mr. Speaker put the question . . . and it was determined in the negative."

The vote on April 17 was 29 affirmative and 46 negative. But it was a first try and however discouraging the result, there was enough support among the legislators to make it seem worthwhile to continue the effort. There would be another convention that summer and more petitions would be submitted. The petition drive would continue for many years, but the constitution of the state would remain unchanged until after the Civil War.[152]

CHAPTER SEVEN

Amistad, *Maryland,* and Albany 1841

The **Amistad** *Case*

On March 9, 1841, the Supreme Court handed down a final decision on the case of the *Amistad* captives: they were free to return to Africa. The federal government, however, under a southern president—John Tyler of Virginia—felt no obligation to expedite their return. The same committee that had provided support for the captives through their long legal fight therefore set out to raise money to charter a ship to take them home. The captives themselves were central to that effort. Taking some of them from place to place around New England, the committee called on the captives to exhibit their knowledge of English, sing hymns in English and songs in their own language, and allow curious Americans to see real Africans close up and contribute to the cost of their return home.

In May, this traveling road show came to New York and "a numerously attended meeting" at the Zion African Methodist Church. James McCune Smith was called on to offer a series of resolutions. These resolved that the meeting had witnessed the liberation of the Mende people "from heathenism, and from a Christian slavery worse than heathenism itself," that their "resistance against the captain and crew of the *Amistad* was a "natural resistance against tyrannical oppression ... [which] the example of the American Revolution has sanctioned as both right and lawful ... [and] that we have reason to bless Providence which cast upon our shores these self-liberated captives." Other clauses expressed appreciation for the work of the support committee and the evidence provided by the sympathy for them of the "common humanity" of the "natives of Africa, and of these United States." Smith, it was reported, "sustained" the resolutions "with a few remarks in his usually clear and forcible manner." Philip Bell also introduced a series of resolutions and supported them "with one of his wonted graphic speeches," and Theodore Wright, the pastor of the Shiloh Presbyterian Church, moved still more resolutions "with his usual flow of eloquence."

After all that, the former captives took the stage and did what people had come to see: they sang American hymns and African songs and read passages from the Bible. After that, the meeting dispersed, "having been richly entertained."[153] It would still be six months before the Mendes were finally able to set sail from New York for Africa.

Maryland and Colonization

Hardly had the Mendes moved on when Black New Yorkers felt a need to express their views on a very different issue. The State of Maryland had found itself troubled by an excess population of free colored people and had taken legislative action to remove them. Almost half the Black population of Maryland was free by this time and 60,000 free Black people seemed to be a threat to the 410,000 white citizens. The legislature had been working for some time to solve the problem with the help of the American Colonization Society. This was not a new problem in 1841; the State of Maryland had been worrying about it for some ten years and passing resolutions in the legislature to encourage free Black residents to move out of the state by limiting their freedom there. After Nat Turner's Rebellion in 1831, the state set a deadline for Black residents to leave the state after gaining their freedom, unless a court of law found them to be of such "extraordinary good conduct and character" that they might be permitted to remain. Any person who was manumitted by a slaveholder had to be reported to the authorities, and county clerks who did not do so could be fined.[154] The

Maryland State Colonization Society was established to encourage free Black residents to leave, and a Republic of Maryland, later incorporated into Liberia, was created in Africa to provide them with a destination.[155]

In 1832, the legislature placed new restrictions on the liberty of free Blacks in order to encourage emigration. They were not permitted to vote, serve on juries, or hold public office. Unemployed free people of color without visible means of support could be re-enslaved at the discretion of local sheriffs and funds were appropriated to support colonization, but never nearly enough for the stated objective.[156] Not everyone was on board with this action, however, and some Marylanders worried about who would do the work if so many free citizens were removed.

In early June of 1841, the Maryland Colonization Society resolved to try harder and passed a series of resolutions clarifying their views on the subject. "Resolved," they agreed, "that the idea that the colored people will ever attain social and political equality in this state is wild and mischievous." That being stated, they expressed hope "that the free colored population of Maryland may see that their best and most permanent interests will be consulted by their emigration from this state" and if they "persist in remaining in Maryland ... They ought to be solemnly warned ... that a day must arrive, when circumstances that cannot be controlled, and which are now maturing, will deprive them of freedom of choice, and leave them no alternative but removal."[157] With that undefined threat looming over the Black people of Maryland, the American Colonization Society decided to use the occasion for a special fundraising effort on July 4th to help those who wished to relocate.

That initiative got the attention of Black residents of other states who took notice and expressed their opinion with meetings and resolutions. In New York City, a committee headed by James McCune Smith called a meeting for June 21 to "gather, and set our brand on this persecution, and send our sympathy to the Marylanders." As a result, "a very large and respectable meeting of colored citizens" assembled in Asbury Church to express their outrage and pass resolutions. A number of speakers came forward before James McCune Smith, "who had been repeatedly called for by the audience," came forward to present resolutions "which he supported with his usual ability."

In particular, Smith told the audience about an incident that had happened only that morning. A girl who had been brought to New York from the South attempted to take advantage of the repeal of the New York State law that had allowed a slave to be kept in the state for up to nine months. As *The Colored American* reported Smith's story:

> [T]he human blood hounds were soon on the track, and in opposition to the late enactment, arrested the poor fugitive. But she was in safe hands; a band of heroic, noble-hearted women wrested her from the grasp of the minions of the law, and again put her on the path of freedom; but the foe was still panting for his victim, and the Doctor was startled by the shrill cry of a female voice, which sounded loud and deep above the din and confusion of the mob: "Kill her! Kill her! KILL HER! Sooner than she shall be again taken back to slavery."

The story, of course, had nothing directly to do with the issue at hand, but it was recent, local, dramatic, and it horrified all those present. What had finally happened to the fugitive girl was not reported but, "[t]he effect [of the story] was electrifying. The audience heartily responded to the sentiment, and one unanimous burst of applause followed. The lateness of the hour obliged the Doctor to curtail his speech." Philip Bell seconded Smith's resolutions which were, perhaps, the most practical of the nine sets that were presented and passed. Smith's resolutions pointed out that the empty treasury of the State of Maryland made the transportation of so many people to Africa a practical impossibility and that the alternative plan of sending them to Canada would succeed only in creating a hostile force in Canada that would endanger American peace. The meeting adjourned at midnight.[158]

Smith was quite right in suggesting that the State of Maryland could not accomplish its goals on the budget available. It could deprive Black people of their rights and it could make the state an uncomfortable place for them to be, but it was unwilling to provide adequate funding for any alternative. Weighing the uncertainties of moving to New York or Canada or Africa, against the known hazards of life in Maryland, most free Black people would settle for the familiar—however uncomfortable. Some Maryland slaves, of course, famously took matters into their own hands. Frederick Douglass and James W. C. Pennington are two of the better-known examples of people who decided not to wait for the legislature, but found ways to escape from Maryland on their own. Harriet Tubman is more famous now than ever for her role as a conductor on the branch of the Underground Railroad that ran north from Maryland. Resolutions passed by the Black residents of New York, on the other hand, would make no real difference to Marylanders Black or white—but they did make a difference to New Yorkers who were just beginning to learn to express themselves and act together in common cause.

The Franchise—Again

That ability to act together was also evident when, two days before the meeting to protest events in Maryland, the first notice was published of the plan for still another meeting to besiege the New York State Legislature with petitions for an unrestricted right to vote. Black New Yorkers had gone through an elaborate effort to gain the franchise during the previous year and had gained the support of the appropriate committee but without result. Under the circumstances, they might well have decided to join Garrison in not even attempting to vote. What they did, however, was very different. Inspired, perhaps, by the efforts of the Liberty Party to battle on against monumental odds and feeling that if the committee was on their side, the legislature soon would be also, they returned to the battle in 1841 with a campaign that rallied Black residents in every part of the state and culminated in a three-day-long state convention in Troy, New York, just seven miles from the state capital in Albany.

In 1840, James McCune Smith had been reluctant to be part of an appeal based on color, but in 1841 his name was near the top of a long list of over fifty sponsors. "Much was accomplished," the call to convention stated, but "our anticipations were not realized." Nevertheless, the committee felt that "the attention of the Assembly was so far turned to the burden of our prayers, as to be disposed to give us a favorable report.... We have been rejected but not spurned." Veterans of political battles might have told the committee that politicians are skilled at providing encouragement even where they have no intention of acting. But the committee members were hopeful:

> Come, brethren, arouse yourselves! Come, in the name of bleeding humanity, come! ... Come from every part of the State; we are in the midst of the last hours of oppressions' battle—with firm steps and strong hearts, establishing our confidence in God. Once more to the breach—with the banner of truth before us—justice and the world on our side—the day must and will be ours.

It has often been said that the legislative process is comparable to making sausage: it's better to look at the end product than the messy steps required to get there. Fortunately, James McCune Smith cared enough about the hoped-for result to be willing to do the tedious work required to reach the goal. Mostly, that required meetings and resolutions. First off, a public meeting was held in New York City and Smith, as usual, played a major part. To provide a focus for the meeting, a resolution was introduced stating that those present at the meeting "do highly approve of the call for a State Convention." They wouldn't have been there if they didn't approve, but it had to be on the record. J. J. Zuille, a New York City printer, introduced the resolution which was then seconded with a supporting speech by James McCune Smith. A second resolution called for a follow-up meeting a week later on Monday, August 9, and a third resolution called for a committee of three to nominate delegates to the convention and report to the next meeting. Zuille, Smith, and a third man, Newport Henry, were appointed to that committee.[159] The follow-up meeting was actually held on August 10 and the nominating committee reported that they recommended a list of "not less than 28" persons to send as delegates to the Troy convention. The names were voted on separately and approved.[160]

The state convention was duly convened on August 25 in the First Presbyterian Church in Troy and called to order by the pastor Henry Highland Garnet. Garnet called on Theodore Wright of the Shiloh Presbyterian Church in New York for an opening prayer and William Rich of Troy was appointed chairman pro tem. A committee appointed to nominate officers of the convention reported immediately that they proposed Austin Stewart of Rochester for president. Stewart was duly elected and proceeded to exhort those present to "speak in such loud and clear tones that your voice will be favorably heard in the Legislature next winter." Such action, he said, was necessary not only for their own benefit, but for "our countrymen, whose sighs and moans come up from the dark prison of slavery." They had come not only to act until they had "freed themselves from partial bondage, but also till every chain shall be stricken off from the poor bondmen of the South."

It was an important point: white Americans—North and South alike—were accustomed to thinking of Black people as slaves. Even in the North, slavery had only recently been ended, but as long as most Black people continued in slavery, all Black people would be affected. It was only one of a multitude of ways in which racial discrimination made a negative impact on society as a whole and which the convention would explore over the course of three days in discussing one resolution after another and searching for ways to express both their hope for a society that would move beyond racial division and their frustration with a society that failed to share their concern.

It is interesting to notice that Henry Garnet, whose congregation was hosting the convention, introduced a resolution calling on people to "agitate, agitate, agitate." Two years later, at a National Convention of Colored Citizens in Buffalo, Garnet tested the patience of many convention members in a speech calling on slaves to "[l]et your motto be RESISTANCE! RESISTANCE! RESISTANCE! No oppressed people have ever secured their liberty without resistance. What kind of resistance you had better make, you must decide by the circumstances that surround you."[161] The parallel use of a triple repetition suggests that Garnet inspired the resolutions in Troy. In Buffalo, the delegates refused to print Garnet's words in the convention report, and he had to print it himself several years later. But clearly, the colored citizens of New York were becoming impatient and Garnet was not alone in favoring strong language. Another resolution introduced that afternoon said, "We consider it criminal in the sight of God and man, longer silently to submit to our indignities, or suffer them to be transmitted to posterity." Here again, there was an implied threat of violence, but no action on that motion is recorded.

The convention moved on from resolutions expressing its opinion to resolutions creating a statewide organization to garner supporting resolutions in every community in the state. Committees were appointed to lead that effort in thirteen upstate counties between Albany and Buffalo. Finally, on Friday afternoon, the convention approved the publication of one letter, "To the Electors of the State of New York," and a second letter, "To the Colored Citizens of the State of New York."

Oddly, in view of the effort he made in promoting the convention, James McCune Smith seems to have been absent. His name appears only in a list of men appointed to the County Committee for New York.

Perhaps there was a medical emergency, or perhaps he simply felt he could not be away from his patients that long. It seems unlikely that he sat through a three-day meeting without speaking. When a meeting was convened in New York City on September 15 to hear a report on the convention, Smith was there. Charles L. Reason reported on the event and read the two letters the convention issued. Smith was one of two who spoke in response. That meeting then called for a "Great District Meeting" to be held on the second Monday of October, and Smith moved that delegates be appointed to that meeting and found himself so appointed.[162] If that meeting was held, there is no record of it, but *The Colored American* reported on a "New York County Convention" that included seven evenings between October 18th and 27th. Those meetings involved 136 delegates at one meeting or another, but the recorded votes on various evenings ranged from twenty-four to thirty-four. James McCune Smith was not an officer of this convention, but he took an active part in the discussion in each of the seven sessions.[163]

The purpose of this convention was, of course, to obtain additional signatures for the petition to be presented to the state legislature, so it seems likely that it was postponed to November 9 when a meeting was held and a resolution was introduced saying in essence that exercising the right of petition demonstrated a love of liberty. That resolution was adopted, but a second resolution created a prolonged debate. Thomas Van Rensselaer, who had been active in the meeting in Troy, introduced a resolution stating that the right to vote is "a right guaranteed to all men by the Supreme Ruler of the Universe." J. J. Zuile, who had also been a delegate to Troy, argued that there was "diversity of opinion" in the state concerning the belief stated and suggested inserting "the Constitution of the State" in place of "the Supreme Ruler of the Universe." Charles L. Reason was uncomfortable with either wording, and James McCune Smith "replied critically" to Reason—whatever that may mean. The motion was then taken, and the original wording was adopted by a majority.[164]

The End of the Year

By the end of 1841, James McCune Smith had been back in the United States for less than four years but in that time, he had established a medical practice, given public lectures on a wide variety of subjects, helped edit a weekly newspaper, and taken a leading role in the political concerns of Black Americans. In late November, he had taken an active part in a "mass meeting" on the subject of the elective franchise. He was, however, only human. In December 1841, *The Colored American* reported that "our learned friend, Dr. James McCune Smith, now lies very low with "inflammation of the lungs."[165] That diagnosis would cover a wide range of ailments from asthma to cancer but when his illness became disabling twenty years later, the diagnosis was "pleurisy" which is an inflammation of the tissue surrounding the lungs. What happened next is unknown because *The Colored American*—with its close attention to the doings of James McCune Smith and his friends—ceased publication at the end of the year. A newspaper needs subscribers and advertisers, but there were too few of either to keep the paper afloat. Smith, with one less major demand on his time—perhaps because of it—survived, but illness would be a recurrent factor in his life.

CHAPTER EIGHT

A Varied Life
1842–1845

Smith and the Legislature

It took some months, of course, for the legislature to respond to the petitions that had come from around the state on the subject of the right to vote, but on the evening of April 2, 1842, five days after Easter, there was a gathering in the legislative chambers in Albany to hear a presentation on the subject by Dr. James McCune Smith. Smith spent the better part of an hour laying out the logic of his position. The legislature had justified its action by suggesting that the tax would encourage colored New Yorkers to work hard so as to meet the property qualification.

Smith showed how illogical that was: "It crushes his industry, and tells him to be industrious—it depreciates his labor, and calls upon him to be laborious—it sends him forth with political and legal inferiority branded upon his forehead, and bids him to elevate himself to the rank of citizenship!" So, too, Smith told the legislators, in words strangely similar to those used to describe American life almost two centuries later, they could not complain that Black people were degraded:

> If the laws of the State have degraded her colored citizens, it is reasonable to expect that they will be found degraded; partly because they are shut out from the free and full exercise of the faculties, and partly because they

may be oppressed with impunity. Your constables, if in search of a culprit, will think twice before they arrest a white man, because they know he has a vote: but they will at once arrest a colored man who even looks suspicious. Thence every colored man who has committed a misdemeanor, is almost sure to be caught, whilst the white man escapes, in many instances.

It was Smith at his best and his audience responded well. Resolutions were offered and "unanimously adopted." They included a statement that the property qualification "is anti-republican, and unjust, and should be blotted from our Constitution." Smith was also asked to furnish a copy of his remarks for publication in the local papers.

Unfortunately, those who had gathered that evening to hear Smith speak were not the people whose votes counted. In fact, the "Committee on privileges and elections, for an amendment of the Constitution, extending the elective franchise to the colored population" had apparently already met and drawn up a very different report. That report, which must have surprised and shocked Smith and his friends, was the exact opposite of the response of the previous year and seems to have been formulated before Smith had even been heard. Titled "Report of the Committee," it is dated "March 29," which was the Tuesday in Easter week and three days before the gathering that had listened to Smith. It must be noticed that this report came from a different committee than the report issued in the previous year, and the members of this committee had a very different, indeed opposite, point of view.

The report of the Committee on Privileges and Elections noted that the first constitution of the state required all citizens to have "a freehold of two hundred and fifty dollars to vote for Senator or Governor," but the number of "free negroes" was so small that it would not have been "a subject for consideration." But with the ending of slavery in the state, "vast hordes of negro voters were brought within the qualifications intended . . . for the white population. The framers of the new Constitution therefore had provided against this unforeseen evil by the adoption of the present freehold qualification." The report goes on to argue that

> [i]f there be not sufficient intelligence, and industry, and self-respect in that class, to induce even a small portion of them to attain the property qualification required, your committee cannot believe there would be more intelligence, more industry, more self-respect, and more improvement by wholly removing a restriction imposed as a motive to ambition, as well as a check to licentiousness. . . . Let the negro show himself worthy of honor and respect and both will instinctively be given; but until that unfortunate class do thus elevate themselves, while the means, the way, and the invitation, are all so freely presented, let not unrestricted political equality be claimed.

The committee imagined that a few thousand Black voters, "an ignorant and degraded portion of the community," voting as a block, might "control the whole result" and adopt "measures, principles, and policy deeply affecting the happiness and prosperity of the two millions of whites." The committee's vivid imagination even led them to fear that "a few hundred negroes of the city of New York, following in the train of those who ride in carriages, and whose boots and shoes they had so often blacked, shall go to the polls and change the political condition of the whole state." Therefore, they judged it "impolitic and inexpedient to grant the prayer of the petitioners."[166]

Making Friends: Frederick Douglass and William Seward—1842
If the action of the New York State Legislature was discouraging, Smith had little time to think about it. After a short trip to Philadelphia to sup-

port anti-slavery efforts there, he was present a few weeks later for the annual meeting of the American Anti-Slavery Society in New York. For the time being, at least, Smith was staying with the Garrisonian side of the division that had taken place a year earlier. In the middle of the meeting, Smith moved a rather dramatic resolution, a proposal to appropriate $2,000 to take a test case to the Supreme Court. That might translate to at least $60,000 in twenty-first-century money and maybe much more. It was a significant expenditure, but to take a test case to the Supreme Court has never been cheap.

Smith's proposal was to test "whether the citizens of each State shall be allowed the privileges and immunities of citizens in the several States." Apparently, Smith imagined that the Supreme Court might rule that if a Black citizen could vote in Massachusetts, then a Black citizen should be allowed to vote in New York. If upheld by the Supreme Court, it would be a neat way around the New York State Legislature. The Massachusetts legislature then would be legislating not simply for citizens of Massachusetts but for all Americans. It would, of course, be a drastic alteration of the federal system on which the Constitution is based.[1*] The meeting had already spent time debating a resolution to alter the Constitution "so as to prevent the national government from sustaining slavery" and another resolution to dissolve the Union on the grounds that free and slave institutions cannot exist under the same Constitution, so Smith's resolution was very much in line with the concerns of the convention. One way or another, the delegates were thinking in terms of the fundamental shape of the nation. It was clear to them, as it would eventually become clear to Abraham Lincoln, that "this government cannot endure, permanently half slave and half free."

It was far from clear to them, however, what should be done to resolve the issue. What happened to the other resolutions is not recorded, but it is recorded that Smith's resolution "after some discussion . . . was laid on the

---

1* *One wonders whether Smith had stopped to think of the consequences if Alabama, by the same logic, could make laws that would apply to the Black citizens of New York.*

table." More interesting than the debate, perhaps, is the fact that among the individuals named as having taken part in it is "Frederick Douglas." Douglass, who was not yet well enough known to have his name spelled correctly, had first spoken to a public meeting only a year earlier. It would be interesting to know whether Douglass supported or opposed Smith's motion at what was probably their first meeting. They would see much more of each other in coming years and become close friends.[167]

A very different relationship—never a friendship—is reflected in a letter sent by James McCune Smith to New York Governor William H. Seward in late December of 1842 "in behalf of the colored citizens of the city and county of New York." Smith had made himself one of the leading spokesmen for the New York Black community, so when Seward's second two-year term as governor was coming to an end, Smith wrote the governor a letter, cosigned by Ulysses B. Vidal and Timothy Seaman. Vidal and Seaman, like Smith, were young men who had been working together to expand the freedom and influence of the Black community. They wrote to Seward in what can only be seen as an attempt to create a useful relationship for the future. Seward was just forty-one years old, and he would obviously be a potential candidate for political office again. Smith and his colleagues wrote to express the "high admiration with which your conduct over the last four years has inspired them." Seward had managed, the letter said, "to separate the principles from the prejudices of political partisanship, and to carry out the former with the firmness and decision of one whom no political elevation could raise above responsibility to his conscience and his God."[168]

In four years in office, Seward had made a difference. He had called for and signed legislation to guarantee fugitive slaves a trial by jury and to repeal the "nine-month law" that allowed slave owners to bring their slaves into New York for up to nine months. With that act, slaves brought into New York became free immediately. Seward had not been able to persuade the legislature to change the suffrage rules since that would have required a constitutional amendment, and the legislature was unwilling to go that far.

Seward did, however, sign two other bills which affected the status of Blacks in the Empire State. An 1840 law empowered the governor "to appoint and employ" agents to negotiate the rescue of free Blacks kidnapped and sold as slaves. In the late antebellum period, New York governors would expend state funds under this law to help free Blacks who had been kidnapped and taken to the South to escape from illegal bondage and return to their home state. Finally, and probably most important of all in long-term impact, a law of 1841 guaranteed public education for all children, regardless of their race.

Seward was both an idealist and a practical politician who knew how far he could go toward translating ideals into reality. Born into a household served by slaves, Seward recalled how he and his siblings had taught the slaves to read. There is some evidence that his home was a station on the Underground Railroad.[169] He was an instinctive supporter of equal rights for Black citizens but also a practical politician who announced himself opposed to Black suffrage when he first ran for governor in 1838. Once elected, however, Seward's instinctive support for Black rights reemerged and by 1846, when he was no longer governor, he was saying that the Black man should have all the privileges of the white. He would give the ballot, he said, "to every man, learned or unlearned, bond or free."[170] The letter from Black New Yorkers expressing appreciation for the modest steps he had taken as governor was intended to encourage him to do more in the future. The letter ended with the hope that "the day is not far distant when your excellency will obey the voice of your fellow-citizens, again calling upon you to occupy your present, or to enter upon a more exalted station in the gift of the people."[171]

It would be five years before Seward was elected to the United States Senate in 1849. He was reelected in 1855, joined the new Republican Party, and became the front-runner for the party's nomination for president in 1860. By that time, his well-known opposition to slavery was one factor that kept him from being nominated because the Republican Party was striving to be as inclusive as possible and, like the older parties, to avoid alienating voters needlessly. When Abraham Lincoln was nominated instead and elected, Seward agreed to join his cabinet where he became a strong voice for the anti-slavery cause. Carefully noting his "sacrifice of some personal advantage," Steward responded briefly but warmly to the letter from Smith and his colleagues.

Equal Education

One of the issues Seward had grappled with—successfully on the whole—was the public education system. Education in America in the early nineteenth century was still a hit-or-miss proposition. In the more settled communities of New England and the Middle Atlantic states, grade schools through eighth grade were often available but frequently charged fees. Wealthier families, especially in the South, hired tutors for their children. When the Manumission Society founded a school for Black children in New York City at the end of the eighteenth century, it was a remarkable step forward. Gradually, a public school system for all children came into being in New York City in the 1830s and a Public School Society, working with both private and public funds, became responsible for most of the city schools. Governor Seward extended the state system of public schools to include New York City, and that system eventually replaced the Public School Society.

The best way to deal with differences of faith and language and race in a publicly supported school system remained unsettled—and still is. Seward at one point favored schools in which children would be taught by teachers of their own faith in their own language. What he insisted on was that all schools be provided with equal funding for all students. Surprisingly, in view of his reluctance to support a "complexional convention," James McCune Smith weighed in with a letter at the end of 1842 in which he laid it down as a rule that "to have manly colored scholars we must have manly and accomplished colored teachers. . . . There is no doubt." He added that "colored teachers succeed better than white ones in spite of the balance of power and monied influence which white trustees fling into the scale of the latter."[172] That viewpoint is still strongly argued by some in the twenty-first century, but it seems out of keeping with Smith's stand on related issues.

Seward's primary concern was to use the influence and power of the state toward equal opportunity for all. By bringing the city schools into the state system, Seward took an important step toward a system in which equality of opportunity would be the primary consideration and white trustees would be less able to put their thumbs on the scales. Historian Jabez Hammond told Seward it was one of "the best and most meritorious acts of your life."[173]

Medical Cases

In spite of his heavy schedule of lectures and his involvement in political activity, Smith was continuing his medical practice. In fact, he was going beyond routine medical care to write up his observations, and this time to have his analysis published in a leading medical journal without the aid of a white intermediary. In February 1844, the recently established *New York Journal of Medicine* published "On the Influence of Opium upon the Catamenial Functions. By James McCune Smith, M.D. of New York." It has been called "the first medical scientific paper published by a black physician in America."[174]

Smith began his report by citing a general opinion: "[I]t is said," that the use of opium does not affect "the reproductive organs of women." He then cited five specific cases he had dealt with over the last six or seven months as well as his "extensive experience in the Lock Hospital at Glasgow" as evidence to the contrary. Case by case he reported on a variety of patients, describing, but not naming, five specific individuals in five rather different situations and the impact on them of varying doses of opium. Four of the five individuals were "courtezans" as were those he had dealt with in Glasgow.[175] Smith reported that, contrary to common opinion, "this unfortunate class have no peculiar liability to *suppressio mensium.*" He put forward his experiences not to argue an opinion but "in the hope that they may attract the attention of medical men to whatever facts may be within their reach."

He wondered what might be the experience of married women and whether the use of opium "in skillfully regulated doses, may not be used as a means to bear women safely through the critical disturbances which may occur at the 'change of life.'" He noticed also that opium seems to inhibit "periodicity" in other areas of life. Hunger, for example, "in the present state of civilized society is a *periodic habit*" that is arrested by the use of opium. Footnotes made reference to a number of authorities ancient and modern. Clear, carefully reasoned, imaginative, it is exactly the sort of reporting that can be helpful to other doctors, expand medical understanding, and improve medical practice.[176]

A Public Debate

Looking as always for a way to speak to the larger community, Smith took note of a lecture given one night in early February 1844 by Orville Dewey, the well-known pastor of a Unitarian Church in New York City, and reported in the morning edition of the *New-York Daily Tribune*. Dewey was a "gradual abolitionist" who had repeated the frequent claim of slave owners that slaves in the South were better off than free Black people in the North, who were "not so well clothed, fed, or so happy."[177] When Dewey declined Smith's offer to debate the subject, Smith wrote again to the *Tribune* to offer evidence that slaves in the South were not, in fact, happier than free Blacks in the North. "There is not," he pointed out, "the case of a single free black, who has gone down South and offered himself a candidate for the enjoyment of slavery. There is no impediment in his way. He has merely to go as far South as Baltimore, walk about the streets, and hold his tongue; the law will do the rest, and he will become a slave. No one has gone." On the contrary, Smith pointed out, a thousand slaves a year were escaping to the North, but it is "a well-known fact that men, whatever the color of their skin, will not in their thousands run away from a good living."[178]

Smith depicted himself as a former admirer of Dewey's, saddened by his willingness to lend the "character of his influence, his character, and his sacred calling, to the support of what I believed to be the cause of injustice, impurity and oppression. I could have wept, I was going to say? I *did* weep as I read that part of your address . . . which relates to American slavery." Dewey represented to Smith the most dangerous opponent of the abolitionist: "a professed minister of the Gospel of Jesus—a man who comes before the people crowned with academic honors . . . whose fame is abroad in the land, and of whose name honorable mention is every where made."

Smith went on at more length about Dewey's reputation and honor and then turned to ask whether Dewey's approval from his audience "was followed by the approbation of your own breast. Did the approbation which followed your performance at the Tabernacle, find an echo in your own spirit, when you had retired to the loneliness and silence of your closet? I think you will find on reflection," Smith told Dewey, "that you have not only been false to the principles which should guide the moral teacher . . . But justly made yourself liable to a charge of slander against . . . our free colored population."

Smith's letter went on for more than two of the paper's long columns. And why this lengthy response? Smith stated his reason clearly: "Orville Dewey at the Broadway Tabernacle is a more dangerous foe to the rights of our enslaved countrymen, then that dignified Senator from the South who declared that hanging would be the doom of any abolitionist, who should be caught within the bounds of the State he represented."[179]

Having opened the subject of comparative conditions North and South, Smith found himself in one of his favorite fields: statistics. A topic that has the capacity to put a good many people to sleep could stimulate Smith's investigating and calculating skills and produce the sort of specific information needed, but usually lacking, in the long-raging debate over slavery. The best-known speakers and writers in that debate—William Lloyd Garrison is the most obvious example—were commonly dismissed by their opponents as fanatics. Smith was determined to avoid that label.

Writing once again to the *New-York Daily Tribune*, Smith began his report by noting: "Figures cannot be charged with fanaticism. Like the everlasting hills, they give cold, silent evidence, unmoved by the clouds and shadows of whatever present may surround them. Let us see what they say." Smith then proceeded to analyze the 1840 census figures, making allowance for slaves in the middle years of life who had escaped to the North or to Canada or who had been removed to Texas and for free Blacks who had "turned white at the North."[180] Omitting the mind-numbing statistics Smith delighted in, the evidence indicated that life expectancy for Black people was significantly shorter in the South than in the North. If the two populations had survived at the same rate, there would have been nearly 180,000 more slaves than, in fact, there were. That number of human beings, then, should be seen as "MURDERED by the system of slavery."

"What mockery is it," Smith exclaimed, "for men to talk of the kindness of the masters in taking care of aged slaves, when death has relieved them of so large a share of the burden!"[181] Smith also produced a much longer and more detailed study titled "The Influence of Climate on Longevity," which was cited by Edward Jarvis, a Massachusetts abolitionist who was awarded the Boylston Prize by Harvard University in 1845. In accepting the award, Jarvis presented a copy of Smith's dissertation to the Boylston Medical Committee.[182]

In a follow-up letter to the *Tribune*, Smith took issue with the suggestion made by the Episcopal bishop of Vermont, among others, that a slave is free to the extent that "he has command over his thoughts." Let those who "wish to gain currency for his brilliant dogma," wrote Smith, "seek some distant rice or cotton plantation, do a hard day's work of compulsory labor, receive thirty-nine lashes well laid on, and then repeat the sentence, 'the slave thinks, therefore' &c and I will believe him to be in earnest."[183]

In April of 1844, still another of Smith's reports to the *New-York Daily Tribune* provided statistics from a report of the trustees of the public schools in New York State. Black and white children were generally in separate schools, so Smith could conveniently compare them and break down the numbers for reading, punctuation, spelling, arithmetic, astronomy, and more. Black children showed slightly higher scores in punctuation and grammar and slate writing, but lagged in the other seven categories including reading, spelling, and geography. Overall, the white children had scored 2.32 on a scale of one to a hundred, while Black children had scored 2.47. Considering that the Black schools had all been established within the last forty years, Smith thought it was a significant achievement and a foreshadowing, perhaps, of greater achievements still to come. "If it be true," he concluded sardonically, "that we have not yet produced any literature worthy the name, it is because we are waiting for the Anglo-Americans to lead the way."[184] Herman Melville at that point had not yet written *Moby Dick* and Smith, of course, had not yet read it. When it appeared in 1851, however, Smith was one of the few Americans who did read and value what is now acknowledged as a pioneering classic. Perhaps it was a first example of what he was "waiting for."

Smith vs. Calhoun and the Census

The skirmish with Dewey over statistics proved to be the prelude to a larger battle in which statistics again were a critical part of Smith's armory. Complicated negotiations were going on involving the United States, Britain, Mexico, and the newborn Republic of Texas. The central issue was whether Texas should be added to the United States with the resulting extension of territory in which slavery would be legal and also a possible war with Mexico. John Tyler, who had become the first accidental president of the United States when William Henry Harrison died after only a few weeks in office,[185] hoped to strengthen his case for nomination to a second term by annexing Texas and calling on John C. Calhoun of South

A Varied Life 1842–1845

Carolina to serve as his secretary of state in the necessary negotiations. Inexplicably, Calhoun took the occasion to write a letter to the British ambassador, Richard Pakenham, defending the institution of slavery in terms that seemed calculated to provoke the anti-slavery forces in the country. Having said that each state was free to decide for itself whether slavery should or should not be allowed, Calhoun then went on, quite unnecessarily, to argue that slavery was in the best interests of the colored people. In states without slavery, wrote Calhoun,

> the condition of the African, instead of being improved, has become worse. They have been invariably sunk into vice and pauperism, accompanied by the bodily and mental inflictions incident thereto—deafness, blindness, insanity, and idiocy—to a degree without example; while, in all other States which have retained the ancient relation between them, they have improved greatly in every respect—in number, comfort, intelligence, and morals.[186]

That would have been enough to excite abolitionists everywhere, but Calhoun went on to provide statistics and to cite particular states as examples:

> Taking the two extremes of North and South—in the State of Maine, the number of negroes returned as deaf and dumb, blind, insane, and idiots, by the census of 1840, is one out of every twelve; and in Florida, by the same returns, is one out of every eleven hundred and five; or ninety-two to one in favor of the slaves of Florida, as compared with the free blacks of Maine.
> In addition, it deserves to be remarked, that in Massachusetts, where the change in the ancient relation of the two races was first made, (now more than sixty

years since,) where the greatest zeal has been exhibited in their behalf, and where their number is comparatively few, (but little more than 5,000 in a population of upwards of 730,000) the condition of the African is amongst the most wretched. By the latest authentic accounts, there was one out of every twenty-one of the black population in jails or houses of correction; and one out of every thirteen was either deaf and dumb, blind, idiot, insane, or in prison. On the other hand, the census and other authentic sources of information establish the fact, that the condition of the African race throughout all the States, where the ancient relation between the two has been retained, enjoys a degree of health and comfort which may well compare with that of the laboring population of any country in Christendom; and it may be added, that in no other condition, or in any other age or country, has the negro race ever attained so high an elevation in morals, intelligence, or civilization.[187]

James McCune Smith and his colleagues could hardly leave such assertions unchallenged. A "mass meeting of the people of color in the city of New York" packed the Philomathean Hall on Monday, April 29, "to consider the calumnies ... uttered ... by John C. Calhoun, Secretary of State, in a letter to the Hon. Richard Pakenham." Smith read extracts from Calhoun's correspondence and various speakers denounced "Calhoun's slanders."

The report on the meeting that appeared in *The Liberator* is signed "Cosmopolite," a pen name used by Philip Bell, and one of the earliest examples of a pattern of pen name use in abolitionist newspapers that would become very common in the next few years.[188] Cosmopolite reported that the most able speaker of the evening was a fugitive slave from Alabama named "Mr. Wright." Wright told the meeting that he had seen slavery "in all its perfection of infamy" and that "if slaves could assemble and send forth their sentiments of the accursed system, there would be a voice that would startle the very echoes." Wright, said Bell/Cosmopolite, "was the star of the evening." After that, the meeting agreed "by acclamation" to appoint a committee of nine to draw up a statement and report back on Friday, May 3. Smith's name was first on the list of those to bring back a report.[189]

When prayers had been said four days later and the minutes of the previous meeting adopted, it was Smith who came forward to present the committee's report. If Calhoun wanted to use statistics, Smith had statistics also, and Smith's statistics raised serious questions about the numbers cited by Calhoun. The census of 1840, on which Calhoun relied, provided numbers, Smith reported, that were "self-contradictory." Smith had already noticed these errors in a letter to the *Tribune* in January 1844.[190] The census reported, for example, that there were 346 Black residents who were insane, blind, deaf, idiots, paupers, and so on in communities in which, according to the same census, there were no Black residents at all.[191] More specifically still, Smith's committee noted that, contrary to Calhoun's claim that one in every six free Black persons was incompetent in one way or another, the statistics for New York and Philadelphia showed about one colored pauper out of every one hundred of population and fewer than one in a thousand to be insane. These figures were roughly the same as those for the white population. As for longevity, Smith's committee had figures that showed only 15.49 percent of those in slavery living past the age of thirty-six while 22.68 percent of free colored individuals reached that age. Comparing intelligence and morals, the committee noted that forty thousand free colored children were in school and that there was one church for every 543 Black individuals in the North, whereas there was no report of Black children in school in the South and only one church for every 2,161 residents, Black and white together.

The committee had three recommendations: 1) that the census figures be reexamined and corrected, 2) that an office be established in Washington to collect information about "the sanitary conditions of each class of inhabitants," and 3) that the Congress undertake a census in 1850 of adults who cannot read and write among the whites, the slaves, and the free people of color in every county of the United States. A memorial summing up these recommendations was adopted unanimously and the meeting was then "eloquently addressed" by H. H. Garnet, Charles B. Ray, Theodore Wright, Julius Morel, and Charles L. Reason. Four more resolutions were then adopted to ensure that the memorial would be signed and sent to the Senate, that all presses throughout the country and the world be requested to publish the memorial, and that "our people in every town and city throughout the United States" would be requested to hold meetings, collect statistics, and publish the facts "refuting the statements of Mr. Calhoun."[192]

Annual Meetings and Divisions

That meeting had been held on Friday, May 3. The following Tuesday, May 7, the American Anti-Slavery Society held its annual meeting and James McCune Smith was there also. The unity of spirit at the previous meeting was entirely missing in the meeting of the Anti-Slavery Society. One New York paper reported that "it was marked by violence, mutual crimination, utter disorder, and final dispersion. The notorious Garrison of Boston, Abby Kelley and two or three others were the principal actor [*sic*]."[193] That was undoubtedly a prejudiced analysis, but a New York clergyman who had given the invocation at the meeting wrote to the papers to report that although he had given the invocation at the meeting, his prayers had been ineffective and he was "unwilling, after the scenes of that day, to be suspected of giving the slightest countenance to the sentiments and spirit there developed." He had tried to heal the division between the New York and New England sections, he wrote, but now recognized that it was not possible.[194]

The American Anti-Slavery Society was celebrating its tenth anniversary and had hoped to mark the occasion with "a fresh declaration of its principles." Those principles included the statement that slavery is "the embodiment of the greatest amount of impiety toward God, and of outrage to man" and that "it convicts the American nation of being perfidious, hypocritical, oppressive and atheistic beyond all parallel or competition in the history of nations since the creation of the world" and that "no harmonious or just political union can possibly exist between freemen and tyrants."

On that basis, the statement of principles went on to deny the possibility of supporting any political party that favored continuing alliance with the slaveholding states and to call on northern voters "to cease sustaining the existing compact, by withdrawing from the polls, and calmly waiting for the time when a righteous government shall supersede the institutions of tyranny." How a righteous government would come into being without the participation of righteous people was not explained.

The society's own summary of the meeting notes that "Wm. A. White," James McCune Smith, and two others opposed the proposed declaration. The debate consumed the rest of the morning and afternoon sessions and was left unresolved. On Friday morning, a resolution was introduced censuring former president John Quincy Adams for reasons not stated. Adams, then serving as a member of Congress, had waged a campaign in Congress to receive petitions for emancipation and had become an increasingly vocal opponent of slavery, but, since he opposed dissolution of the Union, he had become a target of the Anti-Slavery Society. James McCune Smith offered an amendment to the resolution commending Adams for his "noble stand" in support of the right of petition, but that was laid on the table. A member offered a resolution denouncing the Christian church for its hypocrisy and calling on members to withdraw from their churches and "hold her up before the people as hypocritical in profession, infamous in practice ... and one of the greatest obstacles in the way of immediate emancipation." It seems likely that Smith was no longer there since the resolution was passed "without discussion."

Resolutions denouncing the idea of withdrawing from political action were ordered to be placed in the minutes and one condemning the Liberty Party as "an enemy to the slave's cause" was passed. The slate of officers headed by William Lloyd Garrison was approved and the meeting adjourned. When the society held its 1845 annual meeting in New York, Smith was not present. Like the majority of the Black leadership, Smith saw no point either in abstaining from the political process or in dissolving the Union and leaving the northern states with no voice at all in the struggle against slavery in the South. But Garrison and his allies were intent on dissolving the Union, though without taking any active role in the political process.[195]

That, of course, created an impassable gulf between Garrison's Anti-Slavery Society and Smith and his colleagues in New York who were still determined to do everything possible to gain the right to participate in the political process. Ironically, concentration on that goal became a divisive factor within the colored leadership in the state of New York. A fourth annual National Convention of Colored Citizens of the State of New York was held in Rochester in 1843 for the purpose of rallying the Black citizens behind yet another appeal to the state legislature. The records of that convention have disappeared, but when the fifth annual convention came together in Schenectady in early September of 1844, it almost immediately divided over a protest lodged by delegates from New York City. Henry Garnet was the presiding officer of the Schenectady convention, but James McCune Smith, who played a major part in the organization of the convention, moved to create a finance committee and a business committee and proposed a set of rules for the convention's business, all of which was done.

Smith then proposed two resolutions defining the purpose of the convention. The first stated that extending the franchise would be "an act worthy of the people of this great state...because it would be an alliance of *just action* with *patriotic profession.*" The second resolution, however, created difficulties by saying that the franchise should be extended "inasmuch as we have never forfeited it by an opposition to *law*, and have always been and are now willing to bear the burdens of the state." That was opposed by a delegate who told the convention that he was *not* willing to "bear the burdens of the state," if the state withheld the franchise. Smith proposed to add the words "as an equivalent to enjoying equally its privileges," but that was opposed by several delegates as implying a bargain for a right they had never forfeited. That debate used up the rest of the morning session.

When the afternoon session convened, Smith's amendment was adopted but the whole matter was then postponed indefinitely. That was the point at which real trouble broke out. Smith, as chair of the Business Committee, presented a protest from citizens of New York City against the actions of the previous year's convention, and Smith "gave a plain history of the protest" with "an appeal in its favor." What had happened the previous year in Rochester was that the convention had passed a resolution condemning both the Whig and Democratic Parties and stating that "in going to the polls to vote, we will in no case whatever vote with the pro-slavery parties of the land . . . since that would be, in our judgment, giving our suffrages against ourselves."

But the New York delegates held that a convention called to appeal for the right to vote had no business calling on Black citizens to vote for one particular party. They also pointed out that it was "injudicious" to put themselves in the position of "asking from two political parties the power to enable them to overthrow those parties."[196] A New York meeting afterward had called on their delegates to protest what had happened. "An exciting debate" on the subject consumed the remainder of the afternoon session and most of the evening session before it came to a vote. Some held that the fifth convention had no right to amend the actions of the fourth convention while others disagreed with the notion that a convention called for one purpose could not deal with other issues. The motion to record the protest was finally defeated by a vote of 38 to 11. At that point, two members of the New York delegation who were chairing convention committees resigned as members of the convention in protest and so did Smith.

The remaining members of the convention went on to other matters such as continuing to organize petitions for the vote on the local level. The convention also adopted a report "On the Best Means for the promotion of the Enfranchisement of our people," which seemed oddly to adopt the viewpoint of those in the legislature who argued that the right to vote should be earned. "There are some particular pursuits," they said, "which would tend more than others to remove the prejudice which a majority of our fellow citizens cherish toward us." The report listed four specifics: 1) "A general diffusion of Literary, Scientific, and Religious knowledge among the people" by establishing libraries and schools and lectures," 2) "careful education of our youth, and holding out to them additional encouragement, in proportion to the extra difficulties they may encounter," and 3) "by giving our children useful trades, and by patronizing those who may have engaged in useful handicrafts."

Those three proposals were briefly stated, but the fourth proposal went on for at least a dozen paragraphs and suggested a massive strategy for relocating the Black population to rural areas where they could become more self-sufficient and respected by their neighbors in a way not possible in cities. In the country, they said, "every man is known, and even our people who are abused so much in cities are respected almost according to their moral worth.... In conclusion, the committee would advise families and individuals to leave the large cities and repair to the country and by observing the other recommendations in the report, they will use the best and most certain means to promote our happiness and enfranchisement."[197]

This, of course, was almost exactly the plan of action that the legislative committee had suggested a year and a half earlier in turning down the request for the franchise. "Prove you're good enough to vote," they had said, "and we will think about it." Smith and his colleagues had indignantly rejected the idea that a vote has to be earned and so had the convention—until they themselves urged the colored people of New York State to do exactly that. It also strangely foreshadowed a proposal made less than a year later by Gerrit Smith that would have strong support from James McCune Smith. Was Gerrit Smith reading a report of the convention when the idea came to him for what would come to be known as "Timbucto"?

The whole matter came up one more time when the New York delegates reported back to their New York City constituents and found Henry Garnet there. Garnet, who had been the presiding officer of the convention, said he had "come all the way from Troy, one hundred and seventy miles," because he heard "that his character was to be traduced." When Smith demanded to know his authority for saying that he was to be traduced, Garnet refused to give his authority but pointed to the report which had just been read as proof of the fact. Dr. Smith pointed out that the contents of that report were not known till that day to anyone except Mr. Vidal and himself.

A reporter from the *National Anti-Slavery Standard* recorded the ensuing discussion, which brought one further piece of information to light. Apparently, the Rochester meeting had instructed Garnet, as presiding officer, and others to "wait on the Governor and request him to make favorable mention of the extension of the franchise to the people of color, in his annual message," but when the Central Committee waited on Governor Bouck, the governor asked the committee to bring him the minutes of the meeting. This Garnet had been unwilling to do because, of course, those very minutes denounced the party to which Governor Bouck belonged. One of the delegates who had gone with Garnet to meet the governor reported that Garnet, in leaving the meeting, had said, "Pooh! there is no use in going back to that old fellow, he has seen the minutes of the Rochester Convention!!!" So the failure of the Rochester convention to stick to its mandate had prevented Garnet from carrying out its mandate. No wonder the New York City delegates were annoyed.

The reporter concluded, "It was nearly midnight when I left. Mr. Garnet was then speaking, not on the merits of the question, but was making a Liberty Party harangue, and endeavoring to show it to be the duty of all colored men to vote with that party." Many years later, James McCune

Smith recorded his lasting impression of the evening. He was writing an introduction to the historic speech made by Henry Highland Garnet before the Congress of the United States in February 1865. No Black speaker had stood on the dais of the House of Representatives before and Smith, looking back and recalling speeches Garnet had made on other occasions, had only good things to say about his old friend and sometime adversary and the speech he had given on that contentious night long ago:

> In an instant Garnet was up. His tall form seemed to dilate as with uplifted arm and flashing eye he exclaimed, "The eagle screams of liberty, why may not I?" Then followed a masterly argument, interspersed with so much wit, ridicule and sarcasm, and winding up with an appeal to the audience which carried them away with shouts and cheers.
>
> The vote was taken and the protesters, dreadfully voted down, could not get the hang of things, the why and the wherefore for some time afterwards. Mr. Garnet has, on several occasions since then, invited one or more of these gentlemen to try conclusions with them on the platform, but they have not seen their way clear to accept. For one of them, we may add, we speak "by authority."[198]

It's a remarkable tribute to a man with whom Smith had often "tried conclusions." They were two very different men, united sometimes and at fierce odds sometimes, in a common cause.

The *National Anti-Slavery Standard* noticed in reporting the actions of the Schenectady convention that in the vote against recording the protest of Smith and his colleagues, thirty-three of the thirty-eight negative votes represented delegates from Schenectady and Troy with a colored population of less than one thousand, while the eleven "aye" votes represented the twenty thousand Black residents of New York City. That number is probably an exaggeration; a contemporary source puts the Black population of the city in 1845 at thirteen thousand, but the point is still valid. More important, only ninety-one of those thirteen thousand were entitled to vote in state elections. It was that thirteen thousand that Smith and his colleagues represented and whose interests they felt had been betrayed by Garnet and the upstate delegates.[199]

Parties and Publications

Whether to vote and how to vote was an issue that divided the free Black population (and the white population, for that matter) in a number of ways. There were those who wanted to vote for the Liberty Party as a means to end slavery, and there were those who thought it would be more practical to support one of the two major parties. There were those who thought the first objective needed to be opening the polls to all without a property restriction, and there were those who agreed with William Lloyd Garrison that it would be better to abstain from politics entirely. There were also some, particularly in the Liberty Party, who argued that the Constitution was an anti-slavery document so that slavery could be abolished within the terms of the Constitution, and there were those like Garrison and his followers who thought it could not.

Abolitionists in general and the Liberty Party in particular put much stock in the power of Congress to abolish slavery in the District of Columbia. Smith and Pennington saw nothing much to be gained by that even if it could be done—which they doubted. Ten square miles of free soil was a drop in the bucket compared with what remained. Nor would abolishing an interstate trade in slaves make a significant difference. Slavery would remain in place and ways would be found to buy and sell across state lines just as the abolishing of the international slave trade had made little difference in that trade. Equally useless, Smith and Pennington argued, was the priority of the Liberty Party on ending the interstate trade in slaves. Slaves could still be sold within states and family members divided by great distances, and still there would be those who would find ways to sell slaves across any borders "for whilst there is a market, the slave trade will exist, as is proven by the history of that trade, or more truly, piracy." The Liberty Party, they argued, had become simply one more self-seeking band of politicians: "We doubt the sincerity of men who make this bleeding hearts of suffering slaves," Pennington and Smith concluded their essay, "and the sympathies which those slaves excite, a means by which they shall gratify their vaulting ambition. And we speak, in this matter, the views of a very large proportion, of the free colored people of the free states."[200]

CHAPTER NINE

*Timbucto
1846 and Afterward*

Timbucto in New York

On August 1, 1846, Gerrit Smith unveiled a bold initiative designed, among other things, to enable Black citizens to fulfill that hated requirement of the New York State Constitution. He announced that he would give away 120,000 acres of land to three thousand individuals, forty acres of land to any Black male approved by trustees he appointed. James McCune Smith, Charles B. Ray, and Theodore Wright would be the principal trustees and would administer the program in the New York City area. Recipients of the grants would have to be between twenty-one and sixty years old and could not use intoxicating liquor. The land was mostly of poor quality and not worth $250 dollars for forty acres, but Gerrit Smith believed that it would have that value and more if it were cultivated. If improved, it would also, of course, have the potential to make independent citizens of men who were otherwise unable to escape from poverty.

Gerrit Smith's letter spelled out the reasoning that led to his donation and showed a sensitivity to racial issues that McCune Smith would appreciate:

> For years I have indulged the thought, that, when I sold enough land to pay my debts, I would give away the remainder to the poor. . . . I am an agrarian. I would that

every man who desires a farm, might have one. . . . To whom among the poor I shall make these deeds, is a question I did not solve hastily. . . . [F]or a long time, I was at a loss to decide, whether to take my beneficiaries from the meritorious poor generally, or from the meritorious colored poor only.

I could not put a bounty on color. I shrank from the least appearance of doing so: and if I know my heart, it was equally compassionate toward such white and black men as are equal sufferers. In the end, however, I concluded to confine my gifts to colored people . . . I had not come to it, were not the colored people the poorest of the poor, and the most deeply wronged class of our citizens. That they are so is evident, if only from the fact, that the cruel, killing, Heaven-defying prejudice of which they are the victims, has closed against them the avenues to riches and respectability—to happiness and usefulness.[201]

Smith had thought for years of giving land away, but he had also been specifically challenged to do so by George Henry Evans, a well-known labor leader, who had denounced Smith in 1844 as a "slaveholder." By holding such vast tracts of land, Evans argued, Smith was keeping factory workers from using land to gain freedom from a worse state than slavery. Smith had responded immediately that he agreed that the land should be used, but that Black Americans were the poorest of the poor and deserved opportunity first of all.[202] Smith cited also as a reason for his grant the constitutional requirement that colored voters own property in order to vote, and he spelled it out at some length in a letter the following November to McCune Smith, Ray, and Wright. The state had revised the constitution in the spring of that year but failed to remove the property clause in spite of a campaign against it led by McCune Smith and his colleagues:

[H]ow unbrotherly it was to do this wrong! Rich and poor, high and low. Black and white, we are all brothers. Alas! That instead of looking, every man in every other man as a brother—as, indeed, another self—we should be found . . . crushing each other. But do not be disheartened my afflicted, outraged fellow men.

"For a' that, and a' that,
It's comin yet for a' that,
What man to man, the warld a' o'er
Shall brothers be for a' that."[203]

They shall show themselves capable of all that industry, frugality, and self-denial which are necessary to enable them to pay the price. Since they must become landholders, that they may be entitled to vote, they will become landholders. Vote they will, cost what it will, for they have now fresh and conclusive evidence, that it is before the vote only, that the tyrants & dastards who oppose them, will quail.

"The vote, the vote, the mighty vote,
The vote's the weapon of the free."

I fancy that thousands upon thousands of my colored brethren have already been led by the late outrage on their rights, to resolve in the depths of their indignant souls, to quit their City life . . . their self-indulgent life and to betake themselves to tracts of land in our State, which are remote from settlement. . . . On these tracts of land, they will begin a new life, there they will brave the rigors of the wilderness, and make for themselves a hardy and an honorable character. . . . When I came to the conclusion to give away my land to my colored brethren, I regretted, that the greater portion of it is in parts of the State colder and less fertile than most other parts of it. But I am becoming reconciled to what, at first thought, is so great a disadvantage. The chances are ten to one that the settlers on this uninviting land will work out a far better character, than they would, were they to choose their homes on fat land & under genial suns.[204]

McCune Smith might have quibbled with Gerrit Smith's suggestion that city life for Black Americans was a "self-indulgent life," but he responded generously by telling Gerrit Smith that although he had already "borne the taint of fanaticism" he must now be prepared "to be branded as a foolish man: you are accustomed to the scorn and hate of white men; can you bear the cold ingratitude of colored men?" The generosity of Gerrit Smith's plan, McCune Smith wrote, was "incomprehensible" even to him.[205]

Most of the land being offered is in the northeastern quadrant of the Adirondack Mountains of New York state and most of it is now part of an enormous state park, bigger even than such national parks as Yellowstone. It contains stunning scenery and is an excellent area for winter sports. The Winter Olympics were held there at Lake Placid in 1932 and again in 1980. As farmland, however, the area is less than ideal. The mountains, of course, could not be farmed, but even the river valleys contain sandy soil for the most part. Peter Smith, Gerrit's father, at one time owned nearly a million acres in upstate New York and was said to be one of the largest landholders in the whole country.[206] But when Peter Smith's wife died, he lost interest in his real estate business and turned it over to his son, Gerrit. Gerrit Smith, a recent college graduate and widower himself after only seven months of marriage, found himself, still in his early twenties, in charge of an enormous real estate fortune. Managing his father's estate and adding to it himself by shrewd investments, he built up the family fortune.

Slowly he began to use his wealth in support of his social and political views. Always concerned for the disadvantaged, Smith's commitments evolved slowly from an interest in the Colonization Society to membership in the Anti-Slavery Society and then to political engagement first with the Liberty Party and then with the Radical Abolition Party. At a time when Americans of many persuasions were establishing utopian colonies in the wilderness—Thoreau's colony of one at Walden Pond, the Shakers in upstate New York, the Mormons in Illinois and Utah—Gerrit Smith imagined a colony of Black yeomen in the Adirondacks that would transform American thinking about Black people and undercut decisively the southern insistence on the inability of Blacks to be independent.

Had it been available, Gerrit Smith might usefully have studied the theory of civilizations developed by the British historian Arnold Toynbee a century later. Toynbee argued that for civilizations to be born, they must confront and overcome a challenge that provides a golden mean between an excessive challenge that will crush a civilization and too slight a challenge that would cause it to stagnate. Gerrit Smith's Adirondack challenge was, apparently, excessive; there were many Black men interested in it, but few had the skills, resources, and perseverance to survive more than a few years.[207]

Nevertheless, the project was started with high hopes and great enthusiasm. McCune Smith wrote to Gerrit Smith in December to report: "We held a fine meeting on Wednesday night and delivered 10 deeds to a fine set of men. You certainly deprive yourself of a most interesting sight, in declining to see a gathering of the grantees. Tall, stalwart, hard-fisted, they embody a Hope of the Race. We hold another meeting tonight at Brooklyn and in Monday in Westchester."[208]

The "high hopes" for the future generated by the land grant project were more than balanced, however, by the realities of daily life for a Black man in New York City. Only ten days after writing to Gerrit Smith with enthusiasm for his project, he wrote again in a radically different mood. Gerrit

Smith had asked him to write a letter to the colored men of the state, but when McCune Smith thought of it, the bleak reality of their situation overwhelmed him. Seldom has a Black American written so eloquently of the impact of that reality:

> I have not heart to write it. Each succeeding day, that terrible majority falls sadder, heavier, more crushingly on my soul. At times I am so weaned from hope, that I could lay me down and die, with the prayer, that the very memory of this existence should be blotted from my soul. There is in that majority a hate deeper than I had imagined. . . . Labouring under these views, I cannot write a cheering word & will not write a discouraging one.

Smith cites one specific reason for his mood: the necessity of swearing that he was a property owner when he went to vote. No white man had to do that, but James McCune Smith did because of his color.

> My personal influence, manhood—presence at the ballot box is utterly destroyed when the earth-owning oath is thrust at me. The negro *Man* is merged into the negro land-owner. The point of the moral is dipped into poison. It is established by the solemnity of an oath, that this vile earth has rights superior to Manhood's! That this dust of the earth is greater, without—"the breath of life!" What horrible mockery! Is it right to be a party in such blasphemy?

But that train of thought led McCune Smith to spell out for his friend the nature of the perennial challenge:

> The heart of the whites must be changed, thoroughly, entirely, permanently changed. It is well, perhaps, that a temporary political necessity did not produce the outward sign of what is not yet an inward and spirit-owned conviction—the absence of this conviction now stands bared to the gaze, and men, colored men, must go to work to produce that conviction—of the eternal equality of the Human Race—which is the first principle of Good Government—of Bible Politics. This must be done, but how?
>
> Of course, it is mind-work. Physical force has no place in it.

Smith set the letter aside for forty-eight hours before he could continue, and when he came back to it, he had put aside the eternally essential "mind-work" to report on meetings in Westchester, Ulster, and Orange Counties to deliver deeds and to note the "sad fact" that only one of the first seventeen grantees could sign his name. That, in turn, led to a long paragraph discussing the urgent need for schools for colored children and the inability of disenfranchised Black people to insist on enforcement of the law that required schools for Black children.

By the time he came to finish the letter it was New Year's Eve, a year "of crushed hope, of national shame, of ensanguined fields" but also of "two generous Deeds" that ensured that "the Colored People of this State & country" will never forget "how you remembered them in their bonds."[209]

A year later, James McCune Smith wrote of a meeting in New York of some of the settlers who had come back to the city on various missions and reported to Gerrit Smith that "a good spirit prevailed" among them. One of them, William H. Smith, told McCune Smith that it "is better to suffer two years in Franklin, than for ever in New York." He said that when he told his wife that he was going to New York tomorrow and would carry letters to some of her friends that she sat down to write but then exclaimed that she "did not know the day or the month."

"How so?" he asked.

"Oh," she replied, "because I am not forced to remember the landlord's call."[210]

In May 1848, McCune Smith was hopeful for the project and wrote to Gerrit Smith that "[t]here is still slowly but thoroughly organizing here an attack on the soil of Franklin and Essex Counties. As my health appears improved and strong I look with joy to mixing with the strong and hardy men, when they shall have completed their plans."[211]

Eventually, over three thousand titles were distributed and some of the grantees did move north. Men who had been coachmen and barbers and cooks and waiters set out to attempt to wring a living from the land, but if the land was unfriendly, so were some of the neighbors. Local people offered to guide the newcomers to their land, but sometimes showed them barren rocks, and then offered them a few dollars for their deeds. A sworn statement by a certain Elijah B. Jones testified to the local animosity. Jones himself was a supporter of the project and testified that "he would yet read the speeches of Dr. McCune Smith in Congress and live long enough to know that Gerrit Smith occupied the White House at Washington," but he also reported that "there exists in this community much opposition against him, and against the lands being settled by colored people. I have heard the white inhabitants accuse Mr. Lewis of trying to ruin the town, by getting colored people to settle in this town, that the town would be represented by a black supervisor, &c. I have heard much abusive language used towards him in this town, whilst going and returning from surveying." Local residents, Jones testified, believed that the colored people "ought to be banished to Africa, that if Smith and others would let the blacks alone that were here, they could starve them out, and the land would be settled by whites; that they would not live in a town surrounded by colored people, and if he [Lewis] surveyed the land, he would have to go armed, or he would get shot."[212]

Nonetheless, some persisted and established a small community in the town of North Elba, near Lake Placid, that became known as "Timbucto." In November 1848, Gerrit Smith wrote that some twenty or thirty grantees were "comfortably settled" on their land, but three thousand had been granted land and not taken it up.[213] Two years later, McCune Smith found there were "about sixty colored persons in all of all ages and sex" in North Elba and they had "put up several good log houses." A "Mr. Henderson of Troy, a shoe maker, had his sign hanging out" and was apparently doing good business, but a Mr. Landrine, having cleared about two acres, "was vainly striving to reach water, by well digging" when Smith was there but subsequently had given up in despair and was trying to sell his land for four dollars an acre.[214]

Some were wise enough to raise sheep on land that could not be plowed and to establish a wool trade with Canadian communities to the north.[215] In fact, one of the few surviving traces of the project seems to be the tombstone of Lyman Epps, a sheep farmer. Epps helped found the town library and a church and his family remained in the area for a hundred years.[216]

There are few other direct reports of the experience of individuals and no others so positive. The Colored Orphan Asylum records, however, provide two interesting stories. William Smith, a sailor, hoping to build a life for himself, took back the two children he had placed in the orphanage when his wife died and moved to Essex County. Smith apparently had been a farmer in Upper Canada at an earlier stage of his life, so his new beginning may have been more successful. At least the children were not returned to the orphanage. A shoemaker named James Henderson, on the other hand, went to Essex County with his wife and six children to attempt to build a better life, but froze to death in the forest in 1851. His wife then returned to the city and placed her six children in the Orphan Asylum until she was able, six years later, to support them herself.[217]

In 1849, John Brown, not yet known as a radical abolitionist, paid one dollar an acre for 240 acres adjacent to the Gerrit Smith grants and offered his experience as a farmer and surveyor to the little community.[218] But Brown moved on to Kansas, and the combination of poor land, lack of experience, and inadequate resources doomed the experiment. Land cannot be farmed without tools and seed. The ordinary farm in those days was largely self-supporting, raising the food a family needed and earning a little cash income with any surplus, but that required ownership of some chickens, a cow, a mule, and a plow without which land could not be cultivated and a family could not be fed. Many candidates undoubtedly accepted the land title and then realized that, lacking the capital to invest in the animals and tools they needed, they had no way to make use of it. How many defaulted on their land is not known, but enough so that McCune Smith and Charles Ray sent a statement to pastors of Black congregations in 1854 to be read aloud on three Sabbaths. The statement told those who had lost their land by failing to pay taxes for 1849 that they could still redeem it by sending their tax payment to the controller's office in Albany or asking for assistance from Ray or Smith themselves. "The land is growing valuable," the statement said, "on account of the Timber, and the opening of roads." Significantly, the statement did not say that the land was valuable for farming.[219]

James McCune Smith himself accepted title to land in Timbucto and journeyed north in September 1849 to see it. Writing months later to Gerrit Smith, he told him, "I felt myself a 'lord indeed' beneath the lofty spruce and maple and birch, and by the trawling brook which your deed made mine, and would gladly exchange this bustling anxious life for the repose of that majestic country." The land was beautiful, he wrote, but he could not live there himself because he could not serve as doctor to so small a community nor raise his children in a place where there was no school. As it was, however, "the country is yet too sparse to give support to a physician. Until I can make $400 per annum, I must defer settling in the country." He saw one man "miserably—if not criminally—wasting his time" with his wife and children in a clearing of four or five acres. "If we could get about 200 settlers and then cut off all communication with the city . . . things could be made to prosper." But the "critical mass" needed to create momentum and staying power was lacking.[220]

As late as 1859, McCune Smith could still write to Gerrit Smith about a new settler on land recently purchased and tell him that a recent visitor had described things "as being in a flourishing condition."[221] In 2002, however, a local historian told a writer for *The New York Times*: "It was just a small part of our history, a footnote really. The thing was over in no time. Within 20 years most of the families were gone. It just wasn't a successful enterprise."[222]

It might also be said that Gerrit Smith sometimes seemed not really to understand what it meant to be Black in America. He was able to write a letter to Charles B. Ray, Theodore Wright, and J. McCune Smith to tell of his hope that many of his "colored brethren" would be moved to "quit their City life ... their self-indulgent life" to move to the country and "make for themselves a hardy and an honorable character."[223] But two years later, he wrote to Ray:

> The free colored people of this country have lost their self-respect ... and blended themselves, in church relations, with their despisers. Even Dr. James McCune Smith of New York—a gentleman whose rare talents and accomplishments fit him for the highest stations and the most polished circles—even he was once, so far lost to self-respect, as to be found voting for men for civil office, who deny him the right to suffrage and refuse to sit in the same pew, or eat at the same table with him.
>
> "How sad," he continued,
>
> that such men as Doctor Smith and Mr. Douglass, should ever have so undervalued and degraded themselves ... I am aware, that it may be said, in excuse for these

gentlemen that, in what they did, they aimed at the deliverance and elevation of their race. But to this we reply, that even the highest good is not to be sought for, at the expence [sic] of self-respect—that even Heaven itself is not to be crawled into.

But Gerrit Smith was writing from the perspective of the Puritan who would make no compromise and adopt no halfway measures—and would be content with 1 percent of the vote so long as he had avoided any compromise with evil:

> Could I but get the ear of my Northern colored brethren ... I would say to them, "Cultivate self respect—cultivate self respect—cultivate self respect" for by that means, and not without that means, can you peaceably regain your own rights, or the rights of your race at the South. Have no fellowship, political or ecclesiastical, with those who hate or despise you. Turn your backs upon American Christianity and American politics, as upon the Devil himself—for he is their author.[224]

That was the voice of the "come-outer" and purist. But McCune Smith would surely have pointed out that a vote for Governor Seward had meant funding for schools for Black children as well as white and that participation in the politics of the Episcopal Church would win his parish a seat in convention and that slow progress was better than none. Fortunately, Gerrit Smith did not write in such a way to McCune Smith or Frederick Douglass, and they were still able to work together toward common goals. In fact, McCune Smith had written Gerrit Smith several months earlier to say that he had come to agree with his Peterboro friend that there could be no compromises with compromisers in the battle against slavery:

I believe that I am fully up to the doctrine of "No vote for the Slaveholder, nor for any who will vote for a slaveholder to occupy a civil or religious office." I am a late convert, but not the less a firm one. It is a conviction less the result of reading than of a leapt to conclusion from elements in my nature that have thrust themselves forward and I now wonder how the matter required any reasoning. It is self-evident truth containing its proof in its enunciation.

Perhaps Horace Greeley was the immediate cause of this conviction. I have watched him as I once watched Daniel Webster as someone I could look up to. But one fine day, when Black Dan spoke "beneath an October sun,"[2*] "the altar and the God fell into the dust." So when Horace Greeley in the column of his paper wrote a severe condemnation of the War for the Propagandism of Slavery and, in another advocated the claims of a slaveholder for the Presidency, down went Horace in the Dust and up in his place came the clean & hitherto unrecognized truth about voting for slaveholders or their friends.[225]

It seems ungenerous at best for Gerrit Smith, having received that letter, to have written to someone else months later of how McCune Smith had once "degraded himself" by voting for or looking up to such compromising politicians and editors as Daniel Webster and Horace Greeley. Fortunately, McCune Smith never saw his friend's letter. Fortunately also, the friendship of Gerrit Smith and James McCune Smith seems only to have been strengthened by the land grant experience. Writing to Gerrit Smith in

---

[2*] Smith is referring to a speech made by Daniel Webster in Virginia in 1840 in which he said, "[B]eneath an October sun ... that there is no power, direct or indirect, in Congress or the General Government, to interfere, in the slightest degree with the institutions of the South." *The Southern Literary Messenger*, vol. xi, (August 1845), 460.

December 1846, McCune Smith expressed the hope on behalf of himself and his wife that Gerrit Smith would allow them to entertain him and possibly his wife when next they would be in New York. The visit of a white couple to the home of a Black couple would break ground of a different sort and perhaps, in the long run, be more important.

Family Matters

That letter to Gerrit Smith is also the first surviving evidence[226] that James McCune Smith had married a woman named Malvina Barnet and that they had begun a family.[227] The 1850 census lists Malvina as twenty-five years old, so she would have been seventeen or eighteen years old in 1842 or 1843 when she married James McCune Smith and twelve years younger than he. Over the first nineteen years of her marriage, she would bear ten children and see five of them die. That was the typical experience at that time: almost half of all children born died before the age of five.

Smith's letters to Gerrit Smith from that date on almost always close with "my wife joins me in best regards to yourself & family." There are few other references to her. Once, Smith went to a convention he was reluctant to attend because his wife told him he should. Once, he stepped back from buying a book so his wife could have a new chair. Once, she encouraged him to go to a chess tournament in spite of the cost. In 1860, Malvina made a rare appearance in her own right as a "directress" along with at least eight other women at the annual fair on behalf of the Colored Orphan Asylum. She had one child born that year and a two-year-old as well as two older children, ages four and fourteen. Her last child was born in 1862, three years before her husband died.

CHAPTER TEN

St. Philip's Church 1847–1853

Background: Changing the Church

"That all men [that is to say, 'all human beings'] are created equal" is a founding principle of the American experiment, but there has always been a gap between the vision and the reality. American history is in large part the story of the struggle to narrow that gap. The struggle is waged on many fronts, and all of them are interrelated. Whether Marian Anderson could sing in Constitution Hall in Washington or Jackie Robinson could play second base for the Brooklyn Dodgers or Elizabeth Eckford could attend classes at Central High School in Little Rock, Arkansas, are among the specific issues that have contributed to the reshaping of American society and every one of them is an important part of an emerging picture.

The question of the relationship between a Black congregation and the Diocese of New York may seem relatively unimportant, but many of the leading Black and white citizens of New York City were involved in the working out of that question, and its resolution would, therefore, make a significant difference in the ongoing life of the nation's largest city and of the nation as a whole. James McCune Smith had been a member of St. Philip's Church from the time he was baptized as a child, but that church had never been given recognition as a parish of the diocese. The struggle to gain that recognition and have his church recognized as an equal member of the diocese was simply one more aspect of Smith's effort to achieve not so much a color-blind society as a society able to accept the contributions of all its members whatever their color might be.

That story had its beginning only a few years before Smith was born when the Black congregation that had been meeting at Trinity Church began meeting instead in a rented room at the African Free School No. 1 and set in motion the process to have Peter Williams ordained to be their priest. When James McCune Smith was five years old, in 1818, the congregation built its first church, and in 1826, when Smith was thirteen, Williams was ordained a priest. A congregation with a church building and a priest and the ability to pay its bills would normally be admitted to the diocese as an independent parish entitled to vote at diocesan conventions. That, however, is not what happened. Instead, the diocese did not list St. Philip's as a parish of the diocese, nor ask them to send delegates to the convention, nor—significantly—did the members and officers of St. Philip's Church themselves raise the issue for many years.

In view of the various events surrounding his return to the city of his birth and his establishment as a doctor in the community, it would not be surprising if James McCune Smith paid little attention to the fact that the annual convention of the Diocese of New York was taking place in early October of 1837. In fact, the parish leaders themselves seem not to have paid any attention to the event since they were not present. The parish was not listed in the Diocesan Journal nor was their lay leadership. The convention journal did list the pastor of St. Philip's, but it listed him simply as "Peter Williams, (a colored man), rector of St. Philip's Church, New-York, the congregation of which is composed of colored persons." The journal did not list Williams either with the clergy who were present at convention or with the clergy who were not present. Representatives of seven new congregations were recognized and admitted to membership in the convention that year, but St. Philip's was not mentioned. The Diocese of New York had not yet come to terms with the existence of a congregation of Black Episcopalians.

The bishop did, however, visit St. Philip's Church on a regular basis as he visited other parishes, and he showed concern when its building was threatened by rioters. The bishop's response to that riot, already mentioned, had been to take steps to limit Peter Williams's involvement in social action as a member of the Anti-Slavery Society. The bishop returned to that issue in his convention address of 1837. In a long statement within his convention address, the bishop spelled out very carefully his belief that church buildings should not be used for any other purpose than worship: "Her consecrated edifices are *not to be used for any other purposes than those of a holy or religious character*. They are God's houses; and by being made His, have been . . . placed beyond the right of any other disposal." In case any part of that was unclear, the bishop added an extensive footnote admitting that questions might be raised about societies

> designed for the moral reformation of the community . . . Intemperance and other immoralities are great acknowledged public sins . . . and slavery and free masonry[228] are held to be such by many eminent and good men. Societies are formed for purging the land of these iniquities. Is it proper that their business should be transacted and their celebrations held, in our consecrated buildings?

The bishop had two answers to that question. First, there were known to be differences of opinion on these subjects and these differences ought not to be brought into the church. But more importantly, the "Church knows no rule of morals but the Gospel, and no Gospel independent of the Church." Therefore, the church cannot sanction any effort at reform except through the church itself. Even in regard to performances of music, the sharing of refreshments, and "expressions of approbation and disapprobation," the bishop felt it was only necessary to ask "any pious Christian" who might read these notes: "Are they befitting the House of God?"

To him the answer was self-evident, and if his views were widely held and known, he was confident that the church would not again be threatened by unruly mobs. So there was to be a clear line drawn between the church and any divisive social issues and activities, but why was there a line between a Black congregation and the diocese? The bishop did not speak to that, and the question of the relationship between St. Philip's Church and the Diocese of New York would continue to plague the bishop and his successors for ten more years. James McCune Smith might not have been aware of the convention of 1837, but he would become deeply involved in the debate over St. Philip's presence or absence at that convention in years to come.

Again, in 1838, Peter Williams was listed among the clergy of the diocese but not listed in relationship with the convention as either present or not present. In that year, however, it was recorded that the bishop had visited St. Philip's, a church not in union with the diocese, to ordain a young man as deacon. The young man in question, Isaiah DeGrasse, had started work at the General Theological Seminary in New York, but had been forced to withdraw by the bishop and required to study privately out of fear that his presence would inhibit southern support for the seminary. The convention journal did note, however, that the bishop had visited St. Philip's Church and confirmed sixty persons. For the edification of its readers, the journal added: "The Rector and congregation of this Church are colored persons."[229] That, apparently, was sufficient grounds for the diocese to keep St. Philip's in a distant relationship with the other churches, and the parish and its pastor, apparently, were content not to challenge it. Certainly, James McCune Smith was too junior a member of the church and too newly returned from Scotland to make any suggestions of change.

Year after year, St. Philip's Church Vestry did, however, elect delegates to the diocesan convention and year after year the diocese avoided seating them. Sometimes the delegates from St. Philip's may have watched the proceedings from the balcony, the area to which Black worshippers were usually directed in white churches. More often, members of St. Peter's simply stayed home.

Brazilian Slaves: 1847
An incident that illustrated the difficulty the diocese and the parish had in understanding each other occurred when a Brazilian ship entered New York Harbor in 1847. On board the ship were three slaves owned by the ship's captain. State law provided that "every person born within this state, whether white or colored, is FREE; every person who shall hereafter be born within this state, shall be FREE; and every person brought into this state as a slave, except as authorized by this Title, shall be FREE." That seemed clear enough to abolitionists and Black citizens of New York, so when two slaves got themselves off the ship and the captain tried to reclaim his property, the fugitives quickly found advocates to defend them.[230]

John Jay, grandson of the first chief justice of the Supreme Court and a leading member of the Episcopal Church, went to court to obtain a writ of habeas corpus and to anticipate issues raised ten years later in the Dred Scott case. The lawyers for the Brazilian captain argued that a treaty between Brazil and the United States prevented anyone from interfering with his property rights. Further, the captain said, they were members of the crew and members of the crew were under his personal command and no American court could overrule that authority. The judge charged with deciding the case had the slaves remanded to jail while he considered what to do.

While three different judges pondered the case over the next several weeks and arrived at different results, an appeal was made to the vestry of St. Philip's for financial assistance with the legal expenses involved in so complex a case. It seemed reasonable to Sydney H. Gay, the white editor of the *National Anti-Slavery Standard*, to look to Black Americans to be concerned for the fate of Black Brazilians. James McCune Smith was by that time not only a member of the vestry of St. Philip's Church but the clerk (or secretary) of the vestry.

To Smith and his colleagues, it seemed unreasonable to think that the members of St. Philip's Church should be any more concerned about Brazilian slaves than the members of any other New York congregation. It seemed to them that a positive response to this appeal would confirm the white editor and his colleagues in their assumption that Black and white Americans really were different and that Black people cared more about Black people than white people did. It was, perhaps, the struggle against what W. E. B. Du Bois called a "double consciousness—an American, a Negro; two souls, two thoughts, two unreconciled strivings; two warring ideals in one dark body, whose dogged strength alone keeps it from being torn asunder." Smith, like Du Bois, was not interested in losing either soul; he had made that clear in his speech on "The Destiny of the People of Color." Like Du Bois,

> He does not wish to Africanize America, for America has too much to teach the world and Africa. He wouldn't bleach his Negro blood in a flood of white Americanism, for he knows that Negro blood has a message for the world. He simply wishes to make it possible for a man to be both a Negro and an American without being cursed and spit upon by his fellows, without having the doors of opportunity closed roughly in his face.[231]

It was that same perspective that had made Smith reluctant to attend a convention of white New Yorkers. In that situation, he had finally agreed to go and work for his rights. In this situation, his rights were not at issue, but his essential humanity was and he, therefore, took the opportunity to instruct Sydney Gay and John Jay and others of similar good intentions but limited perspective what they needed to understand. The vestry's response is recorded in the vestry minutes as their action, but a recent historian of the parish writes that "the language and sentiments here are once again those of the secretary of the vestry, James McCune Smith." Yet the sentiment was clearly shared, as the vestry minutes use the term "agreed" to indicate a unanimous vote, and there is no record of any discussion or disagreement:

> A letter was received from Sydney H. Gay requesting that this church do join other colored churches in this city in raising One Hundred Dollars for carrying on the suit in the case of the Brazilian slaves. *Moved*, that in the opinion of this Vestry the question is one that concerns all men regardless of complexion, and this vestry cannot by word or deed assent to the doctrine that it is a matter particularly pertaining to colored churches. *Agreed.*[232]

With or without the financial assistance of Black Americans, the legal issues seem not to have been resolved before the Brazilian seamen and their friends took matters into their own hands. The *National Anti-Slavery Standard* reported at the end of the summer:

> The piratical Brazilian master, and his kind friends, the Consul, and his legal adviser, are baffled now completely . . . they must now whistle back their dogs. The game is up. The Brazilians sailed from Boston, on Thursday, of last week, for Haiti.—They are beyond the reach—and they have reason to thank God for it—of the laws of the United States.[233]

Church and Diocese

John Jay was not only a leading voice in the legal proceedings in the Brazilian slave case but also a leading voice for admitting St. Philip's Church to the diocese. Unfortunately, he went at it in a way that tended to antagonize rather than conciliate. The issue, it seemed to him, was simple enough: Should a self-supporting congregation that uses the Episcopal Prayer Book, is ministered to by clergy of the church, and is regularly visited by the bishop to confirm its members be treated in the same way as every other congregation or not? John Jay had already made his views on the larger issue clear by publishing a pamphlet entitled "Thoughts on the Duty of the Episcopal Church in Relation to Slavery." Jay brought resolutions to the convention to say that no congregation should be refused admission to convention "on account of the race, lineage, color, or complexion of the congregation so applying . . . or of the minister presiding over the same nor on account of any social or political qualifications whatsoever."[234]

But this was exactly opposite to the approach favored by James McCune Smith and, on the whole, the vestry and congregation of St. Philip's. Just as they saw no reason for them to be more interested in Brazilian slaves than any other Americans, so they saw no reason to fight for their admission to the diocesan convention as a racial issue. They wanted to be treated like everyone else because it was the right thing to do, not admitted to convention because of a law forbidding them to be treated differently than anyone else.

Through the years that Peter Williams was rector of St. Philip's, there was no effort made by Williams or the vestry to alter the relationship, or lack of relationship, with the diocese. With Williams's death, everything changed. It would be thirty-two years before the parish would be served again by a Black priest. Black clergy were in very short supply in the Episcopal Church. St. Philip's had raised up two candidates for ordination, both of whom had come into conflict with the bishop because of his refusal to support their application to the church's New York City seminary. Isaiah DeGrasse studied privately in New York, was ordained, and served briefly in a smaller Black congregation, but died at the age of twenty-eight in 1841. Alexander Crummell also studied privately, but not in New York. The controversy over his desire to attend the General Theological Seminary had ended in an angry public confrontation.[235] He was ordained in Massachusetts in 1844 and was not yet a priest when St. Philip's needed a successor to Peter

Williams. Still a third potential candidate, Charles Reason, surprised the vestry by complaining to the bishop and vestry after a year of private study that they had not supported his application to the General Theological Seminary as he had expected.

After their experience with DeGrasse and Crummell, the vestry was not happy to be criticized for not fulfilling a promise never made. Reason was summoned to a vestry meeting, and Smith asked him whether he thought the vestry had made any commitment to him concerning the seminary. Reason could only reply, "They did not distinctly promise" any such thing. That settled it as far as the vestry was concerned. Smith wrote to the bishop on behalf of the vestry to say that they were as surprised as he would be and that no such commitment had been made by them.

St. Philip's, therefore, accepted the appointment of a white priest as a temporary solution. The temporary solution became a long-term settlement for lack of acceptable alternatives. The suggestion was made at one point that Crummell be called to serve as assistant to the white priest in charge, apparently in hope that he might then succeed the white priest and become rector. James McCune Smith attempted to negotiate such an arrangement on behalf of the vestry. Unfortunately, the white priest in charge, Alexander Frazer, was uncomfortable with having an assistant chosen for him by the vestry, and Crummell was unhappy with the idea that he would be serving "on approval." Rather than be "put on hold," Crummell went off to England, earned a degree from Queens' College, Cambridge, and went on to serve twenty years as a missionary in Liberia before returning to the United States and a ministry in Washington, DC. Still a fourth Black candidate for ordination in the diocese, Samuel Vreeland Berry, survived the challenges of the ordination process and served as assistant at St. Philip's for over a year. When the vestry then voted to call a white priest as "officiating minister," Berry resigned and left the diocese.

Through the long and difficult period between the death of Peter Williams and the arrival of Hutchens C. Bishop in 1886, the vestry maintained a strong commitment to working with the bishop and to finding a priest, Black or white, able to provide capable leadership and ministry.[236]

Convention Membership: 1845–1853

Peter Williams's death led to an unsettled period in ordained ministry at St. Philip's, but lay leadership finally took the long-delayed step of applying for admission to the diocese. In making his annual report to the diocese the year after Peter Williams's death, Bishop Onderdonk had said of St. Philip's that "[a] better ordered parish the Diocese does not possess." Why, then, had that not been recognized by admitting the representatives of the parish to the convention?

The bishop provided the answer in the preceding sentence: St. Philip's was "a parish composed of Africans and their descendants." That sentence was probably only half true; the parish was almost certainly composed of the descendants of Africans. But that also, of course, is not the full story because many members of St. Philip's were descendants of various European ethnicities as well. Many of those of African descent, however, had still been enslaved in New York state twenty years earlier and were still not seen as free and equal citizens in the minds of many white New Yorkers who had never had a conversation with people like Peter Williams, James McCune Smith, Alexander Crummell, and Philip Bell. White New Yorkers, to be blunt, were fearfully ignorant of their Black neighbors. As a result, St. Philip's Church, under the leadership of Peter Williams, was content to be an Episcopal parish with the ministry of the diocesan bishop and to wait patiently for the right time to take the next step.

In 1845, the vestry began to wonder whether the right time had come. Working together with Alexander Frazer, their white "officiating minister," an application for admission to the convention was prepared and submitted to the convention. The Committee on Incorporation of Parishes accepted the application and promised to report back next year. So, in 1846, James

McCune Smith, serving as clerk of the vestry, and Alexander Elston, one of the wardens, were elected by the vestry to serve as delegates from the parish and the trio of Frazer, Smith, and Elston arrived at the convention at the beginning of the day with high hopes that all would be well. One of the first agenda items was a report from the Committee on Incorporation of Parishes which had received applications from thirteen parishes, rejected one for technical reasons, and reported favorably on the other twelve, including St. Philip's. There was, however, an objection made to including St. Philip's, and the convention found itself forced to debate openly an issue it would much have preferred to avoid.

They found themselves also involved in a complicated parliamentary process. One delegate moved to send the matter to a special committee to report back to the convention. A member of the committee that had recommended St. Philip's admission asked what a short-term committee could learn that the existing committee had not already learned in a year's study. Another delegate had no desire to become involved in so controversial a matter and moved that the convention lay the whole matter on the table "there to lie where for long years it has lain." John Jay, always ready to fan the flames, called for a vote by orders which required each delegate to stand and announce his position and find a majority of both clergy and laity. The lay delegates voted to table the matter but the clergy did not. After further maneuvers, the convention approved the original resolution to form a new committee and hear its report before adjourning the next day.

When the time came, the special committee reported that it recommended that "neither St. Philip's nor any other colored congregation, be admitted into union with this diocese." Such congregations, they believed, should be left simply under the bishop's authority. In their view, it was purely an administrative matter and had no spiritual or theological significance. Church members, like members of any other organization, it seemed to them, could choose with whom they preferred to associate:

> When society is unfortunately divided into classes, when some are intelligent, refined, and elevated, in tone and character, and others are ignorant, coarse, and debased, however unjustly, and when such prejudices exist between them as to prevent social intercourse on equal terms, it would seem inexpedient ... to compel the one class to associate on equal terms in the consultations on the affairs of the Diocese, with those whom they would not admit to their tables, or into their family circles—nay, whom they would not admit into their pews, during public worship.[237]

The fact that these "debased" individuals were often preparing and serving their food and caring for their children seems not to have occurred to the authors. More important, as is so often the case, they saw no connection between their faith and their social and political conduct. They made that very clear in their report:

> If Christian duty require that we should, in all respects, treat equally, all persons, without reference to their social condition, should we not commence the discharge of that duty in our individual and social relations? And is not the fact that we have never so regarded our duty—or have wilfully violated it, sufficient evidence of the existence of a state of society among us that renders an amalgamation of such discordant materials impracticable, if not hazardous to our unity and harmony?[238]

In other words, our unity as Christians derives from our social status, not our faith. The report feared a future in which that viewpoint might be questioned and some would be so bold as to "question ... the Christian character of those whose sentiments do not accord with their own." Perhaps it was still more astonishing that the report went on to suggest that the existence of Black congregations showed that Black people also preferred to worship separately: "The colored people have themselves shown their conviction of this truth, by separating themselves from the whites, and forming distinct congregations where they are not continually humbled by being treated as inferiors."[239]

They seem to have forgotten that it was white Christians who first created the separation by sending Black Christians to the balconies and back pews of their churches. Listening to this report, Smith might well have found himself justified in his reluctance to create separate Black schools and form associations of Black people for any purpose.

At the next meeting of the vestry of St. Philip's Church, delegates Smith and Johnson as well as their priest, Alexander Frazer, were thanked for their efforts. They had not gained the result hoped for, but they had begun a process that would continue. They had not gained admission, but the initial committee vote to admit them and the special committee vote of 3–2 against them let them know that they had considerable support in the diocese.[240]

Perhaps progress had been made, but it baffled Smith how to go forward. In a letter to Gerrit Smith at the end of 1846, James McCune Smith wrote:

> The direction in which our people must labor is a point on which I am not certain. The heart of the whites must be changed, thoroughly, entirely, permanently changed ... and men, colored men, must go to work to produce that conviction—of the eternal equality of the Human Race—which is the first principle of good government—of Bible politics. This must be done, but how?[241]

There have never been easy answers to that most fundamental question, but McCune Smith and his fellow church members continued to work at it in their particular arena.

Smith and Peter Ray were sent as delegates to the next convention in the fall of 1847 undoubtedly with the expectation that the issue of admission would come up again and that favorable action might result. In fact, events took a strange turn when a motion was made to read the reports of the special committee. The clerk began the reading, but it then developed that the majority had had their report printed while the minority had not known that that was an option. This discovery led William Jay, father of John Jay and a delegate from Bedford, to move that action be delayed until both reports could be printed—which put the matter on hold for another year.

The delegates were ready to report this to the next vestry meeting but the vestry had other priorities. There had been deep divisions over the proposal to hire Alexander Crummell as an assistant and at the next parish election there were major changes in the vestry's membership. The senior warden, Thomas Zabriskie, who had served on the vestry for twenty-five of the twenty-eight years of parish life, received only one vote of the fifty-three cast. James McCune Smith received only twelve votes. He continued to be appointed a delegate to convention almost every year but did not return to the vestry until 1855.

Senior members of the vestry were ousted in favor of other parishioners. In May of 1848, Alexander Frazer died and it took the vestry over a year to agree on a replacement. In the meantime, the vestry selected Smith and two others to be delegates to the 1848 fall convention, drew up their own response to the majority report of 1847, probably drafted by Smith, and arranged to have five hundred copies made for distribution at the convention. The majority report had charged that Peter Williams and the first vestry had agreed long ago that, if Williams was ordained, he and his parish would never ask to be seated at the diocesan convention. It was true that Williams had never asked for such admission, but there were members of St. Philip's who were there at the time and knew nothing of such an arrangement. The statement attested that Williams himself, within a year of his death, had denied that such an arrangement was made.

The vestry also wanted the diocese to know that the Dioceses of Rhode Island and New Jersey had admitted Black parishes to their conventions within the last year. In spite of that, the New York Diocesan Convention failed to consider the matter in either of the next two years.[242] In 1850, St. Philip's sent no delegates to the convention, but John Jay called up the majority report and made a long speech refuting it. He was then ruled out of order and no action was taken.[243] James McCune Smith and Henry Scott, the owner of a small business, were chosen, however, when a special convention was called that November for the election of a bishop, and the vestry drafted a special letter urging the importance of including St. Philip's in the selection of their next spiritual leader, and the letter was printed in full in the convention journal. Efforts were made to seat them, but the motion to do so was tabled as out of order, although the convention acted to admit three other parishes.[244]

Again, in 1851, St. Philip's Church sent Smith and Scott as delegates and a motion was made to admit the parish. This time again the motion was tabled after a delegate suggested that it would be best "to avoid an exciting debate."[245] In 1852, William Morris, the white priest serving at St. Philip's, brought the matter up again only to have John Jay irritate the delegates by moving a resolution that convention's failure to do so would be "injurious to the cause of Religion, and most oppressive in its influence on the Colored people." When that resolution was ruled out of order, Jay came back the next day with an even more irritating resolution calling on the diocese to "utterly reject and repudiate" any "distinction or caste based upon natural complexion or social position" as being "absolutely violative of her [the Church's] Catholic unity." Other members objected to any such resolution being put before the convention and, when Jay again insisted on a vote by orders, the chair ruled that the original resolution was out of order. Morris reported back to the vestry that he had sought to have the question of admission taken up on its merits but, when another delegate attempted to link "foreign" matter to the question, he had withdrawn it rather than ignite a controversy. He reported that he received kind remarks from his fellow clergy and their assurance of support when the matter could be brought forward properly.

It would be another year before that could happen, but in September 1853, St. Philip's vestry chose Peter Ray, Henry Scott, and Philip White to serve as delegates and asked William Morris to "urge the admission of the parish." Why Smith was not chosen is mysterious and was, apparently, mysterious to Smith as well. When John Jay wrote to him to ask about convention plans, Smith replied tersely: "The vestry of St. Philip's have elected two delegates to the Diocesan Convention. What further steps or arrangements they have made I am unable to say, as the above is all the Secretary saw fit to communicate in reply to my note of inquiry."[246]

Nevertheless, word went out that history was likely to be made, and four city newspapers and two church newspapers came to tell the story. Oddly, the Committee on Incorporation of Parishes was not called on to report until the second day of the convention, but John Jay took the floor in the afternoon of the first day to move adoption of a new canon (church rule) that would disallow the use of any racial, social, or political criteria for diocesan membership. One delegate pointed out that the canons had no such criteria and Jay's proposal was unnecessary. The convention heard Jay out and amended the minutes the next morning so as to eliminate any record of what Jay had suggested.

That done, the relevant committee put forward the applications of nineteen parishes for admission to convention. Each in turn was duly admitted. They voted last for St. Philip's, and there was no debate, just a vote—and it wasn't even close. Among lay members of convention, the vote was 75–33 and among clergy it was 140–13 to admit St. Philip's. The delegates from St. Philip's came down from the balcony where they had been sitting year after year and took their seats with the other delegates. Smith, oddly, was not a delegate that year, but he was one the next year when a special convention was called to elect a new bishop. He and his colleagues took their seats

St. Philip's Church 1847–1853

with the other five hundred priests and lay people of the convention and reported back that "[t]hey were well received and fraternized with both by clergy and lay people."

The eminent New York diarist and lifelong member of Trinity Church Wall Street, George Templeton Strong, saw it differently. The acceptance of the delegation from St. Philip's did not mean that all New Yorkers were free of prejudice and John Jay had won no friends for them or himself in the process. Strong wrote: "Another Revolution. John Jay's annual motion carried at last, and the nigger delegation admitted into the Diocesan Convention. John Jay must be an unhappy, aching void, as when one's stomach, liver, and other innards have been dexterously taken out."[247]

Undoubtedly, there were many who agreed with Strong in his attitude both toward John Jay and the Black population of New York City.[248] But St. Philip's thereafter would have its delegates to the convention seated with the other delegates, and those other delegates would have an experience outside their normal realm of experience: within the church, at least, they would be dealing with Black Americans as equals.

Craig Townsend, the twenty-first-century chronicler of this history, in summing the matter up and discussing the role of the various actors, says of James McCune Smith that he was "articulate, powerfully faithful, supremely concerned about the advancement of his people, but not always the leader his parish wanted him to be." Townsend cites no evidence for that opinion, but perhaps he is noticing the fact that Smith was usually the clerk of the vestry and never a warden. It was the clerk, however, who gave form to the vestry's opinions and shaped the historical record.

St. Philip's Church is, however, the most concrete and lasting embodiment of James McCune Smith's varied life. Moving in 1909 to its present location on West 134th Street in Harlem, the parish became the largest congregation in the Episcopal Church in the 1950s with nearly four thousand members; among the best known were W. E. B. Du Bois, Thurgood Marshall, and Langston Hughes. A 36,000-square-foot Parish House

Community Center, constructed in 1970 at a cost of $2.5 million, housed the church's day care center, a gymnasium, and space for its community outreach and social services programs.

CHAPTER ELEVEN

The Colored Orphan Asylum 1834–1860

Background

On a quiet day in the spring of 1834, while James McCune Smith was in the midst of his studies in Scotland, two Quaker ladies took a walk on Cherry Street in Lower Manhattan that would make a major impact on Smith's life. Cherry Street was named for a seven-acre cherry orchard that had once stood on the Lower East Side of Manhattan, but that was long gone by 1834. In another generation, the street would be shortened to make way for the Brooklyn Bridge. In the 1830s, it was a mixture of deteriorating tenements and small stores. It was not the best neighborhood in the city, but neither was it one in which two Quaker ladies might not walk to enjoy the spring sunshine.

As the ladies walked along, they came upon a rundown, two-story brick building and saw two small Black children sitting on the front steps. The children were tattered and dirty but smiled up at the elegant ladies. The women stopped to smile back and patted one on the head. Seeing a large woman looking down from the second-floor window, the ladies asked, "Are these your children?"

"No," said the woman, "they are orphans, and I am looking after them until the city finds them a home." Unless such a home could be found, she explained, only the poorhouse was available and the poorhouse offered nothing for the needs of children.

The Quaker women gave the lady some money for clean clothes for the children and promised to return. When they came back a few days later, there were six small children sitting on the steps, all scrubbed and neatly dressed. The caretaker told the ladies that their gift had been more than enough for two, and she had decided to spread their gift to others.[249]

The Quaker ladies, Anna Shotwell and Mary Murray, had discovered a mission.[250] They had some background for such a mission since both their families had been directly involved in the work of the Manumission Society and its creation of the African Free School. That particular mission had ended two years earlier as the city moved to consolidate its school system and the Manumission Society could no longer sustain its educational program. Charitably disposed Quakers were ready for a new challenge.

Shotwell and Murray spent the next two years educating themselves on the lives of the six small orphans and others like them and attempting to educate city officials as well on the need to provide support for children who otherwise were doomed to lives of misery. There were three orphanages for white children in the city, none of them receiving municipal funding, and none that could be persuaded to accept Black children. The women worked to educate their friends on the need and to enlist them in a crusade to do something about it.

On November 26, 1836, fourteen women met with five men in the home of William Shotwell, Anna Shotwell's father, and formed the Association for the Benefit of Colored Orphans. The men were there because the women had no experience in such matters, but it was carefully provided that the men would not be in charge nor would they be responsible for the women's failures: "The husband of any married woman who is or may be a member of the said corporation shall not be liable to the said corporation for any loss occasioned by the neglect or misfeasance of his wife, but if he shall have received any money from his wife belonging to the said corporation, or the same shall have been applied to his use, he shall be accountable therefor."[251]

With a structure in place and officers elected, the women set out to raise funds and find a building. Since no one would rent a house for Black children to occupy, the association was forced to buy a house and a suitable structure was found on West 12th Street near 6th Avenue, a small white cottage shaded by two spreading chestnut trees. They said that the building, formerly a doctor's residence, could accommodate up to fifty children and had a quarter acre of land for play space. It was, they said, "in every way suited to the innocent gambols of the dear parentless children."[252]

Funding for the new enterprise came in donations large and small. Descendants of historic New Yorkers like John Jacob Astor, Peter Stuyvesant, and John Hancock were among the early contributors. A Murray relative in England died and left $150 with another thousand promised if the trustees could raise a matching nine thousand, which they did in short order. Gerrit Smith sent a contribution from his upstate residence. Others with less cash on hand contributed such useful items as a bag of beans and a keg of potatoes.[253]

With a down payment of three thousand dollars and a mortgage for six thousand, the cottage was theirs. They ransacked attics and spare bedrooms for surplus furniture. An appeal was published in *The Colored American* for "old articles of furniture, clothing, or bedding, as may be nearly useless to the donors, and answer all purposes of decency and comfort, to those for whose use they are bestowed." In June 1837, four-year-old Sarah Williams became the first orphan admitted to the asylum and in July, five children were admitted from the cellar of the almshouse. No coachman could be found who would take Black children and several were too small to walk, so Anna Shotwell picked up one and said to Mary Murray and a friend, "I will take one if thee will take the others," and with the three smallest in their arms and followed by two more, they walked the twenty blocks to the orphanage. Seven other children, most of them suffering from malnutrition, came soon after.[254]

The only negative voice in those early days came from the editorial pages of *The Colored American*, co-edited at that point by Samuel Cornish and Smith's old friend Philip Bell. Smith, still in Scotland at that point, would have agreed with them when they wrote:

> The object is a good one, and we doubt not but the motives by which these benevolent ladies are actuated, are of the purest kind, and were their efforts based on solid principles, would be productive of the greatest good.
>
> The line-drawing, wall-building spirit, which pervades our churches, schools, and benevolent institutions, is a bad spirit.... How long will dying men continue to draw cords of caste and lines of demarcation in the family of man, and among the beings of God, made in his own image, and of the same blood? ... we hold separate institutions for colored youth, as being contrary to the principles of the Bible, and at war with the best interests of our colored population.

The editorial ended with an appreciation of "the purity of purpose" of the ladies of the association and published the preamble of the association and a list of its officers.[255] Ironically, serving the children of that orphanage would become one of the most important activities in the life of James McCune Smith, though he would have endorsed the editorial completely as expressing his opinion also.

In October, a visitor from *The Colored American* dropped in on the orphanage with his or her little daughter and was pleased by the visit. The staff consisted of a matron, "a middle aged colored lady, of undoubted piety, and benevolence of heart"; a teacher, "very young ... [but] pious ... and amply qualified"; and a nurse. "The whole place," the visitor reported, "was a pattern of neatness and comfort." The First Annual Report, issued on

December 30, 1837, stated that there were now twenty-five residents and that "[m]ost of them have been rescued from scenes of misery which can only be conceived by those who are acquainted with the extreme wretchedness and degradation of the lower class of our colored population." "How can anyone doubt the value of such a place," the report asked, when there are "souls to be saved, minds to be improved, and characters to be trained to virtue and usefulness?"

Medical Issues

In the annual report, the board included acknowledgment of "the professional services of Dr. MacDonald, and his gratuitous attentions toward those of the little family that have needed the care of a physician."[256] How Dr. MacDonald came to be the attendant physician for the orphanage is not clear, but a minor news item a few months later might have raised at least a small red flag.

Under "News of the Day," *The Colored American* reported: "Another Death from Eating Stramonium." Ann Williams, age eight, a resident in the Colored Orphanage just recovering from whooping cough, had been taken with convulsions and died on a Monday evening. "Doctors MacDonald and Hosack made a postmortem examination of the deceased and in her stomach, found a quantity of stramonium seeds; which . . . left them without a doubt that she had died in consequence of swallowing those seeds, and a verdict was rendered accordingly."[257] It was said that the child had gotten the seeds from an adjacent vacant lot, but since children were not allowed to go beyond the front door without the matron's permission, that judgment can be questioned. It is also true that stramonium "has been used in traditional medicine to relieve asthma symptoms . . . [and that] the tropane alkaloids responsible for both the medicinal and hallucinogenic properties are fatally toxic in only slightly higher amounts than the medicinal dosage, and careless use often results in hospitalizations and deaths."[258] Among the medical systems using stramonium was homeopathy, which was very popular in mid-nineteenth century America—and apparently used by Dr. MacDonald. It would be another year before the problem reappeared in a way that required attention.

James McCune Smith's opinion of homeopathy was revealed in a letter to Gerrit Smith in December 1846. Gerrit Smith had been ill and McCune Smith wrote a letter dealing with several subjects but taking the opportunity to say a few words about homeopathy:

> I regard it as a great compliment to the healing art, that a man of your strong sound sense, after undergoing numerous martyrdoms of knives, & medicaments, still clings to the regulars when the number and persuasiveness of the pathy corps[259] is so great. For my own part, I can scarcely blame the encouragement given by the public to that method of getting well, when I think over the nauseous doses, and painful operations by which we M.D's curse the people.[260]

But the doctor at the Orphan Asylum was a homeopathic practitioner, an advocate of a recently developed system for treating disease on the theory that likes are cured by likes. Homeopaths believe that a medicinal substance that can produce particular symptoms in healthy people can be used to treat illnesses that have similar symptoms, if given in very small doses.

A year later, the trustees reported that sixty-four children had been received, "orphans thirty-three; half orphans twenty-nine." The "half orphans" were children who had been "deserted by their surviving parents" or whose single parent needed to earn a living and so was unable to care for them. Some of these were able to pay "the weekly half dollar for their board." Admission records often show many more half orphans than orphans being admitted.[261] But one aspect of the report foreshadowed trouble. Nine children had died.

> Painful as it has been to consign one little form after another, to its early grave, it is consoling to know that they were not suffered to expire in wretchedness and neglect.... Measles and whooping cough which have prevailed among the orphans to a great extent during the year, have operated very severely, and in some cases fatally, on the more feeble children.... The Managers would here beg leave to refer to a Report made by the physician of the Asylum, in relation to the causes of mortality among the orphans. Its bearing on the arrangements of the house and the management of the children, make it an important document. The duties of the physician have been arduous, and they would tender to Dr. MacDonald, their warm acknowledgments for his humane and persevering attentions.

The report went into great detail about the lives of some of the children who had often found themselves compelled to serve as chimney sweeps or to act as beggars on behalf "of vicious and degraded" adults to eke out a painful existence.

> With constitutions not naturally adapted to bear the extremes of cold to which our climate is liable, hardships and exposure soon render them enfeebled and sickly. Unable to withstand the attacks of any acute disease, they are in most cases early and mercifully summoned to that home, where the "wicked cease from troubling."[262]

The reference to "constitutions not naturally adapted to bear the extremes of cold to which our climate is liable" was another troubling sign of a doctor (and staff?) all too ready to assume that "Black children are different" and better adapted by nature to a more tropical climate.

Two weeks earlier, a celebration of the second anniversary was held and a visitor from *The Colored American* reported that "the children presented a pleasing spectacle, their countenances sprightly and cheerful." The visitor was also pleased by the speech given by a lawyer, one of the advisors to the board, who "referred to the causes which had made this people wretched, as a reason why, they had a claim upon the sympathies of all men; in a word, he not only plead [*sic*] the cause of those orphans, but of the whole colored population." But the visitor was troubled by "one part of the Physician's report, which in our judgment, was erroneous and unsound in principle, and in our estimation, reflected no credit on the doctor."[263]

The Colored American returned to the issue a week later with a blistering critique of the doctor's report:

> [H]ad we no further knowledge of him than what we draw from them, we should not hesitate in attributing, some, of the many deaths which have occurred among the children of the institution, to the indulgence of such erroneous and ruinous sentiments. The hackneyed colonization opinion that the colored people, born and raised in this country have constitutions different from the whites, and with different adaptations, is too absurd to be countenanced. The difference in their mortality, if there be any, may easily be accounted for as the result of natural causes, without the supposition of a different constitutional conformation. Facts go against such a supposition. There are more instances of extreme longevity among the colored people of our country, than among the whites, though their number be but one to six. The colored people of this country, also, have a decided advantage over the native Africans in size and

appearance, while the white Americans, when compared with their European progenitors, have degenerated in both.

Again, the reporter is not named, but one has to wonder whether it was James McCune Smith, especially when the report says, "So much for the Doctor's blunders. We shall professionally say more on this subject."

Few if any New Yorkers other than Smith were in a position to speak "professionally . . . on this subject." For the moment, however, he let Dr. MacDonald's own words condemn him:

> First. As to Peculiarity of Constitution, &c. It is generally admitted that there is a much greater degree of mortality among the colored population of our cities than among the whites. On referring to a report of the Inspector of the city of New York, it is found that four of every hundred of the former, while only two of the same number of the latter, die annually. It is probable that comparatively even a larger number of colored children die; for the same report shows that scrofulous diseases are more fatal among this race than among whites, in the proportion of more than two to one. It is this class of diseases (scrofula in all its varied forms) which proves [fatal] to so many children of African descent.
>
> The experience of the past year has confirmed the writer in an opinion long since expressed, that the diseases of the colored differ in many respects from those of the white inhabitants of our country, and that there would be a greater mortality among the children of the Asylum for Colored Orphans, than among white children of other similar establishments.[264]

At the end of January, *The Colored American* devoted most of the weekly paper to Dr. MacDonald's report and what is, though unsigned, almost certainly James McCune Smith's analysis of it. MacDonald presented a case-by-case report on each death and concluded:

> Careful examination into the history of each case, and reflection on the subject, have brought me to ascribe it to the following circumstances:
>
> 1st, The peculiar constitution and condition of the colored race.
>
> 2nd, The admission of sickly and feeble children.
>
> 3rd, Most of the children admitted, particularly the entire orphans, being the offspring of unhealthy parents.
>
> 4th, Neglect during the early periods of life—improper diet—bad air—and want of clothing—by which means constitutions naturally feeble are greatly impaired.
>
> 5th, The prevalence of epidemic diseases among the children since their admission in the Asylum.

Smith was carefully analytical but scathing in his response:

> Such is the Physician's report of the cases, and such are the causes to which, in his opinion, the uncommon mortality may be attributed. As no deaths occurred during the first year, the mortality in the second year cannot be the result of any general cause, for a general cause being in constant operation, would have made a like proportion of deaths in both years. Of the five causes to which the Doctor ascribes the mortality, the first three are evidently one. For, if there be a peculiarity in the constitution of the colored people causing uncommon mortality, it is plain

that their children must be "feeble and sickly," and the "parents unhealthy."

In search of this peculiarity, let us examine the cases in rotation.

CASE 1. Sidney Johnson. In this case, the Doctor evinces a remarkable anxiety to show cause sufficient for the child's demise. The poor infant which entered the Asylum, "apparently healthy," died a "natural death," and the physician, not satisfied with enumerating probabilities enough to kill any six children living, heroically rushes to the grave, exhumes the corpses of the parents and clothes them with imaginary diseases in order still more satisfactorily to "slay again the slain." Scrofula! Remittent fever!! Teething!!! Shade of Hippocrates! Were not these enough to kill a poor little "Colored American," 12 months old, without raising its parents to answer for the death of their child? Dear, dear Doctor, if providence should ever bless us with a small family, and a hopeful little one becomes sick, we shall certainly employ you as the most satisfactory man in the profession. If the child recovers, you will be able to show that you have snatched it from the very jaws of death, but if you kill—No, if the patient dies, you will smother our grief in wonderment that it did not die nine times instead of one.

The infant died of teething. Now if there be any "peculiarity in the constitution of the colored race," which causes our children to die teething, we may expect to find the fact confirmed by the report of the City Inspector: —on referring to which (Document 134, 1837) p. 476, we find, that of the deaths caused by teething are:

Whites 235

> Colored 7
>
> which gives one colored to 33.57 white. The colored population being to the white as 1 to 16.75, it follows that two white children to one colored die of teething. Hence, if there be any "peculiarity in the constitution of the colored people," anent [concerning] teething, the same is doubled in that of the white.

MacDonald went on to suggest that Black people were not sufficiently acclimated. Smith noted that most Black people had been in the country longer than most white people since there were many recent white immigrants but few new Black arrivals. "We have not been 'transplanted to a comparatively rigorous climate,' but live on the same soil where our ancestors were born, during as many, perhaps more, generations than forbears of Dr. MacDonald's." And if fewer white than Black residents die of consumption, there is a reason for it. Black residents, "who are seized with consumption, die in the city of consumption; whilst the whites fly and obtain a reprieve, or die elsewhere." It is tempting to include the whole of Smith's analysis, but the point has been made. The report concludes with a charitable note:

> For the present, we are done with the report. With its author, we have no personal acquaintance, against him we entertain no feeling of malevolence. He must be a benevolent man, or he would not gratuitously perform the duties of physician to the Asylum. That the views taken by him in his report are erroneous, is manifest from the above statements in figures "which cannot lie," and which administers to him a rebuke more stern than we can pen.

Smith made it all very personal with his closing sentences:

We must confess that it is with painful feelings that we have hurriedly thrown together these remarks. Next to our Maker do we revere Science as the clearest manifestation of his law which he has vouchsafed us. And we have hoped for much Science; born in penury, nursed by persecution, we have fondly dreamed that she would ever rear her head far above the buzz of popular applause, or the clash of conflicting opinion in the moral world; it is therefore almost with the anguish that springs from a blasted hope that we view this first, however flimsy, attempt to demean her to the contemptible office of ministering to public prejudices.[265]

How this played out is, unfortunately, not completely clear from the available records. The official history of the orphanage, published in 1936 to celebrate the one hundredth anniversary, says nothing of any doctor until it speaks of appointing "a colored physician, I. McCunn Smith," in 1847."[266] The association's historiographer obviously may be wrong about the date as well as the name. Other sources give 1843[267] and 1846[268] as the time when James McCune Smith began to serve the orphanage, but Smith had been involved with the orphanage well before that. The criticism of the 1839 medical report published in *The Colored American* indicates extensive knowledge of the institution and in 1841, Smith had lectured on Haiti to raise funds for the orphanage. Whenever it was that Smith began, he would continue to serve as staff doctor for the institution, apparently for a fee of one hundred dollars per year,[269] until shortly before his death in 1865 when his deteriorating heart made it impossible for him to continue. The first matron, the effective supervisor of the asylum, was Black, but it was Smith's presence in the orphanage that created bridges of trust to Black leaders and their communities. With Smith as liaison, Black churches began to hold fundraisers for the asylum and the children began to give concerts for Black citizens.[270] Smith's own lecture was published and sold and contributed over two hundred dollars to the orphanage.[271]

One very practical challenge facing Smith in his new duties was the task of getting to the orphanage. The continued growth of the number of children cared for combined with the distinct limitations of the building on West 12th Street had led the association to look for a site where they could build to their own specifications. The city of New York, finally recognizing the work being done, made a building site available on Fifth Avenue between 43rd and 44th Street. By the end of the century, that would be the middle of midtown Manhattan and some of the most expensive real estate in the world, but in 1842 it was still in the country. The association was able to erect a handsome brick building on the site, keep two or three cows, and plant a vegetable garden.

It was, however, several miles from Smith's home and office. For his first year in the position, he walked the six or seven miles almost every day. A system of horse-drawn streetcars on rails had recently been developed in the city, but the streetcar companies served only white customers. After a year or so, the association obtained "a special dispensation" from the streetcar company and provided Smith with a ticket for his personal use.[272] The special ticket, however, only enabled him to ride the cars provided at long intervals for colored customers. That restriction was later relaxed to allow colored persons to ride if they had procured a ticket or certificate from a company representative who was authorized to grant permits "to such as he deemed respectable." Even that favor may have resulted only from an unfortunate attempt to exclude one of the members of the male advisory committee from the cars, the agent mistaking him about dusk for a colored man.

The issue of equal access to the New York City horse-drawn streetcars on rails was not fully resolved until James W. C. Pennington and others formed an Equal Rights Association in 1855 and fought the issue through the courts.²⁷³ Finally, in 1856, the state supreme court ruled that the city street cars must be open to all. Even then, old habits persisted and Smith complained to a public meeting in 1857 of his inability to reach sick children because he was not allowed to ride.²⁷⁴

An anonymous correspondent, "Spectator," wrote a long letter to *The National Era* in September 1847 to describe Smith's problems with the city transportation system and also to report on a visit to an estate at West Farms in what is now the Bronx. Spectator's report reveals as much about Spectator and contemporary attitudes toward race and poverty as about the children. The directors of the orphanage, Spectator wrote, had been given the use of a wealthy New Yorker's place in the country for the summer so that they could take children there to enjoy the fresh air and open space. The children, "gathered from the lowest dregs of a New York population," were also called on to demonstrate their skills for Spectator and an audience of visitors from the neighborhood.

For two hours the children "astonished" the audience with their knowledge of geography and arithmetic and did exercises and sang "with voices of melody such as characterize the African race." Spectator added that the directors of the orphanage had greater success than other institutions in placing those "prepared to be bound out." They "actually obtain a premium for their colored orphans when they are prepared to be bound out," placed them "with pious farmers," and required that money be set aside at interest annually—five dollars for the first year and more each succeeding year—to be given to the child when of age to set out on their own.²⁷⁵

Children as young as ten or twelve were sometimes "bound out" or indentured but state law required that they spend at least three months every year in school. Some children remained in the orphanage until they were eighteen, and two girls asked for help from the trustees in their desire to move on to Oberlin College so they could become teachers.²⁷⁶

The Board and the Bushman

The annual meeting of the board in 1849 illustrated the problems of a society only beginning to think constructively about racial differences. The children had been called in to perform for the board and the report began well enough with a reflection on the way in which the children's performance had served to dispel prejudice:

> [All] who witnessed the performances of the children, however prejudiced they may have been when they entered the building, [could not have believed] that there was any natural inferiority in the race to which these orphans belonged. We doubt if any public school in the city could make a more creditable exhibition than is yearly given by this Asylum.

But what was the reporter thinking when he went on to say, "Our habits and institutions have made the difference of colour, created by God, a line of separation, and these little orphans are almost as strangers in a strange land among us."

Perhaps the strangest event that evening was the exhibition of a young African bushman who had been picked up near death in the African desert by a trader and left with the American consul Isaac Chase. Over the next four or five years Chase had, with some difficulty, taught the bushman to wear clothes and to speak some English. He had then brought him to America and, for some reason, took him to the meeting of the Orphan Asylum board. The annual meeting report said, "Probably a lower specimen of the African races could not be procured, or one whose circumstances had been more unfavourable to the development of his mere human faculties. Nevertheless the boy spoke English with considerable fluency, and behaved himself altogether like a reasonable creature."

James McCune Smith proceeded to lecture those present at the annual meeting on the geography of Southern Africa and the habits of the bushmen. He was pleased to point out, contrary to those who thought the "facial angle" revealed the relative progress of a racial group, that "his head is well formed, and the facial angle not only excels that of the Caucasian (in what is called the intellectual grade) but equals that which the Greeks gave Jupiter, that is 90 degrees." His eyesight, Smith told his audience, was such that "he can distinguish objects which any one present would require a common telescope to see."

All of which may well have been accurate but seems poorly designed to follow up on a performance by orphan children that had been praised for its dispelling of racial prejudice. Smith, however, saw the life of the bushman as positive witness to human unity:

> [H]ere is living proof that the most barbarous mode of life has not been able to erase from one of God's human creatures the stamp of humanity; that nature at the most can never make man and his offspring so hideous as can Slavery. And we cannot but be grateful to the Almighty Providence which has brought this child from darkness to the light of Christianity.
>
> We have here, too, another link in the grand chain of facts and arguments which go to prove the unity of the human race.[277]

The records tell us that "Henry Bushman," age ten, was admitted to the Orphan Asylum in 1848 and that Isaac Chase had agreed to pay his board. Anna Shotwell wrote that he was a "remarkably innocent and guileless boy" but there is no further record to tell us what became of the little African.[278]

Frederick Douglass visited the orphanage in 1849 and again in 1853 and was given guided tours by James McCune Smith. After his first visit, Douglass reported in very different terms than those of Spectator:

For this visit I am indebted to Dr. J. McCune Smith, the constant Physician of the establishment. We arrived there just as the children were rising from the long dinner table, and were attracted to the room where they were, by their vocal music. They had finished their plain but substantial repast, and were warbling a song of thanksgiving and praise. "Praise God from whom all blessings flow," went upon the wings of a hundred and forty orphan voices. We reached the room in time to catch the closing strain of this precious old hymn, and to see the children as they stood singing it, and were (who would not be?) deeply affected by it. I had often heard this hymn before, and seemed to realize its depth and power, but never until this moment had I been made to feel the unction with which it is capable of being sung. The great God seemed alone to share their thanksgiving. Cut off from earthly parents, they were taught to look to their Father in Heaven as the source of all the blessings they enjoyed and to rely upon him in every time of need. At the close of their hymn I was kindly invited by one of the directresses to make a few remarks to the children. I complied, and addressed them about fifteen minutes, aiming to impress their youthful minds with a sense of the high destiny which awaited them, the responsibilities which were soon to devolve upon them—and the great importance of preparing to meet and discharge worthily their duties and responsibilities. For this I warned them against the vices of lying and indolence,— exhorted them to truthfulness and industry;—showing that while the former leads to shame and ruin, the latter leads to peace, plenty, and happiness. I was listened to with strict attention, and at the close, Dr. Smith took up the theme, and after giving them a little history of myself, the children sang us several songs upon the subject, which we had just been considering. . . . I would gladly say more of this Institution, but time and space will not permit at this writing. I will recur to it at another time. —F. D.[279]

A new hospital wing opened on June 4, 1850, that enabled McCune Smith to isolate sick children and limit the spread of contagious diseases. The wing contained two wards for sick children, a schoolroom for convalescent patients, an apothecary's room, a dining room, a playroom, and a nurse's apartment. The trustees praised Smith for "carefully seeking opportunity of marking the symptoms and arresting the progress of disease, by judicial medical treatment."[280]

The Orphan Asylum would remain a major un-reimbursed commitment in James McCune Smith's life. It was also time consuming. In writing to Gerrit Smith in December 1846, McCune Smith reported: "In addition to my ordinary practice, I have 17 children ill with measles at the Colored Orphan Asylum."[281] In 1847, there were sixty cases of measles among 190 children, and twenty-four died. In 1849, a cholera epidemic that killed over five thousand New Yorkers[282] affected twenty of 211, and eleven died. It is hard to imagine how one man could maintain a general medical practice and care for the orphans as well.

That many of the children were known as half-orphans may have been an important factor in his commitment. The distinction was commonly made at the time between orphans and half-orphans, children with only one parent in the home whose single parent, needing to work to support herself or himself and her or his family, could not always be at home for the child when needed. Some of these parents actually paid the orphanage a monthly fee to care for their child. That McCune Smith himself had been a half-orphan, growing up with only one parent and that one barely able to maintain them, may well have been a factor in his dedication.

CHAPTER TWELVE

The Elective Franchise and Some Family Matters

Looking for Allies

James McCune Smith and Gerrit Smith had met for the first time in the spring of 1838 at a meeting of the American Anti-Slavery Society but had only a passing acquaintance over the next five or six years. When McCune Smith and his colleagues began their campaign against the property requirement in the New York State Constitution they were not sure where Gerrit Smith stood on the issue. So, in July of 1845, using McCune Smith's West Broadway return address, they wrote Gerrit Smith a letter to ask, in very polite and formal terms, where he stood on matters that concerned them: "Sir, the undersigned, colored citizens of the State of New York, being deeply anxious for an extension of the Elective Franchise, take the Liberty of addressing you respectfully to solicit that you will answer the following questions."

They had three questions: Do you think the property requirement is in accordance with the principles of representation in the state constitution? Do you think there is anything in the condition of the colored people that justifies that qualification? Do you think this is a favorable time to remove that qualification? We would like, they told him, "the fullest answer your time permits."[283]

In late December of the same year, McCune Smith and his colleagues Newport Henry, John J. Zuille, Patrick H. Reason, and Thomas Van

Rensselaer wrote a very similar letter to William C. Bloss, another upstate abolitionist who had recently been elected for the first time to the New York State Assembly as a Whig. Bloss had a long record as an abolitionist. He had signed a call for the first New York State Anti-Slavery Convention that was held in Utica in 1833. But, like Gerrit Smith, he was from upstate and he was white. McCune Smith and his friends apparently wanted to know more about these well-intentioned strangers. They had, of course, been campaigning against the property requirement for several years, but now they were reaching out for white support in their struggle. Presumably, they wrote a number of letters that fall seeking individual commitments to their cause.

Bloss mislaid his letter and did not reply until the beginning of March 1846, but when he did, he replied at great length, deeply apologetic. He told them, "No one can rightfully be deprived of citizenship, life, liberty, or property unless he violates the laws. . . . To alienate the equal rights of one of its poorest and meanest citizens even with 'due process of law,' would be to violate the rights, and prejudice the dearest liberties of every citizen of the republic." In writing to Bloss, the committee reworded the second question, asking simply whether he thought the suffrage should be extended to all citizens above twenty-one years of age "(except in cases of insanity and disability for crime) without regard to color?" Bloss strongly affirmed that also and, in response to the third question, he responded that he believed the change should be made as soon as possible.

How many such letters were sent out, there is no way of knowing. The committee was small and the task of writing each one by hand took time. Whether Gerrit Smith responded to his letter is unknown, but he responded in a very different way by initiating his land grant program. It would, of course, not deal directly with the discriminatory clause in the state constitution; it might, in fact, have made it easier for the state to keep that clause in place if a considerable number of Black citizens became landlords and qualified to vote anyway. It seems strange that

The Elective Franchise and Some Family Matters

McCune Smith and his colleagues took up the Gerrit Smith program without raising that question.

Meanwhile, however, a plan had been set in motion to hold a Constitutional Convention in Albany in June 1846 to consider alterations and amendments to the constitution. That meant that those who had been campaigning to change the state constitution would have the opportunity to be part of a larger process of reshaping the document. It had been twenty years since the constitution had been amended to eliminate a property qualification for white voters but leave it in place for Black voters. Now they might realistically hope to eliminate that recently created constitutional distinction between white and Black citizens. With that hope, the Black leadership issued a general appeal in January 1846 to New York voters, "to men of all parties, who love our institutions and their advancement to vote for such delegates as are favorable to an extension of the right of suffrage equally to all." There is, they stated,

> no STATE apart from the PEOPLE—no PEOPLE apart from and ruled by the STATE. The State derives its authority from, and holds it by the will and the voice of the PEOPLE, and has no authority apart from the will of the people. The medium through which the people exercise their will, or express it to those whom they have elected to execute the same, is the ballot box—that is by the exercise of the right of suffrage.

It was part of a long statement, spread across five columns of newsprint in the *National Anti-Slavery Standard* and signed by representatives of county committees in forty-seven of the state's sixty-two counties,[284] evidence of the work that had been going on for a number of years to create a statewide organization. James McCune Smith was one of ten who signed for New York County.[285]

That campaign, for James McCune Smith, was simply one of the many strands of his increasingly complex life. His family, his medical practice, and his pharmacy were, of course, at the center of his life, but the land grant campaign continued to take time as did his commitment to the Colored Orphan Asylum and his role on the vestry of St. Philip's Church. But the creation of effective organizations to promote civil rights and freedom for Black Americans was always a primary commitment demanding his presence at local meetings and regional conventions and the constant letter writing without which nothing would have happened.

Meeting with the Judiciary Committee

The work that began in June continued into September and October as a wide variety of issues came under consideration. James McCune Smith was part of a deputation of colored citizens that brought a petition to the legislature and met with the Committee on the Judiciary. It was Smith again who spoke for the deputation as he had done four years earlier and held the floor for over an hour with a carefully reasoned yet eloquent and even emotional statement of their case.[286] The issue, he told the committee, "notwithstanding its apparent insignificance, lies deeper among the essential elements of our stability and prosperity, than any other which has come before you."

There were four basic principles of democratic government, he said, that are "contravened, contradicted, and annulled by this portion of the constitution:

> One of these principles is, that there shall be no taxation without representation.
>
> Another of those principles is, that manhood and not property, should be represented.
>
> A third principle is, that there shall be no caste, or difference of rank, among the free people of this commonwealth.

A fourth principle is, "that no member of this State shall be disfranchised except by the laws of the land, or a jury of his peers."

Each of these principles, Smith told the committee "is contravened, contradicted, and annulled by this portion of the Constitution"—and he spelled out in detail how that was true. Other states had accepted Black voters. "Will you," he asked the legislators,

> suffer the Empire State to be outstripped in the career of freedom by Massachusetts on the one hand, and Ohio on the other? Oh! if there be any love of country in the humble individual that addresses you, that love has long been wound up in the fair fame of this, his native State. Years ago, when abroad, the only circumstance which could create a feeling of shame for our State, in my mind, was the charge, that in 1777, when it was perilous to life to be a citizen of New-York, she made colored men citizens, and that afterwards, in 1821, when it was safe and honorable to be a citizen, she disfranchised her colored citizens. Let me entreat you, remove this reproach from the fair fame of our noble State!

The committee was persuaded and so reported to the assembly. They told the assembly that they had heard from a delegation of colored citizens and that they supported their request to remove the property qualification for Black citizens from the constitution "nearly unanimously."

The assembly nevertheless spent hours debating the issue and making up its own mind. As the debate continued, Mr. Burr said that he failed to see how it could be determined who was Black and who was not or how it was fair to exclude the child of a white father because his mother was

Black. He had personal stories of hardworking neighbors whose skin was no darker that of "a sun-burnt farmer who claimed to be Anglo-Saxon."

Mr. Russell, on the other hand, "knew that nine-tenths of the people in St. Lawrence County—abolitionists and all . . . believed the Almighty had created the black man inferior to the white man . . . [and] it was our solemn duty, as republicans, to carry out that will, and vote down this proposition."[287]

Finally, that was what the assembly did. Votes were taken at several points and free and equal Black suffrage was defeated each time by a margin of about two to one: "31 aye and 62 no" at one point and "37 aye and 63 no" at another.[288] The issue would return. As late as 1860, Smith was chair of a city committee organizing weekly meetings, publishing tracts, and issuing circulars on the suffrage issue, but when the issue was put to the voters that fall, it was defeated by a vote of almost two to one. Black citizens of New York, like those of the South, had to wait for constitutional amendments after the Civil War to be able to vote without restriction.[289]

Homeopathy Again, 1847

Concerned as he was for the franchise and the Timbucto project, James McCune Smith had medical issues to fight as well. The battle with homeopathic medicine had become a very personal matter when the children at the Orphan Asylum were being given homeopathic treatment. Smith had already raised questions about the treatment the orphans were receiving, and he took that battle out on the public stage as well. *The New York Evening Post* had published an advertisement for homeopathic medicine and drawn attention to it with a "puff editorial" that attempted to demonstrate the value of homeopathic medicine by comparing results obtained at the Colored Orphan Asylum with the records of a Roman Catholic institution called St. Patrick's Orphan Asylum and another orphan asylum for white children called the Leake and Watts Orphan House. The average number of deaths at the Colored Orphanage under homeopathic treatment was,

The Elective Franchise and Some Family Matters

the article claimed, lower than the experience at the other two institutions by a factor of four to one.

Smith would have none of it, and took the time to write a letter to the editor of a medical journal called *The Annalist: A Record of Practical Medicine in the City of New York*. Statistics, as so often, were the basis for Smith's analysis, and he set out to demonstrate that the figures used by the homeopathic doctor were drastically incomplete and misleading. The Colored Orphanage doctor claimed six deaths in five years among 864 children or an average ratio of one in 144. The other three orphanages, using standard medicine, had experienced death in ratios of one in thirty-seven, one in sixty-two, and one in fifty-one. Smith pointed out that there had actually been 867 children admitted to the orphanage in the thirteen years of its existence but only 544 in the last five years. The ratio of deaths would actually, therefore, have been one in ninety. But if the turnover in population were taken into consideration, it would seem that only five had been under homeopathic treatment for the full five years. Smith then added the six who had died to the five who had been under homeopathic care for five years to produce a ratio of one in $1\frac{9}{16}$. But there was more to be said.

Still further analysis showed a very high turnover rate and indications that many of the children taken out of the asylum were taken away because they were ill. "These entries," Smith wrote, "have a suspicious look. They indicate a custom of quietly thrusting away from this charity the very sick children so that they may die elsewhere." This, he wrote, would be a "cold-blooded atrocity" committed for the sake of improving the statistics. Smith had further statistics to cite indicating that the homeopathic figures were completely misleading and that children under care for typhus fever, for example, had died at the orphanage at a rate of one in $6\frac{2}{3}$, while medical reviews reported rates of one in $11\frac{2}{3}$ in one study and one in $49\frac{1}{2}$ in another study. The higher rate had been found in an impoverished district of Liverpool during a famine year complicated by other intestinal diseases. But even there, the reports showed that standard treatment had saved nearly twice as many lives as homeopathy. "Sincerely and truly," Smith concluded, "as against the murderer and the assassin, may the regular practitioner do battle against the most deadly quackery that curses the nineteenth century, in the form of Homeopathy."[290]

Whether the managers of the orphanage read the report or not is unknown, but before the year was over, Smith would become responsible for medical care for the children in the orphanage himself and be able to provide care for the children simply as children, and not as specimens of a different species.[291]

While most doctors in the twenty-first century would agree with McCune Smith in rejecting homeopathic medicine, it remains an available option and Smith understood why. The preceding article in *The Annalist* illustrates that point. A doctor had written to describe his treatment of a patient with an ulcerated lip. The patient had "refused . . . the knife" and had been treated by "a 'celebrated cancer doctor'" who used twelve "plasters" over a period of six weeks that "produced such excruciating pain that he could not sleep for the succeeding 24 hours." The reporting doctor wrote that

> arsenic has long been a favorite application with the profession in these cases, and is also probably the one used by quacks,[292] though many of them deny that they use any *mineral* article. More recently, the chloride of zinc has been recommended by high authority, and in one case of lupus in which I used it, I was pleased with its effects. It is mixed dry with an equal quantity of flour, and then moistened by the addition of a little water. Some recommend its mixture with a larger proportion of flour. You will find directions for its use (and it must be used with caution) in Ranking's *Half-Yearly Abstract, Vol. I*. Our patient declines the use of the knife, and I shall therefore direct for him

the external use of Donovan's liquor (a combination of iodine, arsenic, and mercury), and apply locally the chloride of zinc.

Given these examples of "orthodox" medical practice, it is not surprising (as McCune Smith was not surprised) if many preferred the gentler, though ineffective, methods of homeopathic practitioners. The journal is filled with similar discussions of symptoms and treatments and for a nonspecialist, the impression created is rather like listening to housewives trading favorite recipes: "I tried these ingredients, and this is what happened." James McCune Smith himself wrote in that way to Gerrit Smith:

> I am sorry to hear that you suffer from Haemorroides: down our way a good remedy is found in One Part of Powdered Rosin, 3 parts pure honey and 1/16 of one part Balsam of Copaiba well rubbed up together. Two teaspoons at bed time every night or alternate night: the painful part to be washed or injected with a weak solution of acetate of lead.[293]

Medical knowledge was at a primitive level, but the proliferation of medical journals provided an opportunity—of which McCune Smith took full advantage—to exchange information and learn what "worked" and what did not. The doctors of that time still knew almost nothing about what caused diseases or about the reasons why particular treatments seemed to be effective or failed to be effective. The next generation of doctors would discover the existence of germs and revolutionize the profession.

CHAPTER THIRTEEN

Priorities, Family, and Purified Politics 1845–1850

Choosing Priorities

The decade of the 1840s, especially the last five years of that span of time, found James McCune Smith increasingly involved in such a variety of activities that it is easy to forget that he also had a home and family. The Colored Orphan Asylum, St. Philip's Church, and the Timbucto land grant program all made major demands on the time and energy of a man who was also a full-time doctor and druggist. At one point, he had seventeen children in the asylum down with the measles.[294] He was also a lecturer who spoke on a variety of subjects in various places and provided leadership in the abolition movement and the movements for franchise and civil rights. Nevertheless, he had somehow found time in those same years to marry a wife and father three children. It can hardly be surprising, then, to find a letter from James McCune Smith to Gerrit Smith expressing regret that he could not be present at a convention of the Liberty Party in Buffalo:

> The difficulty in my way is the utter impossibility of arranging one week's absence from my patients: unless I intend to give them up entirely. I have repeatedly found a two days and a half of absence inflict an injury upon my medical (punctual) reputation which months could not

> remove. I am no longer alone: my wife is a fruitful vine through God's blessing, and three little souls look up to me for support and discipline & guidance: what a holy trust! It is my prayer to be spared to train them aright and then fling them on the tide of progress dependent on their own well-developed resources.[295]

A concern for the education of children was also a continuing part of his life. Smith had written about it to the *New-York Daily Tribune* four years earlier. In writing to Gerrit Smith, he referred to that also as a constraint on his time:

> During the few years that I expect to live, I will devote myself to the improvement of colored *children*. There is a great work for the colored people to do in this land: a work not of a day only but of centuries, a generation must be raised up who can recognize the work and who under God will have the mental and moral discipline to essay and do it. I will fling whatever energy I have into the cause of colored children, that they may be better and more thoroughly taught than their parents are.

Having written about the "work . . . of centuries," he went on in a remarkable image to describe his work as comparable to that of the insects that build a coral reef:

> This kind of work suits me because it is very hard, and somewhat noiseless: in the series of metempsychoses I must have had a coral insect for a millio-millio-grandfather, loving to work beneath the tide in a superstructure that someday when the laborer is long dead and forgotten, may

rear itself above the waves and afford rest and habitation
for the creatures of the Good, Good Father of all.[296]

The image is remarkable not only for what it tells us about Smith's modest understanding of the role he hoped to play in his society, but for what it tells us about Smith's appetite for knowledge. The first important study of coral reefs had been published in England by Charles Darwin only six years earlier, and Darwin was still scarcely known in America; his classic study *On the Origin of Species* was still eleven years in the future; yet Smith was able to use his reading of Darwin's work to produce a striking metaphor for his own work. Perhaps "omniverous reading" should also be included in the constraints on McCune Smith's time, constraints which Smith alluded to in still another way at the end of the letter: "These presents are hastily scribbled on a counter amid dealing doses of Epsom salts to say nothing of calomel. There is too much hurry in this city to give a man a chance to think, much less to write. It is a most unnatural, unreasonable state."[297]

Refusal of the request that he go to Buffalo and become involved more deeply in the political realm might have suggested to Smith the possibility of saying no to other demands on his time, but what happened, of course, was the opposite. The political realm was not mentioned above as a major factor in Smith's busy schedule and, indeed, it seems not to have been a significant factor until 1848. But with Gerrit Smith as a friend, McCune Smith would find it harder and harder to resist involvement in that world also.

Gerrit Smith had been deeply involved from the beginning in the affairs of the Liberty Party, a party whose sole object was to abolish slavery. Upstate New York, the area between Albany and Buffalo, was known in those days as the "burned over district" because of the frequency with which waves of religious renewal had burned through its churches and population. Gerrit Smith's home in Peterboro was centrally located in that district. Anti-slavery commitment was almost as deep a conviction in that area as faith itself, and churches were divided again and again as the "come-outer" movement drew members away from churches not willing to commit themselves completely to the destruction of slavery. In one community after another, new churches were formed whose sole reason for being was a commitment to the abolition movement.[298]

The commitment to a perfectionist approach to faith almost inevitably spread to a similar commitment to perfectionism in politics, and the Liberty Party came into existence in 1840 to provide a vehicle for that approach. In 1843, party members gathered in Buffalo for two days and nights under a great white tent used also for revival meetings. There they sang rousing hymns, prayed fervently, and listened as pastors of come-outer churches preached on God's law and the obligations of a sanctified life. When the preaching and prayers were over, the gathering resolved "[t]hat human brotherhood is a cardinal principle of true democracy, as well as of pure Christianity, which spurns all inconsistent limitations; and neither the political party which repudiates it, nor the political system which is not based upon it, can be truly democratic or permanent."[299]

It remains true, however, that political parties are composed of human beings who, however deep their commitment to certain beliefs and even to perfectionism, remain stubbornly imperfect and have trouble dealing with the flaws in others if not the flaws in themselves. Practical politicians were drawn to the new party and success bred failure. The 7,000 votes for James G. Birney in 1840 became 62,000 in 1844 and probably tipped New York State to James K. Polk, the Democratic Party candidate, and away from the more moderate Henry Clay. That was unfortunate in the short term, leading as it did to a war with Mexico and the addition of Texas as another slave state, but it emboldened the Liberty Party to dream of a perfectionist triumph in 1848.

The world, however, was not yet ready for perfection, and the brief moment of success led instead to a division between the perfectionists in the Liberty Party and a new Free Soil Party less concerned for perfection than for political success. Opposition to the spread of slavery into new territories seemed to practical politicians to have a broader appeal than a narrow-minded opposition to slavery everywhere; the Free Soil banner drew moderate anti-slavery voters away from the Whig and Democratic Parties leaving only a core group of committed perfectionists to meet in Buffalo in 1847. Among those present was Frederick Douglass, attending a political convention for the first time and attending in spite of the disapproval of Garrison and his followers, who were committed to abstention from politics. The Garrisonians had tried to persuade Douglass to follow that path, but Douglass was increasingly unwilling. As Douglass watched, the Liberty Party nominated Senator John Hale of New Hampshire rather than Gerrit Smith. Smith's followers, unsatisfied, came together as the National Liberty Party in June 1848 and nominated Smith, and—deviating from their narrow focus on slavery—became the first political party anywhere to declare its commitment to women's suffrage. The purified Liberty Party would draw 2,545 votes, one-tenth of 1 percent of the total, in a year when 2.5 million votes were cast for the major party candidates Zachary Taylor and Lewis Cass, and a quarter million votes for Martin Van Buren and the Free Soil Party. But Gerrit Smith and the National Liberty Party had not compromised their principles.

Gerrit Smith had not been able to draw McCune Smith to his 1848 convention, but he would draw him into the political arena before much longer. It would be a smaller arena because it would reflect Gerrit Smith's views more closely and the evolving views of James McCune Smith as well. Meeting on July 3, 1849, in Cazenovia, New York, just a few miles from Smith's home in Peterboro, the faithful few would adopt in the name of the Liberty Party a series of resolutions that Gerrit Smith presented to them. "Our hope of the establishment of righteous civil governments on the earth," they agreed, "is in the prevalence of Christianity." By which, they quickly explained, "We, of course, do not mean that spurious, or that mistaken Christianity, which upholds unrighteous civil governments, and which votes civil offices into the hands of anti-abolitionists, and land-monopolists, and other enemies of human rights." Subsequent resolutions denounced intoxicating beverages, government debt, and standing armies. In fairness, it should be added that the purists of the Liberty Party could be extremely practical. One resolution suggested that better than sending Bibles to the slaves would be to "supply them with pocket compasses" and "if individual or private self-defence be ever justifiable . . . with pocket-pistols also." Thus provided, the resolution added, they might be able to reach a land where they could "both own the Bible and learn to read it." All these resolutions were passed unanimously.

Family Matters
There were battles to be fought that James McCune Smith believed in, but he could not go to conventions and he told Gerrit Smith exactly why: he had a "day job" and he had a family.

In fact, Smith's family responsibilities extended beyond his wife and three children. The 1850 census listed nine individuals living in Smith's residence, a new house that seems to have been built for his family at 15 North Moore Street.[300] Residents included Smith (age thirty-seven), his wife (age twenty-five), and three children. There were also four others: Smith's mother, Lavinia, and three single women between the ages of forty-seven and fifty-seven with three different last names: Sarah Williams, Amelia Jones, and Mary Hewlett. One might imagine that they were servants except that two of them were still listed five years later and another name had been added, Mary Herman, age nineteen, who alone was listed as "servant."

Five years later, death had claimed two children but another had been added, while the *New York City Directory* still listed one of the three single women, Mary Hewlett, and had added another, Matilda Hamilton, age forty, identified as "sister." Three young people—a man, age nineteen, and two women, ages nineteen and twenty-two—were also listed. The two young women, Sarah and Matilda Hamilton, had the same last name as one of the older women, Matilda Hamilton, and the young man, William Douglas

Hewlett, also had the same last name as an older woman, Mary Hewlett. All three of the young people were listed as "boarder."

It is useful to remember that the definition of family has changed over the years. One dictionary says that "family" is a husband and wife and their children, but also states that an "obsolete" definition is: "All the members of a household living under one roof." In a world without refrigerators and washing machines and electric stoves, families typically included a diversity of individuals who came together to meet their varying needs. The Smith family, as traced through state and federal census reports at five-year intervals, was a large and constantly changing community.[301]

Far from the least of the constant changes was the frequent arrival and departure of the children. Early in 1850, Smith wrote to Gerrit Smith to report that he was "stricken with grief" by the death of his firstborn child, Amy, who died on Christmas Eve, six days short of her sixth birthday. She had been sick for a year with an ailment that was "at times painful and distressing, always obscure, and which she bore with child-like patience." Malvina, McCune Smith went on to say, "was sorely afflicted, and until within a few days I have dreaded a permanent despondency." Now, however, he could report that she was "growing more cheerful," and that was just as well because there were two other children to care for: James, age five, and Henry, age three; there would soon be a third because Anna Gertrude was born just a few months later.[302]

Over the next twelve years, six more children would come at two-year intervals for a total of ten and five would die, three just days and weeks apart in August and September of 1854 in a cholera epidemic. The loss of three children in so short a span of time was a particular burden. Smith wrote later of that summer as "the time of shoreless woe" and of the "eclipse of faith under which I stumbled" and of a book he had read that provided "much of the needed light" that helped him through the crisis. He was so despondent at one point that when he was "spilled" by a horse on a New York street, he wrote that he had "not been able to stir this icy heart to thanksgiving that those steel shod hoofs did not come nearer!"[303] In March of the following year, he wrote to Gerrit Smith that "the first sharp bitterness is past," but "oh it is sad to have no children playing around the hearthstone. I try, and may God give me the Grace to succeed, to look into other little glad eyes, and listen to other little glad voices; and I try to reason myself out of the selfishness that they are not mine. Oh that meeting hereafter!"[304] Five of the ten Smith children would survive their father to be listed in the census of 1870.[305]

The Priority of Education
James McCune Smith had no time to go to Buffalo for political purposes, but he did find time to go to three gatherings in eight months to work for better educational opportunities for colored children. In October of 1847, Smith and James W. C. Pennington served as vice presidents of a National Convention of Colored People in Troy, New York, that dealt with a wide range of issues. In spite of the convention's title, one of the delegates at that meeting had been white and had been sent especially to represent his constituents in Northampton, Massachusetts, who believed in "the importance of abolishing all complexional distinction." He was welcomed with "hearty applause" to join with sixty-five other delegates from nine states from New Hampshire to Kentucky who spent four days debating a range of issues.

Smith brought forward a resolution to recommend the establishment of a national press, and this was favored by a decisive 27 to 8. Whether the resolution made a difference or not is hard to judge, but Frederick Douglass may well have seen it as supportive of his plans, already underway, to establish a new newspaper, *The North Star*, that he would publish before the year was out. The first issue carried a full report of the convention held just eight weeks earlier.[306]

CHAPTER FOURTEEN

Dealing with Douglass and Other Matters 1848–1852

Forming Partnerships

Two important changes took place in the New York landscape in 1848 and both of them could be traced back to a single day eleven years earlier. Frederick Douglass and James McCune Smith had, as previously noticed, both arrived in New York on the same day in 1837. Smith was returning from Scotland and Douglass had just escaped from slavery in Maryland. Smith settled down in New York, but Douglass stayed there just long enough to have his marriage to Anna Murray, who had reached New York ahead of him, solemnized by James W. C. Pennington before moving on to New Bedford in Massachusetts. There Douglass found work in the shipyards and, a few years later, discovered a new life as an orator and advocate for the abolition movement under the auspices of William Lloyd Garrison and the American Anti-Slavery Society. In 1840, Pennington also moved away from New York to take charge of a congregation in Hartford, Connecticut.

Then, by an odd coincidence, Douglass and Pennington both came back to New York City in 1848. Frederick Douglass had settled in upstate Rochester, New York, in 1847 after seven years in New England and almost two years in the British Isles, and founded a newspaper called *The North Star*. In the spring of 1848, he returned to New York City to seek backing for his new paper. Pennington also returned to New York in the spring of

1848 to become pastor of the Shiloh Presbyterian Church. Before long, James McCune Smith, who had stayed in New York, was working closely with both of them.

Establishing a Newspaper

When Douglass came back to the States, it was with the intention of establishing a new life for himself as a publisher. His letters from abroad had attracted attention. Horace Greeley of the *New-York Daily Tribune* had written redundantly that Douglass's letters "for genuine eloquence, would do honor to any writer of the English language, however eloquent" and Thurlow Weed of the *Albany Evening Journal* wrote that they gave Douglass "rank among the most gifted and eloquent men of the age."[307] Rather than resume his life as a traveling witness to slavery's cruelty, Douglass, therefore, resolved to become a writer and publisher and to establish a newspaper in Rochester, New York.

By a fortunate coincidence, a National Convention of Colored People and Their Friends was being held in Troy, New York, from October 6 to 9, 1847, and Douglass was there as a delegate from Massachusetts. James W. C. Pennington and James McCune Smith were two of the three vice presidents of the gathering. Whether it was coincidental or planned is unknown, but it was certainly convenient that a major item of convention business was a proposal to establish a national press. The debate consumed most of the afternoon and evening of the first day and most of the morning of the second day. While Smith and Pennington spoke in favor of the proposal, Douglass, oddly, spoke against it, arguing that although he favored the establishment of a press, he thought that a national press "could not well be sustained. A paper started as a national organ would soon dwindle down to be the organ of a clique and require a creed for the government of the Editor."

In the end, a seven-member committee, including Smith and Pennington, was created "with power and authority to carry out the intention of the Convention." What, exactly, that intention might be was never

Dealing with Douglass and Other Matters 1848–1852

clarified, but the value of a new press of some sort was affirmed. There were already abolitionist newspapers, but there was not a Black-owned paper edited by someone with Douglass's experience and perspective. After the convention, Douglass was able to move on to Rochester with an aroused interest in his project and strengthened relationships with the leaders whose support he would need.[308] The move to Rochester also avoided direct competition with Garrison's newspaper, *The Liberator*, published in Boston, and with the *National Anti-Slavery Standard*, published in New York City.[309] The first issue of *The North Star* was printed in Rochester in December 1847.

The North Star

Douglass understood that financing would be critical, and he had been able to put together a team of supporters including agents in nine states from Maine to Michigan. James McCune Smith was listed as one of two agents for the paper in New York City.[310] Almost immediately after publishing the first few editions, Douglass set off on a "get acquainted tour" around his new home territory and reported his adventures under the title "Gleanings by the Wayside" in the issue of February 11, 1848.

Arriving in Manhattan, Douglass had visited "the Apothecary's Hall of Dr. James McCune Smith in West Broadway" where he found him "preparing medicines, etc., etc., etc., with as much readiness and skill as any other disciple of Galen and Hippocrates." Smith and Douglass might not have met before the convention in the previous fall, and may not have realized that they had nearly crossed paths on the New York docks more than ten years earlier, but Smith was happy to show Douglass his place of business and then take him to visit a public school presided over by a Black teacher, Charles Reason. After that, Douglass made the usual visitors' stops in the city at the Battery, Castle Garden, and Croton Fountain before traveling up to Albany to see the Medical College and to sit briefly in the visitor's gallery of the state legislature. He then followed the course of the Erie Canal through such upstate cities as Schenectady, Utica, and Syracuse on his way back to Rochester.³¹¹ Douglass understood that part of the work of establishing a press was public relations and, just as Douglass's editorial task included building a base of support, so McCune Smith's role in helping to build that base quickly expanded to editorial help as well. In the latter capacity, Smith would become the paper's "New York Correspondent" and write columns under his own name and under the pen names of "Communipaw" and "Wappinumoc."

The first issue of *The North Star* in 1849 laid out a clear and simple statement of policy:

> THE object of the NORTH STAR will be to attack SLAVERY in all its forms and aspects; advocate UNIVERSAL EMANCIPATION; exalt the standard of PUBLIC MORALITY; promote the moral and intellectual improvement of the COLORED PEOPLE; and hasten the day of FREEDOM to the THREE MILLIONS of our ENSLAVED FELLOW COUNTRYMEN.³¹²

In April, Douglass came back again to New York City to do what he could to enlist additional subscribers in the nation's largest metropolis. "The dust and confusion of New York City is not a place I would choose to write from," he told his readers, nor was the human environment all "pleasant breezes and smooth sailing." Douglass was especially annoyed that the trustees of the African Methodist Episcopal Zion Church had charged him thirteen dollars to use their building for a meeting. The pastor of Zion Church, however, had let him use the pulpit for his message on Sunday morning and so had other pastors. In particular, Douglass had his old relationship with James W. C. Pennington, who willingly opened the Shiloh Church for a large meeting. Pennington and Smith were among those who spoke there on behalf of the new paper.

Dealing with Douglass and Other Matters 1848–1852

The Friday meeting at the Shiloh Church in support of the paper was followed by a Monday meeting in opposition to the Colonization Society that drew an audience of over a thousand and showed such enthusiasm that another meeting was held the next night. Douglass, Pennington, and Smith were among the speakers. Smith spoke last and gave what Douglass called "one of the neatest speeches to which I ever listened." The anti-Colonization Society meetings were instigated by word from Alexander Crummell, in England again, that an agent of the Colonization Society had recently arrived from the United States to report that "immense numbers" of colored Americans were eager to emigrate to Liberia. The New York meetings were designed to send a message to the contrary. As James W. C. Pennington put it, "The time has come when we must commence and fight the same battle over again." George Downing moved resolutions to say that "the testimony of our generation of the people of colour is entirely, uniformly, and absolutely against the scheme of African Colonization and that this solemn testimony . . . should be abundant evidence to all men that we will not remove to Africa except by the exercise of force."[313] All of that, of course, was in addition to Douglass's main objective of enlisting subscribers. On that subject, he spoke also in Brooklyn and Newark before returning to Rochester.[314]

Douglass on His Own

A few weeks later, McCune Smith wrote to Gerrit Smith to comment on the impression Douglass had made in New York. McCune Smith was not yet well enough acquainted with Douglass to have noticed how he spelled his name, but he had analyzed him well in more important ways:

> I love Frederick Douglas [*sic*] for his whole souled *outness*; that is the secret of his noble thoughts & far reaching sympathies: you will be surprised to hear me say that only since his Editorial career has he become a

colored man! I have read his paper very carefully and find phase after phase develops itself as regularly as in one newly born among us. The church question, the school question, separate institutions, are questions that he enters upon and argues about as our weary but active young men thought about and argued about years ago, when we had literary societies.[315]

As James McCune Smith saw it, Douglass "with his wounds yet unhealed, fell among the Garrisonians—a glorious waif to those most ardent reformers."[316] Garrison and his friends had loved employing Douglass to talk about slavery and his direct experience of its horrors, but they had actively discouraged him from exploring other subjects or even expanding his vocabulary to sound less as people expected an uneducated slave to sound. In his introduction to Douglass's autobiography, *My Bondage and My Freedom*, Smith wrote of how

> these gentlemen, although proud of Frederick Douglass, failed to fathom, and bring out to the light of day, the highest qualities of his mind; the force of their own education stood in their own way: they did not delve into the mind of a colored man for capacities which the pride of race led them to believe to be restricted to their own Saxon blood.

All they wanted and expected from him "on the platform or in the lecture desk" was "a pathetic narrative of his own experiences of slavery."[317] But Douglass, with an editor's chair, was free at last to think for himself and come to his own conclusions as, McCune Smith suggested, he and others had done long ago. From McCune Smith's point of view, the arena of action was the city and Douglass needed to be in closer touch with the urban centers where issues were being debated and leaders could come together to act. Douglass, however, remained equally convinced that he could serve best by living outside the city and making regular visits.

He was back again in the spring of 1849 for a large meeting at the Shiloh Church at which he spoke with his usual eloquence, and his friends offered their continuing support. Smith brought the meeting to a close with a series of resolutions, "unanimously adopted," endorsing *The North Star* as "living proof of the fitness of slaves for liberty and enfranchisement" and stating that it was "the special duty of the free colored citizens of these United States to support *The North Star*, as the defender of their cause, and that of the slave." George Downing added a resolution creating a committee to solicit subscriptions to *The North Star*. An interesting addition to the familiar names on the list of committee members is that of "Mrs. J. M. Smith."[318] Unfortunately, Malvina appears on the record only as a committee member for the Orphan Asylum and Douglass's newspaper and in one of her husband's columns; that she could take on these roles while producing and raising children indicates a woman worth knowing better.

Support for the paper was always a struggle. Douglass's own earnings as a lecturer provided a major source of funding since there were never enough subscriptions to balance the budget. James McCune Smith would continue to urge support of the paper in whatever way he could. In 1854, for just one example, he sponsored a resolution adopted unanimously by the New York Literary and Productive Union, a largely Black organization, "[t]hat we recognize in *Frederick Douglass' Paper*, the organ of the enslaved and down-trodden throughout this land—an instrument, which proves beyond gainsaying, the practicability, the safety, and the glory of Emancipation, and of Self-Emancipation."[319] But that, of itself, brought no funds. The paper remained located in Rochester. Douglass had no real experience of city life and no desire to learn.[320]

Black Doctor

The Compromise of 1850

The critical event of that year, however, was the passage in Washington of a series of bills known collectively as the Compromise of 1850. Daniel Webster brought his considerable influence to bear on behalf of the legislation with a Senate speech in March, and the Congress proceeded to enact a number of measures intended to calm the growing tension between North and South. It was too late, however, for a mutually acceptable compromise, and for James McCune Smith and his friends there was nothing compromising about it. It was a devastating threat to the freedom not only of Black citizens but, indeed, to the freedom of white citizens as well. It suspended, Smith pointed out, one of the most fundamental guarantees of freedom, the "habeas corpus" act. He speculated on what would happen if, under the terms of this law, Daniel Webster himself, frequently described as "a large dark man" and even as "Black Dan," were to be apprehended and carried off into slavery in Alabama.[321]

The new Fugitive Slave Act became law in September of 1850, and Smith drew up a statement signed by a Committee of Thirteen that was widely published in the following weeks. "By this enactment," he wrote, "the personal liberty of every American citizen is seriously periled, if not entirely taken away." Now, he pointed out, any person brought before the newly created "Commissioners" could, on the oath of one person, be deprived of their liberty and sent South into slavery whether they had ever been a slave or not, indeed whether they were Black or white since some slaves were white to all appearance. Under this law, the right to a trial by jury was eliminated and "all the safeguards of personal liberty, all the foundation elements of modern civilization are at once swept away." This law, he wrote, is

> dehumanizing in letting your fellow human being be carried off into slavery and calling on you to help carry them off: no matter, if he says he is free, no matter if she screams for the last sight of her own children: good citi-

zen, club him, choke her shrieks, and hurry them away to fulfill the compromises of the constitution and the law of our free and happy land![322]

"So far from allaying" the agitation and division in the country, said Smith for the committee, "it has served to excite that agitation beyond all former experience" and created "sterner and more unfraternal opposition" between the two sections of the Union "than has happened since the foundation of the Republic."

> But this slave bill, so insulting in its nature, so shameless in its exactions, not only fails as a measure of compromise, it also fails as a technical remedy for the great evil of which the south complains.... Now and ever, men and women will continue to flee from unrequited toil so long as there are footsteps and carriage roads and railways reaching from Mason & Dixon's line to our northern frontier. Let our Congress tear up these roads, blot out the northern star, sear human sympathy from the human heart, and crush out the Divine inspiration to be free which comes with every breath into the human bosom—and it will have only begun to make provision to arrest the escape of persons from unpaid labor![323]

Opposition to the legislation included the creation of what would be called "sanctuary cities" in the twenty-first century. The Chicago Common Council, for example, denounced the law as unconstitutional and instructed the city police to refuse to cooperate with federal authorities in the arrest of fugitives.[324]

William Lloyd Garrison and his followers saw the new laws as further evidence that the American Constitution was a pro-slavery document, but

Frederick Douglass, at the same time, reversed himself and announced that he now believed that the Constitution was an anti-slavery document. James McCune Smith had long held that position and opposed the Garrisonian call for disunion. Douglass, in his new upstate home, studied the matter and debated it with Gerrit Smith, James McCune Smith, William Goodell, and others. Finally, at the May meeting of the American Anti-Slavery Society in 1851, Douglass announced that he had come to "the firm conviction that the Constitution, construed in the light of well established rules of legal interpretation, might be made consistent in its details with the noble purposes avowed in its preamble; and that hereafter we should insist upon the application of such rules to that instrument, and demand that it be wielded in behalf of emancipation."

Garrison, for whom Douglass proclaimed "a veneration only inferior in degree to that which we owe to our conscience and to our God," was outraged and exclaimed, "There is roguery somewhere!" But Douglass had come to believe it wrong "to give slavery the slightest protection," as the Garrisonians did by calling the Constitution a pro-slavery document. After all, if it is a pro-slavery document, the Garrisonians were right in seeing no way to overthrow southern slavery and in advocating disunion, but that left millions in slavery and without hope. Smith and Douglass and other Black leaders were unwilling to accept that. Rather, Douglass now held the slave system to be "a system of lawless violence" and insisted that "it never was lawful, and never can be made so." That analysis brought slavery within the realm of politics and made it "the first duty of every American citizen, whose conscience permits so to do, to use his political as well as his moral power for its overthrow."[325]

But Smith and his colleagues also had a larger concern than southern slavery. They cared about their rights as free Black citizens and were aware of a battle being fought out daily in relation to the conditions of Black workers in New York City. Smith, concerned as usual for the healing of society as much as individuals, was a member of a "Committee on the Social Condition of the

Colored Race" whose report called attention to the way accumulated capital was "slowly invading every calling in the city from washing and ironing[3*] to palace steamers." That accumulated power, he wrote for the committee, "must tend more and more to grind the face of the poor in the cities, and render them more and more the slaves of lower wages and higher rents."[326] Such slavery was not, Smith might have added, a "complexional" matter.

The Christiana Riot

Positions were hardening, and a minor incident in a small town in Pennsylvania was evidence that people on both sides were ready to fight. In September 1851, in the small town of Christiana on the Pennsylvania side of the Mason-Dixon Line, Edward Gorsuch, a Maryland slaveholder, came looking for slaves of his who had been taken in by William Parker, also a fugitive slave, who had settled in that area a dozen years before and become a valued member of the community. Gorsuch came with a United States marshal with two assistants as well as two members of his family and two neighbors. It was only a small army, but it drew attention in the quiet rural community and Parker's neighbors were ready for it. What exactly happened was disputed, but shots were fired, Gorsuch was killed, and others were injured. The leading figures in the episode escaped, but a number of arrests were made and a trial was held.

James W. C. Pennington and James McCune Smith were among the leaders in raising funds for the defense. A "small but spirited meeting" was held at the Shiloh Church to raise money "to defend the Christiana Patriots" and Smith sent a report to what was now *Frederick Douglass' Paper*.[327] In November "a large enthusiastic meeting of colored citizens" was held and McCune Smith presented resolutions accusing the Congress of "breaking the public faith" and asserting that it was the members of Congress, not those arrested, who were guilty of "an act of treason."[328]

[3*] *If Smith's mother had earned a living by washing and ironing, it is not surprising that he would cite that by way of illustration.*

After that, more meetings were held and funds were raised also in Philadelphia and Chicago; $250 came in even from San Francisco.[329] Eventually, thirty-eight citizens, thirty-five of them Black, were indicted for treason and President Fillmore instructed Secretary of State Daniel Webster to employ all the resources of the federal government to secure convictions. The first individual put on trial, however, was acquitted by the jury after fifteen minutes and the others were eventually released after three months in jail— though broken in health and deeply in debt.[330] But other individuals here and there were still gathered up and carried to the South by newly empowered slave catchers. It was not despite the Compromise of 1850 but because of it that tensions between North and South continued to grow.

Colonization and Horace Greeley

The African Colonization Society never seemed to gain the momentum needed to become the major force its backers hoped for, but also it never seemed to go away. By 1849, Horace Greeley had become a significant voice in the newspaper world. He had founded the *New-York Daily Tribune* and made it the most widely circulated newspaper in the country. He had also given support to the American Colonization Society. When Daniel Webster spoke for that society in March 1851, Greeley followed up with what James McCune Smith characterized as "an incessant and ruffian volume of abuse . . . [and] with a flourish of a whip that would do credit to a negro driver, has laid it on without stint, reason or mercy." When Greeley added that "he wanted to know" if anyone meant to fight, Smith "sent him a calmly worded request to have privilege of reply" only to have Greeley back out with a torrent of abuse. Smith answered Greeley anyway in a lengthy two-part essay published in the *National Anti-Slavery Standard*. "Neither you nor I, in the hurry of city life," said Smith to Greeley, can provide the needed study of "the Race History of Man, Climatology, Psychology, and, indeed, breadth of thought" required to do justice to "this great problem," but Smith did hope to "jot down glances" at it.

Dealing with Douglass and Other Matters 1848–1852

First of all, Smith wanted Greeley to understand that the subject of colonization had been around for a long time and that it had been rejected by the Black population from the very beginning. When the organization of the American Colonization Society was announced in 1817, "at least thirteen years before Garrison began the publication of *The Liberator*, nay, while you and he were yet children," meetings were held in Philadelphia and New York denouncing the colonization scheme as "unchristian and unjust."

Next, Smith wanted to quarrel with Greeley's use of the term "the African race." Africa, Smith pointed out, is a large continent and produces "every variety of human kind from milk white to jet black, the Caucasian, Mongolian and Negro type. It is a misnomer, then, not to say a slight upon white men and Moors, to style the small and poor specimen of Africa that has reached these shores 'The African Race.'" But these specimens, having been mixed with the various types of European, have produced a mixture that is "an American race, if you will, but surely not the African." The "child playing at my elbow," Smith wrote, has forbears that "may be named Korymantse in Africa, Carib and Iroquois in America, Spanish, French, and old Puritan in Europe. And this child has a white skin, grey eyes, and flaxen hair. Will you brush up your Ethnography and tell us how and why this child is to be classed with the African race?"

Greeley had argued that Black people were "a degraded class," only capable of employment as servants. Smith reminded him that "the Divine authority of our Saviour has linked the highest human greatness with the meanest of human employments."[331] Greeley should also remember, Smith told him, that most Black Americans were slaves themselves or were the children of slaves. To say they cannot be elevated is to "manifest either a beetle-headed ignorance or a voluntary blindness." Meanwhile Smith pointed to Black justices of the peace in Massachusetts and Black captains of ships on the high seas as evidence of Black progress. "From these and a thousand kindred facts, we blacks know that our degradation is passing away in this the land of our birth." And furthermore: "We blacks are not yet done grinning at your asking us yesterday, if we really mean to fight rather than go to Africa and be baked. Why, man, we do nothing else but fight all our days in this land, and if you can point out any new thing for us to do, rather than go to Africa, we will do that also."

Part two of Smith's response to Greeley focused on the question of racial mixing, which Greeley had deplored but which Smith saw as a means of progress. Smith pointed to historical examples of isolated human strains that failed to advance and other societies in which various human types had come together to produce something new and better. The "Anglo-Saxon race," he asked Greeley to notice, enshrines racial mixing in its very title. Taking always the long view, Smith imagined an America a hundred years in the future that would want to know how it was that "this laughing, dancing, 'Jim Crow' people which the builders reject, will have become the cornerstone of the Republic."[332] Here he was looking again at the "Destiny of the People of Color" as he had done in a much fuller way ten years earlier, but this time the vision was somewhat earthier. Greeley had written a few days earlier that "intermingling with the blacks is naturally revolting to the whites." In other words, Smith responded,

> the hundred thousand whites who will pass this night in the embrace of black women, in the South, are committing a crime against Nature. Now, sir, you know that the South produces mulattoes every hour.... It is a libel to call that connexion a curse, because society at the South tolerates it; it is a libel against Nature to call it revolting, because the Creator had long since solemnized and made holy this connexion.... No, sir! These Southerners do nothing revolting to Nature, to God, nor to themselves, in this matter. They simply obey that Higher law of Progress which demands as its first condition, the free admixture of varieties of human kind.

This admixture, Smith suggested, had already taken place and continues. If it is "revolting" as Greeley had said, "Where did the browns, the mulattoes, and the quadroons come from? . . . We are yours; you are ours. 'What God hath joined together, let no man put asunder.'" All the ingredients, Smith pointed out, are here in America: the energy of the English, the cool sagacity of the Scot, the keen intellectual sagacity of the Gaul, the subtle genius of the German, as well as the climate and the territory. "The work goes bravely on," Smith told Greeley, but "take out of your heart that leprous prejudice against his creatures. . . . Fall in, man! Pray for a larger heart, and you will begin to understand the why and the wherefore of a black man's endurance."[333] By way of icing on the cake, Smith cited Shakespeare as an authority. The witches in *Macbeth* had sung of the mixing of colors:

> Black spirits and white, red spirits and gray;
> Mingle, mingle, mingle, you that mingle may.[334]

James McCune Smith and Frederick Douglass' Paper

In Smith's attack on Greeley, we begin to see the emergence of a somewhat different voice in Smith's writing, a voice more down to earth and colloquial. Douglass described his writing as "racy."[335] He was writing now for a larger audience and speaking directly to readers who would, perhaps, be more likely to respond to humor than to earnest eloquence. Greeley's *Tribune*, however, was less likely to give Smith space than *Frederick Douglass' Paper*. A month after Smith's letter to Greeley, *Frederick Douglass' Paper* printed a "Letter from Dr. James McCune Smith." A few months later letters from Smith would begin to appear under the byline "From Our New York Correspondent," and early in 1852, Smith would adopt "Communipaw" as a pen name for occasional use. Sometimes he also reversed the name and signed himself "Wappinumoc."[336] Wappinumoc was presented as "a young Sacem" who "comes to the rescue of poor old Communipaw."[337]

But what was this odd name "Communipaw"? It was, first of all, a native American settlement in northern New Jersey, across the Hudson River from Manhattan. It is still commemorated in the name of an unincorporated village and of a street in the area. Washington Irving had written a satirical history of New York some forty years earlier that was widely read and in which he claimed that the first Dutch settlement was in Communipaw. Irving calls it "the egg from whence was hatched the mighty city of New Yorke" and depicts the original Dutch settlers still there, still puffing their clay pipes. It has been suggested that Communipaw appealed to Smith as a pen name because it was an interracial community of Dutch, Native American, and Black residents. But perhaps Smith used the name simply to create the character of a somewhat distanced observer able to look at his community with the perspective of an outsider. "I am a plain Dutch negro," Smith as Communipaw wrote on one occasion, "well known in the flats . . . and am lineal descendant from one of the folly fellows who Washington Irving alludes to in his sketch book, as shining and laughing on our side of Buttermilk Channel."[338]

Whatever the source of the name, Smith used it for almost ten years. As the New York Correspondent and Communipaw, McCune Smith wrote about pressing issues and idle fancies as the Spirit moved him and frequently engaged in public jousting with Douglass's "Brooklyn Correspondent," a schoolteacher and civil leader whose real name was William J. Wilson and who often used the pen name, Ethiop. That aspect of Smith's writing career, however, deserves a separate chapter.

Smith's involvement with *Frederick Douglass' Paper* had a more practical side as well. In October 1851, he outlined a proposal for semiweekly publication to be financed by an appeal for special gifts from subscribers and an increased subscription price of three dollars to be phased in over the next two years. The Colonization Society, Smith noted, was now publishing a weekly journal. "Craven are we," Smith wrote, "if our organ do not put on another barrel and fire two rounds to their one—all the while looking forward to

Dealing with Douglass and Other Matters 1848–1852

the early day when we shall have a six-shooter—that is, a daily." "We want more of you," Smith wrote to Douglass. "And if you could secure a New York Correspondent, who would furnish each number of your paper with something from hereabouts, it would doubtless increase your circulation in this city." With the New Year, that suggestion was carried out: though the paper remained a weekly, Smith found himself installed as the "New York Correspondent" he had asked for and writing a regular column and signing himself as Communipaw.[339]

Colonization and Washington Hunt

The Christiana jury's verdict was handed down in mid-December, but the excitement surrounding it had hardly died down when the new governor of New York, Washington Hunt, began his second year in office in early January 1852 by calling on the state legislature in his annual message to make a "liberal appropriation" for the work of the Colonization Society so as to remove the Black population of the state. Black people, Hunt told the legislature, were unable to play a useful part in the life of the state:

> Debarred from all participation in public employments, rejected from most of the institutions of learning and religion, governed by laws which they have no share in framing, having been denied the right of suffrage by a vast popular majority, shut out from social intercourse and condemned to a life of servility and drudgery, their condition amongst us is deplorable in the extreme.... The instincts of nature, too powerful to be counteracted by the refinements of abstract reasoning, proclaim that the two races must be sooner or later separated.[340]

Black New Yorkers, caught off guard, were astounded. They had been passing resolutions against the Colonization Society for twenty years and, in spite of Horace Greeley, had reason to believe that their stand against it was well-known and generally respected. Unexpected or not, the Black population had a structure in place to respond—and they did respond promptly both at the state and local level.

The Committee of Thirteen immediately came together and denounced what they called a "nefarious design" and a "most flagitious appeal" and summoned "the colored men of the State" to a convention in Albany on the twentieth of the month. Meanwhile, the same committee convened a meeting at the Abyssinian Baptist Church in Manhattan on January 13. This time the invitation had urged, more inclusively, "Come one, come all—maidens and mothers, brothers and sisters, fathers and all—come, come, and proclaim to the world your unanimous resolve not to leave the country."

That gathering was opened with a prayer by James W. C. Pennington in which he "denounced the foul system of colonization . . . and trusted that the villainous policy would be frustrated." George T. Downing, McCune Smith's companion in the youthful street battles of the Five Points neighborhood and now the wealthy owner of New York's most prestigious oyster restaurant, quickly moved a series of resolutions stating that

> we see no reasonable grounds for the continuation of the American Colonization Society . . . [nothing] shall induce us . . . to sell the cause of our oppressed brethren and forsake the land of our birth, and the glory of our moral greatness by an ignominious flight to the pestilential shores of Africa . . . colonization is not and cannot be a remedy to the anguished American heart for the wrongs perpetrated upon American citizens on account of the colour of their skin.[341]

But the meeting in Albany, which the committee deemed "necessary even at this inclement season of the year," went through the governor's statement point by point in what was a precise and careful dissection of his argument. "Had these animadversions come from the Colonization Society," the Albany gathering said, "we should have borne them in silence, for 'tis their vocation... but when the chief officer of our State makes these assertions, they assume the prominence of historic truths, and appear before the world and posterity with an authority which will win for them the common belief, if they be permitted to pass uncontradicted."

Therefore, they set out to contradict them. Are Black people, they asked themselves, "debarred from all participation in public employment?" Of course not! Black men sail in government vessels, they have always been employed in the public stores in New York, they hold elective office in Essex County, they have refused office in Oneida, and they have received a fair number of votes for other offices. Are they "rejected from most of the institutions of religion and learning?" Yes, but only because of the influence of young men of the South, who have succeeded in closing these institutions to young Black men to prevent them from demonstrating their abilities. Are we "shut out from social intercourse?" Here the framers of the response enjoyed pointing out to the governor that his experience of "social intercourse" was apparently much more limited than theirs: "It may not be within the experience of his excellency, but we can assure him ... that social intercourse can exist apart from the class of our fellow-citizens who monopolize the higher offices in the gift of the people."

But the notion that Black people were "condemned to a life of servility and drudgery" and that their condition was "deplorable in the extreme" produced an inventory of Black achievement and some sardonic speculation about the "servility and drudgery" that might be the lot of the governor and his associates:

> Throughout the State of New York, colored men are occupied, or employed, as farmers, blacksmiths, engineers, carpenters, shoemakers, merchant tailors, professors, cler-

gymen, editors, teachers, physicians, lumber dealers, in short, in every calling, except the highly salaried offices of government; how far the last named employment may condemn a man to a life of servility and drudgery, we cannot say from experience, however distinct may be our opinion derived from observation. In regard to all the other occupations, we say, because we know, that they bind no chains upon our persons nor upon our souls.

They went on to cite the *New-York Daily Tribune* as a "respectable authority" for the statement that "colored beggars are extremely scarce in New York." The convention had statistics to show that public expenditures for the colored poor were only one-fiftieth of the total amount spent in the most recent year. The report also provided dollars and cents statistics as to the value of Black-owned businesses and real estate and noted that while the Black population had increased by 25 percent in the last twenty years, the value of their property and investments had increased by 100 percent. The governor might have annoyed the Black population with his ignorant evaluation of their situation, but he had also given them an opportunity to do a bit of legitimate boasting.[342]

The Committee of Thirteen also sent the governor a detailed financial report on the affairs of the Colonization Society showing that they had more than enough funds on hand to provide for the few Black people interested in going to Africa. In fact, their numbers showed that the bulk of society funds were expended on salaries and other expenses and that very little was actually used to send anyone to Africa. They suggested to the governor that any funds the state provided to send people to Africa would be likelier used for salaries of officers as well. "Sir," they wrote, "with these facts at your command, the undersigned feel sure that you will not permit the public funds of the State to be thus squandered." Thirteen names are listed at the end of the letter, but James McCune Smith was the one with by far the most experience in letter writing and cogent reasoning and it seems likely that he took the lead in producing the document.[343]

Perhaps because of the flurry of colonizationist activity, Gerrit Smith, James McCune Smith, and other state leaders met in Rochester in March 1852 to create a New York State Anti-Slavery Society. A one-page constitution was adopted listing six "truths" it would promulgate and practice, among them: that slaveholding is sinful, that it is wrong to apologize for it, and "that prejudice against color is wicked." Why a state society was needed was, perhaps, explained by the fact that a proposal to make the new society an "Auxiliary to the American Anti-Slavery Society" was rejected after lengthy discussion with only one vote in its favor. The New Yorkers were obviously no longer comfortable with Garrison's American Anti-Slavery Society and the American and Foreign Anti-Slavery Society created by the schism in 1840 had failed to create a viable alternative. A literal reading of Scripture and opposition to women in leadership roles made too narrow a basis for a broadly popular movement and many of those who disagreed with Garrison's policies disagreed also with the evangelical narrowness of the Tappan brothers who provided the funding and guiding hands of the new organization. Both of the anti-slavery societies also had white leadership. The New York State Anti-Slavery Society also chose a white presiding officer, Gerrit Smith, but James McCune Smith was chosen to be one of seventeen regional vice presidents, and Frederick Douglass was chosen to be corresponding secretary.

There is, however, no evidence that the New York State Anti-Slavery Society ever met again.[344] It was part of a widening search for effective methods to confront the evil of human slavery, but none of the organizations created in response to the obvious need seemed able to build an effective national movement that could bring about real change.

CHAPTER FIFTEEN

Smith as a Writer
Communipaw, Ethiop, and Others

Frederick Douglass' Paper and Communipaw

Frederick Douglass' Paper was obviously one of the most prominent voices in the national debate, but Douglass was wise enough to welcome other voices than his own. James McCune Smith soon became a regular contributor with a column headed, "Our New York Correspondent." Smith wrote the column under the pen name Communipaw and the anonymity seemed to release an aspect of his character not otherwise so evident. The relationship with another anonymous writer, Ethiop, "Our Brooklyn Correspondent," could be prickly at times as they enjoyed disparaging each other, but it could also dredge up long-buried and humorous memories. When one caustic letter from Ethiop ended by using "the touching, winning, deprecatory, insinuating, melting, heart-of-stone-softening expression, 'dear Communipaw,'" Smith/Communipaw wrote that it brought "to my swimming eyes," a vivid memory of a childhood experience in the African School. "One of us . . . I shan't say who, had played hookey" and had come to school prepared by several layers of paper in their pants for a good thrashing by Headmaster Charles Andrews. Unfortunately, Andrew's "quick ear" detected the insulation and, stripping it off, "laid on with a mischievous vigor which brought from the boy a hundred exclamations of 'Oh! Oh! Oh! Mr. Andrews, I'll never! Oh! Mr. Andrews,' and finally 'dear Mr. Andrews! My dear Mr. Andrews!' which brought down the house; even Charley Andrews could cut no more. Neither can I."[345]

But that was only a digression from a serious debate between the two pseudonymous columnists as to the relative value of money for the advancement of Black people. Smith/Communipaw was arguing that "our present real can only be bettered by a 'nobler ideal'" and that money is not that nobler ideal, but rather "liberty, equality, human brotherhood . . . and we can only reach it by the right development of character here where God has placed us. . . . I take it that Alexander Crummel has done more for the advancement of our people, by his true manhood, than any coloured man could do by the amassing of gold." Communipaw cited the negative example of Jeremiah Hamilton, a Black millionaire, who had amassed a fortune by various unscrupulous maneuvers. Hamilton was able to compete with Cornelius Vanderbilt for control of a transit company and was said to be the richest Black man in America when he died in 1875.[346] But Hamilton, Communipaw wrote, "fled from his identity (to use the elegant phraseology of Ethiop) like a dog with a tin kettle tied to his tail."[347]

Communipaw was not the same writer as James McCune Smith. Smith could be eloquent, but also scholarly in his use of language. Communipaw, on the other hand, was quick to go for the colloquial terms, sarcastically referred to here as the "elegant phraseology"—sometimes borrowed from Ethiop—that the sophisticated Smith was unlikely to employ.

Humor could also be used sometimes with more effectiveness than a tirade. McCune Smith had excoriated Horace Greeley more than once in the pages of the *National Anti-Slavery Standard* and elsewhere, but when he took to the lists as Communipaw, the detached and humorous observer, he could treat Greeley with a pitying contempt. He told of going to a program where Horace Greeley (who usually wore white) sat on the platform: "Happy Horace Greeley, there he sat on that sofa on the platform aforesaid, like a huge carter potato in a bed of mignonette." Communipaw added zest and flavor to Smith's more academic style.[348]

It can be safely assumed that Communipaw and Ethiop, or Smith and Wilson, knew each other perfectly well though they pretended not to. New York and Brooklyn were not that far apart even before the Brooklyn Bridge was built, but the pretense of not knowing provided readers with some useful word pictures of James McCune Smith from Ethiop's pen. In one letter "From our Brooklyn Correspondent," for example, he wrote: "I should also have mentioned, I have had the pleasure of an introduction to Doctor James McCune Smith. The Doctor is a fine fellow I judge; lively, good natured and keen, with much of 'the laughing devil in his eye;' relishes a good joke and tells a good story, and ought to be, and I doubt not is, the soul and centre of wit, fun, and learning in Gotham." That's a vivid and valuable word picture of Smith not found elsewhere.[349]

That description of Smith is, by the way, further confirmation that the essay, "The Washerwoman," is a depiction of Smith's mother. In writing that essay, Smith/Communipaw had described the washerwoman's boy as having "a 'laughing devil' in his eye." By using the same term to describe Smith in his essay a few weeks later, Ethiop/Wilson seems to be letting Communipaw/Smith know that he had noticed that self-description and saw the boy whose mother was the washerwoman behind the man who had portrayed his mother in his essay.

An imaginary character encouraged, of course, imaginary thinking; Communipaw was free to indulge his imagination in a way the doctor might not have done. In one of his early letters, Communipaw pondered references to the "solitary ship" that brought the Puritans to New England and wondered whether the day would come "half a century hence when a black president shall hold court at the White House" and "some succulent antiquarian may fish up from the musty parchments in Annapolis the title of that vessel which brought the first human cargo to the American continent from the coast of Guinea."

That is a remarkable guess—though off by a century. It was, in fact, over a century and a half before the first Black president would "hold court" at the White House, and just a bit earlier than that, in the late 1990s, that a "succulent antiquarian" at Boston University discovered that the first slaves in the present United States came from a Portuguese ship that had been robbed of its human cargo by two English ships flying a Dutch flag. Within a few days of each other, in 1619, those two ships, the *Treasurer* and the *White Lion*, brought their human cargo to Jamestown and traded them for provisions.[350]

"It becomes us to be meek," Smith, as Communipaw, wrote to Douglass, affecting a colloquial style, "but don't the last 'solitary ship' kick up a bigger dust in the year of grace 1852 than ever the May Flower did?"[351] Certainly a case could be made that the consequences of those two ships at Jamestown were of equal or greater magnitude for American society than the Mayflower, and now we know, as James McCune Smith, alias Communipaw, predicted we would, how it all began.

Communipaw and the Anglo-Saxons

As an imaginary character, Smith—writing as Communipaw—may also have felt freer to castigate a reputed abolitionist like Theodore Parker for his partial blindness. Parker had taken in fugitive slaves, written a scathing letter to a southern slaveholder, and advocated disobeying the Fugitive Slave Act of 1850, but Parker shared some at least of the unthinking prejudices of the southern slaveholder and revealed them when he spoke at the Tabernacle in New York on "the Anglo-Saxons and their Influence." Parker, like most people, could compartmentalize his ideas, and he was probably not thinking much about slavery when he thought about the Anglo-Saxons. He was also probably not aware that James McCune Smith would be in his audience and ready to take note of any inaccurate or injudicious remarks. Had he thought more carefully, he might not have attributed "trial by jury" to Anglo-Saxon origins, and he surely would not have said: "The Anglo-Saxon is not cruel."

Smith delegated the response to Wappinumoc, who was able to cite Hale's *The History of the Common Law of England* and Crabb's *A History of English Law* to testify that trial by jury was "universal among all the northern tribes of Europe from the very remotest antiquity" and that the Normans had trial by jury before they ever set foot in England. As for the statement, "The Anglo-Saxon is not cruel," Wappinumoc could refer his readers to such basic texts as *American Slavery As It Is: Testimony of a Thousand Witnesses*, published fourteen years earlier by Theodore Weld; his wife, Angelina Grimké; and her sister, Sarah Grimké, and widely distributed. The Grimké sisters, born and brought up in South Carolina, were eyewitnesses of the cruelty of slavery and provided firsthand testimonials and personal narratives from both freedmen and whites of the horrors of the slave system. Parker had very likely read the book, but he had not stopped to think that many of the slaveholders depicted there were probably of Anglo-Saxon origin. The Grimkés' book, Wappinumoc wrote, proves

> that Anglo-Saxons, south of Mason and Dixon's line, lash naked and defenceless women, maim and bruise, and brand, with hot iron, poor dumb men, tear husbands from their wives, sucking infants from their mothers, and then go down on their knees and 'thank God that they are not as other men:' and the Reverend Theodore Parker, a transcendental priest of this Anglo-Saxon phariseaism lays his hands upon their heads and solemnly says, 'Blessed are ye, for ye are not cruel!' . . . To a more whining, canting, at-truth squinting, piece of self-adulation it has seldom been my misfortune to listen."[352]

Wappinumoc/Communipaw was not always amused or amusing, and he was free to speak his mind in a way that Smith might not have felt able to do.

Heads of the Colored People

James McCune Smith, writing as Communipaw, was at his most innovative and controversial in a series of columns that he wrote for Frederick Douglass' Paper and titled "Heads of the Colored People." Ten columns with that title were published at intervals over a span of almost three years, sometimes only two or three weeks apart but twice with longer gaps, one of seven months and one of well over a year. Smith set the series in broad and ambitious terms: harking back to the ancient Greeks, he invoked the spirit of the poet Anacreon, and the spirit of the seventeenth- and eighteenth-century Republic of Letters that linked leading thinkers in Europe and America. Smith proposed to show his readers some of the residents of "the outermost enclosure leading to the Republic of Letters."

If the subjects of Smith's portraits were unlikely to read his columns, many of those who did read them disliked them. The literate and successful Black residents of New York, Smith's readers, wanted to hear inspirational stories about successful careers in the world of business, about artists and businessmen, doctors and lawyers. Instead, Smith showed them, among others, a news vendor, a bootblack, a washerwoman, and a gravedigger. It was a faithful portrayal of Black residents as they were, not as they would be—and were beginning to be. There were, it should be pointed out, many other stories that could have been told of men who had not achieved even the modest success of the bootblack and news vendor, men and women who had only their physical strength to offer and who pushed and hauled carts full of produce and trash around the city, who swept floors and dug ditches, heated flat irons and hauled laundry. Smith himself had spent four years pumping the blacksmith's bellows. James W. C. Pennington had driven a lawyer's carriage and cared for the lawyer's horse. Communipaw's "Heads" had done better than that, but not much. Douglass's readers, however, were the educated elite and they wanted to read about themselves, or, at least, about others like themselves. Douglass might have pointed out to his readers that Smith's portraits were almost entirely positive stories of progress, lives established on the bottom rung of the ladder, but established nonetheless: not slaves, but free, and building lives that were secure.

Portrait Number One, dated March 25, 1852, was "The Black Newsvender," a man selling newspapers on the street corner for a few pennies. He had a wife and a family and a decent income. Was that not something to be celebrated?[353] The news vendor's story was perhaps the most intimate and personal of the whole series. It was done in large part as an interview, so allowing the news vendor to speak for himself:

> Com.[Communipaw] — Good morning, sir; have you a family?
> News Vender — Yes, a wife and two children; one of them, you recollect, was sick ...
> Com. — Where was you born?
> News Vender — In Virginia; came from there some years ago and followed the sea, until two years and a half ago, since which time I have sold papers ...
> Com. — You *came* from Virginia—free, of course?
> News Vender — Why—yes—I—made myself free.
> Com. — Have you no fear of being arrested and taken back?
> News Vender — Not now (sadly looking at his maimed legs.) When I stood six feet two in my stockings, and heard talk of Virginians hereabouts, I would go straight to the dock, take ship, and be away two or three months; but now—what would they want with me?

As the conversation continued, Communipaw learned that the news vendor lost his legs when they were frozen in a storm at sea on Christmas Eve two years earlier and Communipaw/Smith realized it was the same day on which his firstborn child died at the age of six. In a burst of emotion, Communipaw promised that the news vendor would have a shop and that Smith would contribute to the purchase of his first stock of supplies in memory of the child who died. Smith ended the essay by drawing attention to the hope that lies in the story "for all who like him are battling against slavery and caste."[354]

So also, the second column in the series depicts the bootblack, an illiterate former slave, as a man who has carved a niche for himself in a hard world and is determined that his children will have a better life. He had hoped for boys who would become storekeepers, but girls arrived instead. Redirecting his hopes, he saw to it that they were educated and became schoolteachers. Once again, the story was one of hope and progress, though those portrayed were near the bottom of the occupational ladder.[355]

The washerwoman's story, third in the series, was told impersonally, but seems almost certain to be that of Smith's own mother. The circumstances were hard, but here again, the story was one of successful determination to create a stable home against all the odds. The washerwoman may be hard-pressed to survive, but she was surviving and was raising her son in freedom.[356]

With that third story, Frederick Douglass published his editorial dissent. He would not defend the columnist who portrayed what Douglass saw as "contented degradation." He warned his columnist that readers wanted to know who this "Communipaw" might be so they could vent their displeasure on him. Communipaw should be prepared, Douglass told him, to "come in violent contact with a broomstick" or to feel "a few drops of moderately hot 'suds' upon his neatly attired person."[357]

It may be that Smith had already written and submitted the fourth essay in the series when Douglass printed his warning. Certainly, the next essay yielded nothing to the threats; indeed, it was the darkest study of them all. "The Sexton" is shown discharging his duties as gravedigger, working at night, and the subject of rumors of nefarious deeds. Smith would, of course, have remembered the tales of grave robbers in Scotland in the years just before his arrival, but similar tales were told of "resurrectionists" at work in New York. The Doctors' Riot of 1788 occurred when evidence was found of such activity in Trinity Churchyard. In the same year, Black residents petitioned the city authorities to end the stealing of corpses from the "Negros [*sic*] Burial Ground." That burial ground was later taken over by St. Philip's Church and the sexton of St. Philip's became gravedigger to the city's Black population.

All the ingredients were present for a tale of Gothic horrors, and Edgar Allan Poe, who had died just three years earlier, had shown that such tales could be popular. Smith, an omnivorous reader, would surely have read "The Murders in the Rue Morgue," "The Pit and the Pendulum," and other tales Poe had written of mystery and the macabre, but he told the story of the sexton with a lighter hand. We are told that the sexton, described in fearsome terms—gigantic height, bowed legs, prominent staring eyes—worked mainly at night, that the graveyard somehow was never full, and that a tallow factory beside the graveyard seemed always to have an ample supply of raw material. The St. Philip's vestry heard rumors of dark deeds and conducted an investigation but returned satisfied with what they had learned. The graveyard was a good source of income for the church and the vestry had no interest in rocking the boat. But Smith built his ominous narrative toward an unexpected and amusing climax. As organizer of the New York African Society for Mutual Relief, the sexton had locked himself in with a colleague and settled down to keep vigil over the corpse of the first deceased member of the society. Toward midnight, they heard a series of raps and then saw the linen over the body rise and fall. Terrified and unable to open the door, they headed for the chimney and scrambled up. The neighbors, hearing the racket and convinced that the sexton was feasting on the corpse, burst in, snatched the sheet from the body, and found the deceased man's favorite spaniel thumping its tail beside its master's remains.[358]

Smith's critics would surely not have liked the portrait of a Black gravedigger in their concern for a more positive picture of New York's Black residents, but what would they have made of the humorous ending? Whatever the readers' response, there was a six-month hiatus between the sexton's tale and the next published portrait for the "Heads of the Colored People."

Whatever the reason for the long delay, "The Steward," essay number five in the "Heads of the Colored People," would have done little to mollify the critics. "The Steward," the officer on a passenger ship, did cut a more elegant figure surely than those in the earlier portrayals. While the ship was in port, the steward appeared in a splendid morning gown and red slippers as he showed passengers to their cabins. On the other hand, when the ship was under way, he was servant to all, subject to the beck and call of any passenger or crew member who summoned him. Yet when the ship came into port and the garbage was lowered over the side and carried away to a certain place, the steward would find a need to go ashore and visit a tradesman's store and negotiate with watch dealers for the thousands of dollars' worth of watches that had somehow been salvaged from underneath the trash. Other mysterious packages were lowered over the stern to small boats that came alongside. As in several of these columns, Communipaw ended his picture of his subject and then went on at great length about other things, in this case schools in the Five Points.

The remaining columns seem even less clearly focused. Unlike earlier columns, the essay headed "The Editor" is not about the editor as a single individual, but rather is a collection of comments about the role of an editor and how much time must be spent by any editor in raising money, and a sampling of the appeals that must be made. After a great deal of this, there was one paragraph that showed us one editor at work, dictating to his wife because he himself cannot read or write. Douglass, of course, could read and write though his spelling was uncertain, but it was an annoyance to Smith that Douglass and Julia Griffiths, his managing editor, so often misread and misspelled what he had written.[359]

An editor might have suggested that Communipaw's essays needed to be tightened up and better focused. It seems surprising that Douglass apparently made no effort to do that or to modify Smith's rather negative depiction of an editor, but Douglass was often away from the office raising money, and it seems likely in any event that neither he nor his co-editor, Julia Griffiths, would have wanted to suggest substantial rewriting of material from so important a supporter and contributor.

It was well over six months before the next two "Heads" appeared in September 1853, and in the interim, another of Smith's children, Henry, had died like his sister at the age of six. Smith as Communipaw wrote that the sketches had been interrupted

> by the long and painful illness of one whose little chair is vacant by my hearthstone, whose little grave is filled on the hillside; and again and again, as I sit by my easel, brush in hand, spirit fingers weave his golden hair upon the canvas, and those sad eyes light upon me, and spirit voices break the stillness of the night, in cadences now light and airy, now sobbing in keen agony.[360]

John Stauffer, in his compilation of *The Works of James McCune Smith*, comments on Smith's use of irony and his "experimental" avoidance of the sentimental style of the day.[361] But the frequent death of children made sentimental writing a very natural pattern in the Victorian world, and Smith could not avoid revealing the pain he felt, if not in the body of his essays, at least in his introductory comments.

In the next two "Heads," Communipaw's essays never did succeed in focusing on one individual. His essay on "The Inventor" seems to suggest that Douglass had assigned the title but that Smith/Communipaw had been doubtful from the beginning that a Black inventor could be found: "When you announced your 'workshop,' dear Mr. Editor, I had doubts as to its practicality." That white craftsmen refused to take on Black apprentices, he pointed out, was a major obstacle to the development of a skilled cohort of potential "inventors." The essay cited a carpenter in Alabama whose skillful work on the state capitol building had earned him his freedom, and cited another carpenter in Brooklyn. One paragraph began, "But what has all this to do with one inventor?" and then talked about standing on the banks of the Morris Canal watching a boy netting crab, which surely had nothing to do with inventors. Another paragraph began with an incomplete sentence: "But then one inventor." It proceeded to describe a church outing. It seems clear that the writer was having difficulty keeping his work in focus.[362]

The essay on "The Whitewasher" also, though it has much to say about whitewashers in general, managed to focus on a single whitewasher only briefly. After that, almost a year went by with no further essays, and then disaster overwhelmed the Smith family. In the space of five weeks, three children died, probably in the cholera epidemic of that year.[363] Frederick Douglass Smith, three months old; Peter Williams Smith, a two-year-old; and Anna Gertrude, four and a half, all died between August 13 and September 19. Only James, age nine, survived. When Communipaw resumed his writing, the original plan had essentially been abandoned. The title, "The Schoolmaster," headed two essays, but only passing reference was made to a schoolmaster, and that only toward the end of the second essay. For Smith, there was no avoiding the sentimental when he set out to write again: "The leaves are falling in our lane; and the trees, stripped and gaunt, seem prepared to wrestle with the coming storms; and the blossoms are withered, and the little feet no longer patter in our door-way, and Oh, I am aweary, aweary!"[364]

Nor could Smith carry on the plan to write about a schoolmaster with the inevitable picture of a schoolroom filled with children. The title, "Heads of the Colored People—No. X: The Schoolmaster," remained in place, but the essay began with the quoted lament and continued with several paragraphs about the Crimean War before switching abruptly to the tragic story of a Black stewardess. The story of Anna Downer, who kept pumping as the ship went down, is an inspiring story of heroism—perhaps the sort of story Douglass's readers were looking for when the series began—but Anna Downer was not a schoolteacher. She did, however, not only provide the sort of appealing story Douglass wanted, but also, in the story of a sinking ship, an appropriate image for the United States for which "we must work as Anna Downer did, as long *as we can move our arms*! We may not save the ship, but like that noble woman, we may leave a deathless name."

Two closing sentences of the column about Anna Downer expressed the hope that the "Schoolmaster" could be dealt with on another occasion and that "my friend," the editor, "will keep calm." Once again, however, the title was subverted by subjects of more immediate interest to the writer, who had paid a visit to Baliere's Bookstore and needed to talk about a book he had found there that demeaned the free Black population of the northern states. Communipaw brought his knowledge of census figures to bear against the book before finding another book that he and his friend "Fylbel" clubbed together to buy. A final paragraph set out to deal with the nominal subject by describing a schoolteacher met in a remote region of New Hampshire, but ended, "(to be continued.)"

There is no complete file of the *Frederick Douglass' Paper*, but there is no evidence that any further columns were written for the "Heads of the Colored People." James McCune Smith had more immediate issues to deal with, not least the effort to make a real and immediate difference in the lives of Black Americans through the convention movement and political parties. The existing evidence suggests that Douglass asked Smith to write a series of portraits of Black citizens, assuming that he would select the most distinguished. Douglass had recently been in New York and visited churches and business places where he had met successful leaders of the community. "Why will not my New York correspondent," he asked, "bring some of the real '*heads of the colored people*' before our readers?"

But Douglass continued to print what his most talented writer submitted even as Smith struggled to find time to concentrate on the work he had agreed to do in the midst of his own work and personal tragedy. The result was wildly uneven but included brilliant glimpses of the ordinary people with whom, as a doctor, Smith, if not Douglass, was in daily contact.

CHAPTER SIXTEEN

The Convention of 1853 and the Industrial School

The National Convention in Rochester

Nine National Conventions of Colored Americans had been held since the first such gathering in 1830. A plan for an industrial school or manual arts school had been proposed by that very first convention and by almost every convention afterward.[365] The tenth national convention and first in five years called to meet in 1853 in Rochester, New York, set out to go significantly further than previous conventions by creating a specific plan for such a school and a National Council to serve Black Americans on a continuing basis. The invitation to the convention was eloquent in its appeal:

> We have gross and flagrant wrongs against which, if we are men of spirit we are bound to protest. We have high and holy rights, which every instinct of human nature and every sentiment of manly virtue bid us to preserve and protect to the full extent of our ability. We have opportunities to improve—difficulties peculiar to our condition to meet—mistakes and errors of our own to correct—and therefore we need the accumulated knowledge, the united character, and the combined wisdom of our people to make us (under God) sufficient for these things.

The call to convention went on to list specific issues that needed to be dealt with, and first of all the Fugitive Slave Act of 1850, which it called "the most cruel, unconstitutional, and scandalous outrage of modern times." Beyond that it listed

> the proscriptive legislation of several states with a view to drive our people from their borders—the exclusion of our children from schools supported by our money —the prohibition of the exercise of the franchise—the exclusion of colored citizens from the jury box—the social barriers erected against our learning trades—the wily and vigorous efforts of the American Colonization Society to employ the arm of government to expel us from our native land.

And finally, the call cited "the propitious awakening to the fact of our condition at home and abroad, which has followed the publication of 'Uncle Tom's Cabin,' call trumpet-tongued for our union, cooperation and action in the premises." Harriet Beecher Stowe's novel had changed everything by letting ordinary northern citizens see vividly what slavery was like and had given enormous impetus to demands for abolition.

But perhaps the most interesting item on the convention's agenda was not a protest but a constructive proposal for a National Council to give the Black population of the country a voice with "permanent existence." With that agenda, the convention was called to order on Wednesday, July 6, in Corinthian Hall, an auditorium erected just four years earlier and rented for three days for sixty dollars.[366] Corinthian Hall was noted already for having hosted one of Frederick Douglass's most famous speeches, "The Meaning of July Fourth for the Negro," which was given there a year and a day before the convention began.[367]

James McCune Smith was the organizing officer of the convention's first day in spite of the fact that his six-year-old son, Henry, had died only a few weeks earlier.[368] It was he who read the "Call for the Convention," he who moved that the signers of the call be considered de facto members of convention, and he who moved that a committee of eight be appointed to nominate officers for the convention. Smith was duly appointed to chair that committee, and he reported back at the opening of the afternoon session. Nominated and elected to serve as president was James W. C. Pennington. Pennington had been a recently escaped fugitive slave at the first National Convention of the Free Persons of Color twenty-four years earlier, but he was now the Yale-educated pastor of a large New York congregation and possessor of an honorary doctorate from the University of Heidelberg in Germany. He was one of only two delegates in Rochester who had been present at the first convention.[369]

The highlight of the first afternoon session was a speech by Frederick Douglass as chair of the Committee on Declaration of Sentiments. "We are Americans," said Douglass, "and as Americans we would speak to Americans. . . .

> We ask that in our native land, we shall not be treated as strangers, and worse than strangers. We ask that, being friends of America, we should not be treated as enemies of America. . . . We ask that the doors of the school-house, the workshop, the church, the college, shall be thrown open as freely to our children as to the children of the other members of the community. . . . We ask that as justice knows no rich, no poor, no black, no white but, like the government of God, renders alike to every man reward or punishment according as his works shall be— the white and black man may stand on an equal footing before the laws of the land.[370]

Douglass went on to argue his case for equal treatment under the Constitution:

> By birth, we are American citizens; by the principles of the Declaration of Independence, we are citizens; within the meaning of the United States Constitution, we are American citizens; by the facts of history, and the admissions of American statesmen, we are American citizens; by the hardships and trials endured; by the courage and fidelity displayed by our ancestors in defending the liberties and in achieving the independence of our land, we are American citizens.

Over ten pages of the fifty-six-page report of the convention were given to Douglass's opening oration. Delegates might have been justified in feeling that they had already gotten their money's worth when Douglass sat down, but James McCune Smith then stood up to challenge them with a two-page report on creating a National Council of the Colored People and providing an ongoing structure to make a difference. That brought the afternoon to a close, but there was still an evening session that received a six-page report from the Committee on Social Relations and Polity. That report, perhaps inevitably somewhat moralistic and negative in its comparisons of Black and white households, proved controversial. It ended by calling first for "[a]n increased number of better regulated homes among us" and last for "more enlightened views of the high and holy principles of morals and religion." The hour being late, the debate was brief and the report was referred to the committee for amendment. When it came back the next day, there was further debate and a rejected motion to "strike out obnoxious passages," but finally, the report itself was rejected by a margin of two to one. Some previous conventions had focused their attention on moral reform, but the delegates in Rochester had a different agenda.

The morning and afternoon of the second day were spent on that debate and a variety of procedural and organizational matters. The convention then moved on to consider Smith's proposal for a National Council. He "made a few eloquent remarks," and the council agreed to consider the proposal by sections. Frederick Douglass spoke first on the need for such a structure. Then a complicated debate began with rival speakers claiming the floor and making attempts to reword various passages, but the debate was suspended to hear a report of the Committee on Manual Labor School. This subject had been proposed in the very beginning of the convention movement and had come to the fore most recently at a convention in Troy in 1847. Now a committee called for the creation of still another committee for the "maturing of a plan" to erect, at an appropriate place,

> a school of a high intellectual grade, having incorporated an Agricultural Professorship, or an equivalent thereto, a professorship to superintend the practical application of mathematics and natural philosophy to surveying, mechanics and engineering, the following branches of industry: general smithing, turning, wheel-wrighting and cabinet-making; and a general work-shop in which may be combined such application of skill in wood, iron, and other material as to produce a variety of saleable articles, with suitable buildings and machinery for producing the same.

The committee, believing that fifty thousand dollars would be needed to acquire land and erect buildings, proposed the issuing of stock at ten dollars a share with a board of directors. Another one hundred thousand dollars would then be raised as an endowment. A further proposal for a Department of Industry for Females was provided "only in outline," but the suggestion was made that "the straw-hat business in some of its branches, paper box making, and similar occupations might from time to time be connected."

The idea was not unrealistic; only two years later in 1855, a white abolitionist, John Gregg Fee, created Berea College in Kentucky, which survived the Civil War and still exists as a tuition-free college for students who want to earn their way. In 1853, however, there were not yet among the Black population the experience and resources to make such an institution a reality.

Frederick Douglass followed the committee's report by reading a very long letter he had written to Harriet Beecher Stowe in response to her question as to how she might be most helpful to the colored population. Douglass, like the committee, pointed to an industrial school where young men could gain the skills they could not acquire as apprentices since white artisans would not take them on. "At this moment," Douglass wrote, "I can more easily get my son into a lawyer's office to study law, than I can into a blacksmith's shop, to blow the bellows, and to wield the sledge hammer. Denied the means of learning useful trades, we are pressed into the narrowest limits to obtain a livelihood."[371] But Douglass made no specific proposal and the reading of the letter did nothing to advance the work of the convention.

Oddly, McCune Smith, writing as Wappinumoc four months earlier, had questioned the value of an industrial college. In his opinion, there was no dearth of Black mechanics, but rather a dearth of such mechanics who could earn a living at their trade. "I can at this moment," he wrote, "name boot-makers, engineers, carpet-makers, tailors, coopers, &c., first class workmen, all black, who have turned waiters or barbers; and is it worth while to raise up another crop for the same menial callings?" Frederick Douglass presumably had read Smith's column in his own paper but obviously thought differently on both subjects.[372]

The afternoon and evening of the third day were spent in large part in modifying the language of the proposals for a National Council and an industrial school. Brooklyn delegate William J. Wilson, writing later as Ethiop, described in amusement how the delegates had grappled with the

The Convention of 1853 and the Industrial School

National Council proposal: "[A] member who fancied ... he saw a hole in the plan would get up to apply a patch; then another would rise to piece out an invisible corner; here a member would attempt to clip off an excrescence; there one would supply a deficiency; this one would come forward to enlarge—that one to curtail.... Each operator, performing long enough only to clop his own fingers." But James McCune Smith "with his usual tact and ability" had "brought it safely through" and would find himself installed as president of this new organization. All such gatherings can be sometimes tedious, but even *The New York Times* admitted that "the Convention is earning the reputation of being practical and business-like."[373]

The first National Negro Convention had taken almost two weeks in two sessions to produce resolutions condemning the Colonization Society and commending settlement in Canada. The Rochester meeting took a far more positive stance and used just three days to call attention to the promise of America's founding documents and to protest the nation's failure to keep the promise and provide an equal place in society for Black and white alike. Ignorance, Ethiop believed, was to blame. "Our white fellow-countrymen do not know us," he said, in a summary that may still be true for many. "They are strangers to our character, ignorant of our capacity, oblivious of our history and progress." To remedy this problem, he pointed "with pride and hope, to men of education and refinement ... mechanics, farmers, merchants, teachers, ministers, doctors, lawyers, editors and authors against whose progress the concentrated energies of American prejudice have proved quite unavailing."[374]

Overcoming the ignorance of white Americans would provide a national agenda for generations to come. Meanwhile, the convention set out to provide new opportunities for Black citizens to make a difference by creating an ongoing structure with delegates and dues and a proposal to raise tens of thousands of dollars to create an industrial school. The industrial school, admittedly, did not come to fruition, but the fact that the delegates could even envision such projects and take specific steps toward realizing them reflects the significant growth in ambition and confidence since the early days of the convention movement. *Frederick Douglass' Paper* called the gathering "unquestionably a great convention—perhaps the most extraordinary, in many particulars, ever held in the United States. The talent, zeal, and eloquence displayed took our citizens by surprise; and we confess ourselves, even with our expectations, more than gratified." The paper listed James McCune Smith, James W. C. Pennington, Amos Beman, and over a dozen others and boasted that such an assembly of "men of mark could not be brought together in any place, in any circumstances, without producing a sensation—and a sensation they did produce amongst us."[375]

After the Convention

On the following Friday, James W. C. Pennington opened the meeting rooms of the Shiloh Church to let James McCune Smith and other delegates talk about what had happened in Rochester. Pennington, relaxed and confident, opened the meeting by telling some amusing anecdotes, and then four Ohio delegates who were visiting the city gave their impressions. Resolutions were then passed endorsing the work of the convention and creating a committee to move forward with plans to elect delegates to the newly created National Council.[376] James McCune Smith was appointed president of the council and two delegates were appointed from each of ten states, though only six states had been represented at the convention. As a first step, an organizational meeting was called for New York on November 23.

September balanced the hopeful signs of progress with an incident that brought Smith face to face with the reality of the unchanged world around him when he attempted to attend a Whole World's Temperance Conference in New York City. Smith, who called himself "an old-fashioned Temperance man . . . relying on my own unpledged will to keep me temperate in all things," had been chosen to serve as a delegate from the Fifth Ward Temperance Alliance and arrived at the Metropolitan Hall at

10:00 a.m. on the first day of the meeting. He identified himself to a policeman and was admitted. Shortly after that, a member of the Credentials Committee appeared and chastised the policeman for allowing Smith to come in since his credentials were not in order. When Smith asked what credentials he needed, he was told, "That will depend on the action of the Committee." Smith then crossed the street and found a table in a friendly tavern where no credentials were requested and sat down to write a report to the *New-York Daily Tribune*. He had intended, he told the paper, to call the attention of the delegates to the relationship between the rum trade and "its twin brother, the Slave Trade." The trade in rum, he wanted the delegates to understand, was simply one part of a complicated economic system on which many people in New England and Europe depended and it involved slaves as well as rum. Unable to speak to the delegates, Smith addressed the larger audience that read the newspaper, but the incident was an unpleasant reminder of the way Black lives could be suddenly disrupted by the invisible barriers that separated Black from white throughout the North.

A Lecture on Immigration
Although he was coping with family tragedy, maintaining his practice, and organizing a new national structure for colored Americans, James McCune Smith traveled back to Rochester in the week before the first meeting of the National Council at the invitation of the Rochester Ladies' Anti-Slavery Society to give a major address entitled "The German Invasion." Immigration to America has tended to come in waves and provide an issue for politicians to use in various ways. In the 1850s, eight hundred thousand immigrants from Germany arrived in New York City as a result of war and tumult in their homeland, and by 1855, only two cities in the world, Berlin and Vienna, had more German residents than New York. Possibly tongue-in-cheek, Smith imagined a future presidential inauguration in which "a man shall uncover his head on the Capitol steps, and deliver an Inaugural in good *High Dutch*" and "some remnant of Anglo-Saxondom

shall move in the House, that a few hundred thousands of the President's Message shall be printed in the English language." He imagined a day when Broadway shops "shall hang out signs declaring, 'English spoken here.'" But Smith argued that such invasions are a good thing. He quoted "an old writer" as saying that "England owes her civilization more to the frequency with which she has been invaded, than to any other cause."

A reporter for *Frederick Douglass' Paper*, possibly Frederick Douglass himself, called the lecture a "chaste, finished, comprehensive, and highly instructive discourse." Smith's approach was generally evenhanded and scholarly. He began by analyzing the way in which successive invasions of England by Romans, Saxons, and Normans had enriched the English character, and suggested that similarly the consecutive invasions of North America in more recent times by Spanish, French, Negro, English, Irish, and German immigrants had provided valuable enrichment to the American character, especially in offsetting the decline in character that had followed the arrival of the first English settlers in New England. Smith cited the Salem witch trials as evidence of the deterioration of English character in the harsh circumstances of the New World and the need for new ethnic strains. The mixture of racial and ethnic groups is good, Smith maintained, and he cited Fulton's steamboat as the perfect illustration. When "the waters of the Hudson first foamed beneath the impulse of the first engine driven by heated air ... it was an Englishman who furnished the capital" and "the only thing American was the *locus* in which the Swede and French science, and English capital might meet and fuse." Fulton himself "was Irish in all except the accident of birth.... It is on this fact," he continued, "that our land, presents a grand trysting place for the human to meet and commune with his brother human; and ... our institutions present a certain facileness of invasion, that all our present greatness and future progress depend."

In an age of immigration, Americans inevitably wondered about its impact on the country and many reacted fearfully to change. The Know-Nothing Party built on that fear and briefly became a major party in 1854 and 1855. Black Americans, in particular, might have reacted in anger to the Irish who pushed them out of entry-level jobs and the Germans who seemed to preempt small business opportunities in bars and grocery stores, but neither Douglass nor Smith, their most prominent leaders, seemed interested in attacking others. Smith, on the contrary, collected statistics and offered a generally positive perspective on the value of bringing together people with different characteristics and backgrounds. In a later essay, Smith pointed to one aspect of the German influence that made a lasting impact that most Americans of most ethnicities now take for granted:

> The German character is visibly gaining a strong influence on our New York Society, especially in the matter of social enjoyments on the Festival Days. Christmas feels differently from the Christmas of twenty years ago. It is the Jubilee of the little folks, and the Christmas tree is already an Institution among us. New York, for once, seems at leisure, resting itself, rationally enjoying itself during an entire week.[377]

Committee on the Manual Labor School

To help make the proposed manual labor school happen, Smith had proposed a National Council of the Colored People and Smith, as so often happens to one who proposes, had been put in charge of the proposal. He called a first meeting for November and nine members duly came together representing five states.

Reporting later as Communipaw, Smith took an optimistic view of things and wrote of "the fine, vigorous spirit, the harmony and determination to work which marked this, the first meeting of the National Council." It was agreed that the council's offices would be in New York City. A committee was also appointed for the proposed manual labor school and it was agreed that the school would be located within a hundred miles of Erie,

Pennsylvania. The council then adjourned to meet in Cleveland in May of 1854. The next day, they met again as the Committee on the Manual Labor School and organized themselves under the laws of the State of New York. Frederick Douglass was appointed their agent to receive and solicit funds and a committee of Smith, Douglass, and Amos G. Beman of Connecticut was appointed to draw up a plan for the school.[378]

In March of the next year, the committee produced, as requested, a "plan for the organization of the school." They proposed that the school should have at least two hundred acres of land and that three-quarters of the land would forever be used for agricultural purposes. Every branch of literature would be taught, and for every branch of literature, there would be one branch of "handicraft." Students would spend half their time in handicrafts or on the farm. "There shall be," they said, "a foundation fund of thirty thousand dollars" and twenty thousand would be acquired by selling two thousand shares at ten dollars each; ten thousand more was to come from donations "to be solicited from friends of the cause." The shares were to be payable at 10 percent quarterly—so for just one dollar every few months shares could be purchased. That translates, however, to twenty-five or thirty dollars in twenty-first-century money and $250–$300 in two or three years, and some two thousand contributors would need to be found who were able and willing to contribute at that level among the poorest citizens of the country. Of course, there were some Black citizens who were well off and some white citizens who would be supportive, but to find two thousand such was a challenge that proved to be beyond the reach of the committee.[379]

Part of the problem was that the very idea of a labor or industrial school was encountering opposition and misunderstanding. Smith's own commitment to the project was, in fact, uncertain. Writing later that year to Gerrit Smith he said, "Our Industrial School has been regarded by me as desirable, rather as a nucleus about which to gather an *esprit du corps*... among 'our people' than as a specially desirable thing in itself, which it is only to a certain extent."[380] In other words, he thought it was important as a project that would be valuable in bringing people together and providing evidence of what Black people could do, rather than as something that was important in its own right.

Frederick Douglass wrote about all this in his paper and expressed deep regret that illness had kept him away from the National Council meeting. He was confident, he wrote, that the work of establishing an industrial school would go forward. But one thing more was needed and it was not available: the executive ability to create an organization that could raise funds and administer a program. The leadership group among the free colored population was still too small and too lacking in expertise and experience to make such things happen. Even in small matters, it was easy to call for something to take place, but hard to bring it to pass.

Even though the National Colored Convention could not provide Smith with the data he needed, his ability to deal with statistics was beginning to be widely recognized. In early May of 1854, the American Geographical Society led by George Bancroft, a distinguished historian, diplomat, and politician, elected James McCune Smith to membership and listened to his address on the subject of improving the methods used in taking a census of New York State.[381]

CHAPTER SEVENTEEN

A Rising Tide of Anger 1854–1855

Searching for Unity

Why was it, James McCune Smith began to wonder, that after more than twenty years of conventions and speeches and appeals and protests, there was so little evidence of progress? The answer, he suggested, was that Black people were "not equally oppressed." For one thing, laws and public opinion varied from state to state, and for another, not all Black people were equally Black. Massachusetts offered perfect equality while Pennsylvania offered almost no rights, and New York and Ohio and Midwestern states were somewhere between. When Ohio offered the vote to quadroons, citizens with only one Black grandparent, some residents thought they should take advantage of the opportunity to vote, while others denounced them for being "willing contributors to their own degradation." Opposition to the colonization program had been unifying and Smith had hoped the industrial school would be unifying, but New Yorkers had different issues than Bostonians or Philadelphians and common causes would often be only local. New Yorkers found a common cause that summer in the transportation system.[382]

Streetcars

On Sunday, July 16, 1854, Elizabeth Jennings, a twenty-four-year-old schoolteacher, set out to go with a friend, Sarah E. Adams, to the church where she was the organist. The trustees of the Colored Orphan Asylum had made arrangements some eight years earlier for James McCune Smith to use the streetcars, but the system as a whole remained segregated. Colored citizens could, however, use the "whites only" cars if no one objected, and Jennings had been doing so on Sunday mornings for some months without a problem. This time there was a problem. She walked with her friend to the corner and held up her hand; the streetcar stopped, and the two young women boarded. On this particular Sunday, however, the conductor, Edward Moss, objected. She would have to get off, he said, and wait for the next car. While they argued, the next car came up, but Jennings was told they had no room. She told the conductor that she was already late and could not wait any longer. Moss replied that she could come aboard but would have to leave if other passengers objected. Jennings replied that she had never before been insulted on her way to church and told Moss that he was a "good for nothing impudent fellow for insulting decent people." It was a hot summer Sunday and tempers were obviously short. As Jennings later described it, Moss first pulled Sarah Adams off the car,

> she all the while screaming for him to let go. He then said that 'I should come out and he would put me out.' I told him not to lay his hands on me. He took hold of me and I took hold of the window sash and held on. He pulled me until he broke my grasp and I took hold of his coat and held on to that. He also broke my grasp from that.... He then ordered the driver to fasten his horses, which he did, and come and help him put me out. They then both seized hold of me by the arms and pulled and dragged me flat down on the bottom of the platform, so that my feet hung one way and my head the other, nearly on the ground. I screamed murder with all my voice and my companion screamed out, 'You'll kill her; don't kill her.'

The driver then let go of me and went to his horses; I went again in the car, and the conductor said, you shall sweat for this; then told the driver to drive as fast as he could and not to take another passenger in the car; to drive until he saw an officer or a Station House. They found an officer on the corner of Walker and Bowery, and the conductor told him that his orders from the agent were to admit colored persons if the passengers did not object, but if they did, not to let them ride.... The officer, without listening to anything I had to say, thrust me out and then pushed me, and tauntingly told me to get redress if I could; this the conductor also told me, and gave me some name and number of his car; he wrote his name Moss and the car No. 7, but I looked and saw No. 6 on the back of the car; after dragging me off the car he drove me right away like a dog, saying not to be talking there or raising a mob or fight.[383]

By that time, it was too late to play the organ for the church service and Jennings was too bruised to play in any event. She went home to nurse her bruises and tell her father what had happened. Thomas Jennings, Elizabeth's father, was a druggist and a leading abolitionist who had been present at the first National Negro Convention. The next day, Thomas Jennings contacted James W. C. Pennington, James McCune Smith, and others and organized a protest meeting at Pennington's church. A clerk read Elizabeth Jennings's account of the previous day since she was too shaken to attend. Resolutions were passed and copies were sent to the major New York papers as well as *Frederick Douglass' Paper*. But Thomas Jennings also took the next step, seeking legal counsel and contacting a former member of Congress who referred him to Chester A. Arthur, a junior member of his firm only recently admitted to the bar, but also a future president of the United States.

It took seven months for the case to be heard and a judgment to come down, but the jury decided against the streetcar company, and the judge ruled that "Colored persons if sober, well-behaved and free from disease, had the same rights as others and could neither be excluded by any rules of the Company, nor by force or violence." Arthur had asked for $500 in damages and a majority of the jury favored giving Jennings the full amount, but a persuasive minority talked them down to $225 and $22.50 in costs. Nevertheless, a point had been made and the Third Avenue Company ordered its cars integrated the next day. Other rail companies ignored the verdict and other cases had to be brought, but a very small yet very significant first step had been taken toward removing the barriers between races in the northern states. To continue removing such barriers, Jennings, Pennington, Smith, and others created a Legal Rights Association, and it was not long before Pennington himself was thrown off a streetcar and brought his own case.

Pennington had well-qualified lawyers, but they lost his case in spite of taking so minimal a position that Smith thought it was "badly got up." Pennington's lawyer opened by stating that they "did not seek nor claim social equality with the whites." To Smith that seemed like "asking for a verdict by withdrawing his client's plea—denying his belief in that very equality which he sought to gain." Smith wondered whether the fact that the legislature still refused to give Black and white citizens equal access to the ballot might impact the case. He also wondered whether the fact that the judge in the case was brother to the counsel for the railroad company might have influenced the outcome.[384] But other cases were brought as well, and eventually the state supreme court issued a ruling that all lines must treat all passengers equally.[385]

Smith's Family: Three More Deaths

That decision, however, was still several years ahead. Meanwhile, cholera struck the city again in the late summer of 1854 and Smith lost three children before it was over. The story of those deaths was told earlier and how

A Rising Tide of Anger 1854–1855

Smith found himself not caring whether he survived being thrown from a carriage. The first of those deaths was on August 18, the second on Sunday, August 27, and the third on September 19. On Friday, September 1, in the midst of such devastating events in his immediate family, the National Council met and somehow James McCune Smith managed to be there and preside.

He continued also to read widely, and not only about racial matters. Death in the family impacted his reading. Early in the summer he had read a recently published book titled *More Worlds Than One* by the English scientist David Brewster, and later, "when mid-summer came and its bereavements," he read *Conversations on the Plurality of Worlds* by the earlier French scientist Bernard le Bouvier de Fontenelle, the book to which Brewster's book was a response. He wrote that he found de Fontenelle more helpful. "In the time of shoreless woe," it "afforded much of the needed light to remove the eclipse of faith under which I stumbled."[386]

A Hard Winter and Different Perspectives

The winter of 1854–1855 was a hard one. Ethiop saw it differently than Communipaw and was angry about it. He summed his anger up in words that might still be written in New York City in the twenty-first century:

> Winter, with his icy and firm grip is freezing and pinching the life of many a poor wayfarer here, in Gotham; and to stay his ravage ... soup kitchens have been brought into requisition by the rich, and soup ladled out daily to thousands of soft hungry creatures. Gotham is, I believe, the metropolis of America, the boasted center of civilization, the seat of material prosperity, the focus of moral, mental and religious light. Palaces, towers and spires, in gorgeous array, benignly smile up in the face of heaven, as much as to say, Behold our perfection! Looking down from thence,

and viewing Gotham for this point, might it not be well to get the Historical Society, or, better, the Geographical Society of which friend Communipaw is a member, to inquire of some of the world's strolling scribblers to ascertain how many of the indigent women of Kamshatka and Nootka Sound have been dressed in calico gowns to keep life from going out by frost, and how many soup houses have been set up in Timbuktoo, Ethiopia, &c., to feed starving wretches this year. Let some one of them get up a paper upon the subject, for comparison's sake. Also, let that portion of the religious world, about Gotham, whose business it is to mould her institutions to its own notion, and hence responsible for what we have, I say, let it get up a tract upon soup kitchens, and starvation, rags and wretchedness in general, in the year of grace, 1855, in the middle of Gotham, the focus of religious light in America.

Communipaw, Ethiop went on to suggest, might better pay attention to this aspect of the world than simply add up numbers while finding time to write about visiting elegant bookstores and to discuss the latest poetry from England. "Belonging, as I do, to the toiling masses, I have no back office with cushioned easy chairs, nor idle time for reading of that sort . . . would it not be better for him to exhibit to the public a little less of his inordinate passion for fictitious reading, mere trash and verbiage that leaves the mind no better than it finds it?"[387]

Wilson (Ethiop) was angry. So was James McCune Smith, but his anger was differently focused. He had personal tragedy to deal with on the one hand, and ambitions for the Black population on the other hand. Those ambitions apparently went beyond the horizon of his contemporaries, with the result, not surprisingly, that there was a growing sense of anger and frustration in Smith's writing also.

A Rising Tide of Anger 1854–1855

Early in 1855, that frustration led to an angry exchange with Garrison's Anti-Slavery Society in the pages of that society's New York newspaper, the *National Anti-Slavery Standard*. The controversy seems to have begun late in December of the previous year with an attack by McCune Smith on what he called "the Garrison Society." Smith accused it of many things, such as hypocrisy in not inviting Black speakers to its platform, but he summed it up with the broad, general charge "that American Abolitionists do not, as organizations, treat black men as men." Oliver Johnson, editor of the *Standard*, replied at length and involved Frederick Douglass in the exchange. *Frederick Douglass' Paper* reprinted Smith's charges and Johnson's countercharges along with responses from Smith and Douglass that dealt with everything from broad issues of abolition strategy to the salary of the *Standard*'s editor and the price charged an unaccompanied lady for admission to the Abolition Society's lectures. Smith, perhaps, came closest to seeing the ultimate issue when Johnson accused him of "mendacious assaults" and Smith did not deny the charge, but explained his position:

> You seem, Mr. Oliver Johnson, at a loss for the reason of my "mendacious assaults." Let me tell you. With you, slavery is a matter of intellectual contemplation; with me, it is positive endurance; the iron enters into my soul, and the chains clank on my limbs daily, hourly: I undergo depths of oppression which the slave in the cotton field never dreams of, of which you can form no conception —"the terrible ordeal which we free colored men and women are passing every moment of our existence" an ordeal twisting a real human heart from trustfulness in anything human.[388]

Oliver Johnson was a Quaker and an abolitionist with good intentions, but he was also a white man who was well paid for his work as an editor.

Smith, on the other hand, had been born in slavery, and lived daily with the insecurity and indignity of being Black in a racist society. Unlike Johnson, he was not paid for his writing. Both men were dedicated to the abolition cause but could not, out of their different experiences of life, trust each other or find ways to work together. Oliver Johnson might not have been able to understand how Black people were feeling, but Frederick Douglass made it very clear in an editorial: "We are *pitied* by the American A. S. Society, and are *despised* by the American people; both must be supplanted by a feeling of *respect*."[389]

In a letter to Gerrit Smith later that winter, McCune Smith pointed to New York Governor William Seward as a case in point. Seward was a man of high principles who had become involved some years earlier in the case of William Freeman. Freeman was an African American who was accused of breaking into a house after his release from prison and stabbing four people to death. Seward, having long been an advocate of prison reform and better treatment for the insane, sought to prevent Freeman from being executed by using the relatively new defense of insanity. Freeman was convicted, but Seward gained a reversal on appeal. There was no second Freeman trial, as officials were convinced of his insanity. Freeman died in prison within a year. In the Freeman case, invoking mental illness and racial issues, Seward argued, "[H]e is still your brother, and mine, in form and color accepted and approved by his Father, and yours, and mine, and bears equally with us the proudest inheritance of our race—the image of our Maker. Hold him then to be a Man." Two centuries later, the expression used was "Black Lives Matter."

Abolitionists respected Seward for taking so principled a position, but James McCune Smith in his letter to Gerrit Smith told him, "My spiritual quarrel with Seward began in the very act for which you commend him. In defending Freeman, he used an expression about "inferiority of race" which I can forgive in no man. And I gave up all hope of him when I read that sentence, because no man can fight the true anti-slavery fight who does not believe that all men are equal. Hence I have waged war against the Garrisonians, and will, until they admit this doctrine. It is a strange omission in the Constitution of the American Anti-Slavery Society that no mention is made of Racial Equality either of slaves or of free blacks, as the aim of that society."[390]

In February 1855, Smith took time to review the relationship between Black Americans and the Garrisonians. White Americans might imagine that Garrison had begun the abolition movement. Smith wanted them to know that Black Americans had been there first. He noted the steps toward an abolition movement that preceded Garrison's involvement: the organization of the New York African Society for Mutual Relief in 1809, a meeting in 1817 in Philadelphia to establish the claim of Black people to be Americans and resist the Colonization Society, the creation of a Black press with *Freedom's Journal* in New York in 1827. He pointed to the organization of the Philomathean Society in New York and a companion society in Philadelphia with lectures and debates. "Hence, when in 1830–31, Mr. Garrison came among them, he found the Colored People already a 'power on the earth.'" And Garrison, he noted, was a gradualist, writing in *The Liberator* that "[i]mmediate Abolition does not mean that the slaves shall immediately exercise the rights of suffrage or be eligible to any office ... or be free from the benevolent restraints of guardianship."

Smith also cited the long and useless effort to create a "manual labor school for colored youth." Garrison had gone to England in 1833 with the "principal object ... to obtain funds for the establishment of a MANUAL LABOR SCHOOL FOR THE EDUCATION OF THE COLORED YOUTH OF OUR COUNTRY."[391] He had returned with over $1,500 given for that purpose, but as Smith noted, "Twenty odd years elapsed since these pledges were made and published: how have they been fulfilled? Twenty years have elapsed, during which the American Anti-Slavery Society has expended at least half a million of dollars, in agencies, editors' salaries, newspaper publishing, &c., &c., and controlled two millions of dollars more in the business relations of its supporters . . . how many colored youth has this organization or any portion of it, or its supporters, helped to 'trades' or to the higher departments of business as clerks, or editors, or merchants?" Smith went on in this vein for another column and concluded by suggesting that if Black people had not supported the Anti-Slavery Society, the society had only itself to blame because it had "deserted the free people of color." "Have we," he asked, "come to a parting of the ways forever?"[392]

Black Religion and White
The American Anti-Slavery Society increasingly angered James McCune Smith and his colleagues. It seemed to them that the senior Anti-Slavery Society was growing more and more irrelevant: that they were concerning themselves with theories while Black Americans were dealing with the reality of racism and being kept from taking their rightful place in society. Oliver Johnson at the *National Anti-Slavery Standard*, perhaps especially because the paper was published in New York and Johnson lived there, had a special ability to irritate Smith. A statement Johnson published in January simmered on Smith's back burner for four months and then produced a typical historical-philosophical-ethnological response from Smith as Communipaw that set the matter in the context not only of American history but of a broader anthropology.

Johnson "opens up a mine," Smith wrote, "of ethnological discussion of new and startling interest." "The truth is," Johnson had written, "that colored people are kept out of anti-slavery societies [for the reason] that many of them are either pro-slavery in feeling, or indifferent to the wrongs of the slave. To a great extent they are wedded to sectarianism, or misguided by priest-craft, or swayed by fear of public opinion."[393] That statement, responded Smith, "is downright slander for which there is no excuse." The true reason colored Americans are not much involved in the American Anti-Slavery Society, Smith told Johnson, is "that they do not recognize our manhood: do not uphold our social, intellectual, and spiritual equality. They had nothing to *teach* us in the matters of Anti-Slavery."

Smith went on from that beginning to provide a brief history of religion among Black and white Americans, noting the near simultaneous arrival of the Negro in Jamestown and the Puritans on Plymouth Rock in 1619–1620.[394] As usual, Smith has much to say about the interplay of climate and culture, suggesting that the harsh New England climate had turned Congregationalists into Unitarians while the Presbyterians in New Jersey and Roman Catholics in Maryland remained essentially unchanged in a more familiar climate. "The Negro," Smith wrote, "rejects Unitarianism; there is nothing in it which supplies the wants of his spiritual nature. Its cold, evasive Saxon exclusiveness chills the warm instincts and prompting of his nature . . . The nature of the religion of the American Anti-Slavery Society coincides with that of New England; it is Unitarianism, a sort of intellectual, or religion of the head." There are but two churches "well-thronged" in this land, Smith told Johnson and readers of *Frederick Douglass' Paper*, "the Papal church by the Celts, and the Methodist churches by the blacks." Finally, Smith pointed to the history of the African Methodist Bethel Church in Philadelphia and suggested that "brother Johnson go with bared head and reverential heart, and before its altars let him seek of the One True God there worshipped, forgiveness for the sin of having, whether ignorantly or maliciously, borne false witness against his brother man."[395]

"A person finds joy in giving an apt reply" says the Bible,[396] and Smith undoubtedly enjoyed responding aptly to Johnson, but the conflict between the American Abolition Society and Black leadership did nothing to advance the common cause. The feud was, nevertheless, still going on in October with Johnson refusing to publish notices of New York meetings and Smith likening Johnson to a turkey buzzard. "Go home," Smith told Johnson in *Fredrick Douglass' Paper*, "get a nice cool bath, then tie the wet bandage around your burning brow, and if you have such a thing about the house, open the Bible and read certain portions of St. Paul's epistles, and I am no doc if you don't feel better."[397]

Black Is Beautiful

The evidence of anger and impatience was balanced to some degree by the arrival in New York of the first Black singer to draw widespread attention. Elizabeth Greenfield had been born in slavery in Mississippi but her owner moved to Philadelphia, became a Quaker, and set Greenfield free to develop a natural voice of great range and power. Singing first for small audiences, she moved on to a concert tour that took her to New York and eventually to Europe. A reviewer in Buffalo, New York, wrote that she had "a voice of great purity and flexibility, and of extraordinary compass; singing the notes in alto, with brilliancy and sweetness, and descending to the bass notes with a power and volume perfectly astonishing." Jenny Lind, advertised as "the Swedish Nightingale," had toured America in 1850 and 1851, so it was inevitable that Greenfield should have been advertised as "the African Nightingale" and "the Black Swan." When she went to New York, her concert was limited, ironically, to a white audience, but James W. C. Pennington and others protested and a second concert was scheduled open to all. McCune Smith reported to *Frederick Douglass' Paper* that the second audience drew an audience of "upwards of two thousand . . . of whom at least six hundred were colored. . . . Never," he wrote, "was the [Broadway] Tabernacle so thoroughly speckled with mixed complexions." But Smith took the occasion to look at a far larger issue and sound a note that anticipated the "Black is beautiful" movement of the 1960s.

> There is one thing our people must learn, and the victory is won: we must learn to love respect and glory in our Negro nature! Why are we clothed in black skins unless it be to ennoble God Almighty's black man? And how can we do this while we suffer the atmosphere of

prejudice to penetrate our souls and shape our thoughts? Since the world began, no nobler, fuller, more complete man has been thrown upon its stage than the Negro. We are only beginning to contribute our share to the common progress, and see with what tropical exuberance we fling it down . . .

And here the bills announced that the BLACK SWAN . . . "reaches thirty-one clear notes in the scale, a greater compass of voice than any other mortal has ever reached." There we have Negro exuberance again! Tropical nature vindicated in this child of the sun.[398]

From a different perspective, Smith also saw the performance as an illustration of the challenge confronting him and other Black people as they tried to claim their fair place in the American pageant. "The colored man," he wrote, "must do impractible things before he is admitted to a place in society. He must speak like a Douglass, write like a [Alexander] Dumas, and sing like the Black Swan before he could be recognized as a human being."[399]

The National Council

1855 was a year of conventions, especially for New Yorkers. By the time the year was over, James McCune Smith had attended conventions in Philadelphia, Troy, Syracuse, New York City, and Boston. He was present in a leadership role in all of those and, of course, was present and presiding at National Council meetings as well and would have had other local meetings. All of them came against a background of increasing anger and impatience.

The felt need for a changed attitude among Black and white alike was evident in the summons McCune Smith sent to the members of the National Council in calling them to a meeting in New York in May of 1855. Smith asked them not simply to be present, but to prove "that although among the oppressed and down-trodden, you are prepared to resist and overcome oppression in your own behalf, and in behalf of your bleeding brethren of the South who, being manacled and dumb, rely upon you to struggle for their rescue from Slavery and ignorance."

To publish this in the newspaper was to amplify the challenge to the members; this was not a private matter in which they could succeed or fail without being noticed. Smith made sure that their response would be noticed in his public summons to them.[400] That summons linked abolition and elevation; what happened in the North affected what happened in the South, and vice versa. It was not only the slaves, but the free population as well who were the focus of attention in May of 1855. Free Black citizens were beginning to realize that the emphasis on abolition had left them out. The National Council therefore agreed at its second meeting that another national convention should be called together to focus attention on the situation of the free Black population. No one knew, of course, that a Civil War was only six years away and that American society would be changed forever, but there was a growing impatience with the slow and almost imperceptible changes taking place and a feeling that more drastic change was necessary. Not everyone was ready to pick up a gun and join John Brown in Kansas, but otherwise peaceful citizens like Gerrit Smith were willing to fund Brown's efforts, and James McCune Smith's growing impatience was evident in his exhortations to work together to make a real difference in the North.

The Industrial School Again

But inching forward was hardly better than neglect. The Committee on the Industrial College met in May also and passed two resolutions, one requesting Frederick Douglass to write a letter and one asking James McCune Smith to write a letter. The letters were sent to potential agents for the school who could bring important skills to the project, but bolder steps were needed and Smith knew it. When the council itself met that same day, Smith, as presiding officer, told them the school was needed as evidence of their capability: "There is no use further holding these Councils and passing first-rate resolutions, unless we do something tangible and show our people what may be accomplished. It is said this plan is impractical. The colored man must do impractical things before he is admitted to a place in society."

But as the meeting proceeded, it became evident that there was neither a will nor a way to pursue the dream of an industrial school. The amount of money needed was daunting and there was no agreement that a program of the sort envisioned could actually achieve its goal. One after another, speakers expressed doubts until Frederick Douglass sounded the death knell, angrily telling his colleagues that "if they voted down the proposition . . . they were incompetent to do anything to help themselves . . . that all efforts to elevate the free colored people while Slavery existed in America are useless. I expect to see the school voted down and will say no more." So the school project was voted down and the council accomplished nothing of importance except to call for another convention in the fall.[401]

If the National Council meeting would not support the industrial school, there was still one thing James McCune Smith could do to help young Black Americans gain skills: advertise. Small ads began appearing in *Frederick Douglass' Paper*: "WANTED a situation, or apprenticeship for a colored lad, aged 16—prompt, active, can read and write, and now understands cane chair work: a place in a country village in New York or a New England State preferred. Apply to J. McCune Smith, 55 West Broadway, N.Y. City." If a school could not be built to train hundreds, Smith might still be able to help one individual at a time.[402]

Radical Abolitionists

Whatever the new National Council structure or individual ads might or might not accomplish, these were not the only tools available to abolitionists. There was still, potentially at least, the ballot. That process was failing to deal with slavery because both of the two major parties, Whigs and Democrats, needed to win voters in southern states and, therefore, were unwilling to deal directly with slavery. The Liberty Party alternative had failed to gain widespread support. The newly formed Republican Party seemed not to offer a better alternative since it promised not to interfere with slavery where it already existed. Worse yet, William Loyd Garrison and the Anti-Slavery Society, the loudest anti-slavery voice in the land, had ruled out use of the ballot in favor of moral persuasion and had little to say about civil rights at all.

In this situation, Gerrit Smith, James McCune Smith, and others felt a need for some new political alignment that would oppose slavery in the South and work for civil rights in the North. The Convention of Radical Political Abolitionists—called to assemble in Syracuse, New York, at the end of June—was their next attempt to provide leadership for activists. Eight names were signed to the call to convention: Gerrit Smith, James McCune Smith, and Frederick Douglass among them.[403]

When radical abolitionists assembled in response to that call, James McCune Smith was chosen to preside. It was the first time a Black American had presided at a national political convention and the convention thanked him before adjourning for the "urbanity" with which he had done so. But the radicalism of these abolitionists was about ideas, not actions, and especially about the divisions within the abolition movement itself. They were anxious most of all to push back harder against William Lloyd Garrison's American Anti-Slavery Society and its strong belief that slavery was allowed by the Constitution. Delegates in Syracuse were equally sure that the Constitution itself outlawed slavery, but they were not equally sure how to act. "We have come here," Smith told the delegates, "to inaugurate a great movement."

But those present had very different agendas. When John Brown addressed the convention, he appealed for men and means to defend freedom in Kansas. "His remarks deeply stirred the hearts of the audience," and they took up a collection of sixty dollars "to aid in the objects . . . pistols and all." But Lewis Tappan, always dedicated to the abolition cause and always nervous of anything that went further than statements, "disclaimed all sympathy with the war spirit as an auxiliary to the cause of abolition." The convention adopted statements, but its only concrete action was to establish a central committee with an office in New York to raise funds and distribute literature. It may have been the first national political convention realistic enough to nominate no one for president or vice president, but 1855 was not an election year anyway. So the convention was held and statements were made, but those involved still remained a tiny fragment of the population.[404]

Looking for Leaders

James McCune Smith himself may have offered the best diagnosis of the difficulty in pointing to the gap between the leaders of the convention movement and the population they aspired to lead. Any short list of leaders among the colored population before the Civil War would inevitably have included James McCune Smith, but Smith wrote as Communipaw to deny "that the colored people in the United States now have, or ever had, leaders." He offered several reasons why he believed this to be so, but suggested, in effect, that there could be no leaders without followers and the colored population was unwilling to turn to colored leadership. He may have been telling of his own experience when he wrote, "Let any man among us, set up a creditable business in the midst of a colored neighborhood, and he will find, as others have found, that his brethren, so far from supporting him and holding up his hands, will, on the contrary, pass his door to trade with the whites." It is sometimes suggested without evidence that Smith had white patients; it seems likelier that there were Black patients who turned to a prestigious white doctor rather than the Black doctor in their neighborhood.

So, also, Smith suggested, "the colored men who assemble in conventions, write addresses, pass first rate resolutions, &c., . . . have never had the masses to support them, nor even to give an approving cheer or God's speed to their well meant efforts." The problem was not, he suggested, the lack of a will to rise, but a leadership that was too ambitious: "[T]hey have looked upon the enterprises of the whites, and laying their plans of the same scale, and have called on an ignorant, poverty-stricken, and divided people to accomplish the work. The consequence has always been disheartening failures."[405] Certainly that had been Smith's experience.

My Bondage and My Freedom

If Black Americans had a leader at all in those years before the Civil War, no one had better claim to that title than Frederick Douglass. James W. C. Pennington was a pastor; James McCune Smith was a doctor; committed though they were to the abolition movement, it could never be the center of their attention. They had jobs to do. Frederick Douglass, on the other hand, was a full-time abolitionist. Primarily as a writer and speaker, Douglass had made himself the best-known name among Black Americans. He was an inspiring speaker; at the Rochester convention, delegates who had wandered outside for a break from the sometimes tedious proceedings hurried back inside when word came that "Douglass is up."

Looking always for more ways to promote the abolition cause, James McCune Smith urged that Douglass write a new and more complete biography. Douglass had written of his experience of slavery and his escape to freedom in *Narrative of the Life of Frederick Douglass, an American Slave*, published in 1845. The book had been a bestseller and made Douglass famous, but ten years had gone by and it seemed to Smith that a more complete, up-to-date biography would be useful. Douglass was reluctant at first to do anything which might "make me liable to imputation of self-seeking public notoriety, for its own sake," but, on further thought, told Smith that he had come to see that the whole slave system was now "at the bar of public opinion—not only of this country, but of the whole civilized world—for judgment" and, therefore, that any writings that might "enlighten the public mind, by revealing the true nature of the slave system, are in order, and can scarcely be innocently withheld."[406]

So in the summer of 1855, Douglass brought out the second of three versions of his autobiography, this one titled *My Bondage and My Freedom*. His first biography was, as the title, *Narrative of the Life of Frederick Douglass*, says, simply a story of the events of his life. *My Bondage and My Freedom*, on the other hand, ponders more deeply the implications of slavery and freedom. James McCune Smith, having urged Douglass to write the book, wrote a lengthy introduction and said:

> WHEN a man raises himself from the lowest condition in society to the highest, mankind pay him the tribute of their admiration; when he accomplishes this elevation by native energy, guided by prudence and wisdom, their admiration is increased; but when his course, onward and upward, excellent in itself, furthermore proves as possible, what had hitherto been regarded as an impossible, reform, then he becomes a burning and a shining light, on which the aged may look with gladness, the young with hope, and the down-trodden, as a representative of what they may themselves become. To such a man, dear reader, it is my privilege to introduce you.[407]

Toward the end of his introduction, Smith also wrote, "I shall place this book in the hands of the only child spared me, bidding him to strive and emulate its noble example."[408, 409]

Meetings and More Meetings
Between January 1 and November 15, 1855, James McCune Smith attended twenty-four meetings, not including probable monthly meetings of the vestry of St. Philip's and the inevitable planning meetings and com-

mittee meetings in relation to this list of meetings important enough to be noticed in printed records. In most of them, Smith was presiding or secretary. Five of the meetings were held outside New York in Syracuse, Troy, Boston, and Philadelphia, and would have taken the better part of a day both going and coming back. Three of the meetings took place over three days. And, of course, he was still keeping up a medical practice.

Busy as he was with organizing and attending meetings, Smith found time that summer to write a satirical word about mid-nineteenth century police tactics that was published in *Frederick Douglass' Paper* and might still have some relevance. The mayor, he wrote,

> has announced the 'reorganization of the *Optical Department of the Police*. The Optician in Chief will have his office located in the coal-hole of the old City Hall, from which hall light is rigidly excluded: here police-men are inspected in the following manner: the M.P. is brought in from outer sunlight, placed in the center of the room, and a gong struck close to his head: being asked if he heard anything, if he says "no," it is satisfactory: light is then let in, and right before him is placed a white man beating a colored one: he is asked, "do you see anything?" If he answers "no," it is satisfactory: then the tableau changes to a drunken row, in which notorious bullies, under indictment for manslaughter, are beating screaming females: "do you see anything?" "no" satisfactory: if he says "yes," and starts to rescue the women, he is seized, thrust back, and sent to undergo drill in Mercer Street or the Five Points. The next tableau is a furious fight between half a dozen Irishmen and more a-coming: if the candidate leans back, buttons his coat over his star and looks another way, he is pronounced all right, and in a fair way to get a silver medal with a speech from the Mayor.[410]

A Rising Tide of Anger 1854–1855

National Convention 1855

What turned out to be the last National Convention of the Free People of Color before the Civil War met in October 1855 in Philadelphia and heard two reports on the proposal for a "Mechanical School." Smith, finally seeming to accept the inevitable, wrote an essay for *Frederick Douglass' Paper* suggesting that it was simply not in the nature of young Black men to be mechanical:

> [W]e are an aesthetic people: we have an inborn love of art: how much this explains! Poor black humanity, too poor to have marbled halls and pictured galleries of its own . . . would rather be a doorkeeper in the temples of art, then a rawboned angular struggle with wiry independence! Poor black humanity, preferring the ease and luxury of a barber's shop and it's lute, or viol, or tambour . . . from whose souls has sprung the music of this land . . . Our industrial difficulty is accounted for. It was Athens, not Sparta, Italy, not Holland, which gave birth to the children of art: the reason why our youth do not learn trades, why our people are not mechanics, lies not in the difficulty of learning trades, or of pursuing them. No! It is in our essentially aesthetic or art-nature. I find it in elevating our people, we have a heavier labor than we thought of: we have to raise the whole social fabric along with them whites as well as blacks: and some of us will get the back ache if we lift too high in the jump.[411]

Black New Yorkers and Black Philadelphians had often found themselves at odds in the past, and Smith was afraid they would be again at this convention. He wanted to stay home. Looking back, he wrote that "I could not see very clearly what good could be accomplished by the Convention;

but my better half insisted, as a personal favor that I should go ... and, as a dutiful husband, I went." Later Malvina explained to him that there were some who "would have charged me with cowardice had I stayed away." It was, he said later, "three days of the very hardest mental labor I ever performed."

When the convention met, it was quickly obvious that it disliked the industrial school project. A committee cited a fundamental obstacle in the lack of capital, but also questioned whether such a scheme was practical anyway: they believed that three to five years would be needed to train people in certain skills and that such a variety of skills was needed that it was impractical to think of creating a school that could encompass those skills and combine teaching them with any ordinary college program, but McCune Smith, still not ready to give up on the idea of a school, opposed the report and it was not adopted.

Smith may not have accomplished what he had hoped for, but one delegate who was there, in writing to *Frederick Douglass' Paper* on another matter, provided a remarkable picture of Smith's personality and parliamentary abilities:

> Smith's resolutions ... were originally offered as a substitute, but the quick sighted Dr. Smith, finding that they failed to command the necessary support to carry them, (in substitution of the original,) suggested that the original be modified in one of its terms, and then as a compromise that his resolutions be attached thereto as an amplifying amendment. This Dr. Smith did in a very polite, dexterous, and dignified manner, accompanied with his bewitching smiles which it was difficult to resist; those of us opposing his resolutions responded to his suggestions, glad to pay homage to the good sense which prompted the Doctor thus to submit them and thereby harmonize the convention on this subject.[412]

Nevertheless, when it was over, Smith remembered later that he had gotten out of Philadelphia "as fast as I could." He said that it was after that event that people began asking for him as "'the old man,' and one impertinent youngster actually called me 'Pop.'" When "I looked in the glass," Smith wrote, "I found . . . my three days fight in Philadelphia had turned my dark hair gray!"[413]

The convention adopted overwhelmingly a statement that the Constitution of the United States is "aggressively Abolition" and gives power to Congress to abolish slavery. Therefore, Smith told his readers, they should vote "to urge your Representative to carry out this glorious and benign doctrine." Smith signed the letter, as he often did, "your brother in bonds."[414]

CHAPTER EIGHTEEN

The Approaching Crisis 1856–1860

Health Problems

When Smith became aware of his health problems it is impossible to say, but as a doctor, he would have been more aware of his own health than someone without his training. Even so, it is only in his letters to Gerrit Smith that we find McCune Smith writing candidly of that awareness. In 1848, when he was just a month past his thirty-fifth birthday, McCune Smith wrote to his friend of "the few years I expect to live," raising the question: What did he know, and when did he know it? He ended that letter with the hope that he would be able to visit the Adirondack land "as my health appears improved." The two comments together would seem to reflect a serious health episode and an awareness that there was no real cure for his problem.

A Challenge and Rejection

Smith did, of course, continue to be involved in abolition issues at some level. In January 1856, he joined with other officers of the New York Abolition Society in writing a letter to the American Anti-Slavery Society challenging the latter society to a debate on the constitutionality of slavery. The New York Abolition Society laid the subject out under four headings and offered to pay for a hall in New York and divide equally any profit from the venture. Lewis Tappan, William Goodell, Simeon Jocelyn, and

James McCune Smith signed the letter. Smith's name is last and it seems likely that he drafted the letter. The Anti-Slavery Society responded less than three weeks later that they had no interest in such a discussion since they believed most people agreed with them that the legality of slavery in the slave states was "self-evident . . . and we do not feel called upon . . . to expose ourselves to the just ridicule with which such a discussion must be regarded by all well-informed and intelligent persons," and, furthermore, they added, in a bit of needless nastiness, they rejected the proposal since such a debate "might seem to recognize as genuine abolitionists and honorable antagonists, men in no wise entitled to be so regarded."[415] Such were the divisions in the anti-slavery ranks in an election year not long before the outbreak of war.

Smith as an Essayist

Whatever the state of his health or the abolition movement or nation, Smith continued to write and to examine subjects as diverse as pens and pyramids. The breadth and depth of his interests is constantly surprising. He would comment on the Chinese empire in one paragraph and in another discuss the Latin historian Tacitus. He would discuss the building of the ancient Temple of Luxor and in the next paragraph investigate the revolution of the moon on its axis. No subject seemed uninteresting to him. In another age, his essays would be collected and published for admirers of his style and imagination.[416]

In a column published in September 1856, Smith wrote of how he had exchanged an old pen for a new one. Those were the days (which some still living remember) when small children were taught how to dip a pen in an inkwell and use it to draw elegantly curved letters. One's pen expressed one's personality and could not be easily replaced. Nevertheless, Smith had "dropped in" at the jeweler's shop on Canal Street and allowed himself to be persuaded to relinquish his old pen and go out with a new one:

> [B]efore I left, we had traded pens; he getting decidedly the better of the bargain, for that old stump of Gold which has written so many Communipaws is his, and this new pen, handsome, well made, fluent is all that I got in return: I think the diamond point of the old pen has been pretty well worn down, and the solid stump which has been the means of many communications between us, is remorselessly set down in his ledger, "old gold 31 1/4 cents!"—There is no telling now what will become of that dear old pen: whether a new diamond point will be ground on it, and it will be dignified with a new and golden handle: or whether it will "go to pot" with other old gold and mix its ultimate particles with what will be changed into a beautiful finger ring, or maybe a lady's ear drop, or infant's bracelet clasp, or a flaming breast-pin. Whatever be its fate, may good betide the dear old stump![417]

That elegant paragraph, set in motion by a visit to Canal Street, was immediately followed by a meditation on the simple unmarked graves in the Quaker burial ground just east of the Bowery on Houston Street. That led in turn to reflections on African burial customs and the builders of the pyramids. A "P.S." returned to the subject of the pen in order to propose a conspiracy theory. Noting that "Brother William H. Day," an abolitionist editor from Ohio had been in town, Communipaw suggested that he "doubtless gave our jeweller a commission to buy that pen at any cost ... to see if he can write with it: let him be careful how he uses it," Smith warned, "for it will sometimes kick in harness."[418]

It is remarkable that a man who cared as much as did James McCune Smith about American politics could write a column with so little reference to current events just a few short weeks before the election of 1856. Even when the election was over, he made no direct reference to it in his writing but waited a month for his next column and then cast doubt on the value of writing anything at all by quoting a cynical Chinese proverb: "A man may as well amuse himself with his pen as with his kite—if it please him as well—it is all a matter of taste." "How," Smith asked, "can any man with proper self-respect ever again take up his pen, when once he reads that abominable Chinese saying?" But Smith had to acknowledge its "lurking truthfulness": "Of the reams of foolscap scribbled over today for the Press, how much would be better employed if hoisted in the air at one end of a string, while the scribblers held the other?"

The nearest Smith came to a direct comment on the election was to suggest that there was not much difference between our "free institutions" and those of the Chinese:

> [T]he Mantchou Tartars who keep us down are a few southern slaveholders, who like the Tartars in China, command our armies, our fleets, and our money chests. . . . Indeed, the painfullest analogy between the Chinese and ourselves is contained in the fact, that in both, *material well being* seems the end of national existence, and so long as trade is left alone, despotic tyranny may play any fantastic tricks whatever before high heaven.

Smith picked up the "kite string" reference again at the end of his column. He had moved on to a renewed attack on those New England abolitionists who liked to ascribe everything good to their "Anglo-Saxon heritage." Smith had engaged with them on that subject before,[419] but perhaps Wendell Phillips and Theodore Parker did not read *Frederick Douglass' Paper* or had missed the issue of March 25, 1853. That issue reported a speech that Phillips had given at a Women's Rights Convention in which he asserted that Tacitus had written that the Saxons consulted their women on all great occasions. On the contrary, Smith/Communipaw wrote, Tacitus said no such thing; in fact, "Tacitus never wrote a word about the Saxon, in such of his works as have reached the present time." The Saxons, Smith went on to say, "did not emerge from obscurity until almost a century after the last date recorded by Tacitus" and what Tacitus wrote about was the German nation which "consulted their women as they did the neighing of horses ... and as many half barbarous tribes have in all ages."

Chess and Charity

Increasingly limited physically, Smith continued to pursue a wide range of interests. In 1857, the city was in a financial crisis, and Smith was well aware of it, and aware also of the unpredictability of the stock market. He wrote of the "masters arrested in their golden dreams of profit" as "surging to and fro under impulses they no more understood and could no more govern than the iron waves in the howling storm" and compared them to the equally frantic poor who rush to the savings banks or gather in bread mobs. But in a quiet corner in the midst of the storm—"at the center of the vortex," as Smith put it—and probably unnoticed by most of the panicked city dwellers, rich or poor, a chess match took place between a renowned German player, Louis Paulsen, and a young American challenger, Paul Morphy.

Smith desperately wanted to go, but the admission charge for the week was one dollar. "Was it prudent," Smith asked himself, "with the bank account at low water" to "throw away" a dollar? He debated the matter with himself for three days and then "held a family council with *die frau* who at once decided we must go." That seems to be an editorial "we" since there is no further reference to Malvina, but the reader learns that "we" managed with "a little skillful elbowing" to be seated beside the board. Although he paid close attention to the game, Smith took note of the fact that the officers of the Chess Congress "did not hesitate or refuse to admit a negro" though there were southerners present and there was "the danger of the dissolution of the Union before their eyes." Smith also thought he detected a "brunette hue" in the American (who won the match) that made him suspect that he was not "the only Carthaginian in the room." It was the physical and psychological aspects of the game, however, that interested Smith the most. It is, he decided, a useful game for young men and an amusement for others, requiring physical as well as mental strength, but not a pastime that produced deep and original thinking.[420]

The financial crisis had to take second place temporarily to the chess match, but Smith was a member from the time he came back from Scotland until the organization was dissolved shortly before his death of the Steward's and Cook's Marine Benevolent Society of New York, an organization whose name would not automatically convey its purpose "to relieve the distressed and soften the frowns of poverty, by a timely aid to the afflicted." Only in his obituary do we learn that Smith was treasurer of that society from 1836, the year of his return from Scotland, until 1863 when it was disbanded—perhaps because Smith could no longer play his central part in the society's work.[421] Smith could write lightheartedly of the dollar he squandered on admission to a chess match, but he never says a word about his stewardship of significant funds for the poor.

The Calm Before the Storm
Thoughtful Americans, North or South, in the election year of 1856 knew very well that the bonds that held the country together were being tested as never before. Most elected leaders, North and South, still hoped for peace and most of those opposed to slavery were, like Lincoln, willing to accept slavery in the South as the price of peace. With the next election eight months away, Smith surveyed the political scene and found nothing hopeful in it. William Seward, serving his second term as senator from New York, had joined the new Republican Party and had the strong support of Horace Greeley and his *New-York Daily Tribune*.

An Indifference to Politics
James McCune Smith apparently found nothing in any of the political options available to engage his interest. In a column published just a month

before the election, he turned his attention away from politics to both a wider perspective and a much narrower one. Perhaps he had been reading archeology or architecture; his column of October 3 began with a cynical reflection on the great mansions and churches going up on Fifth Avenue—where many still stand. "Even our scientific architects," Smith wrote, "erect in the Fifth Avenue palaces and churches, which imitate the beauty of Grecian temples, and, in the teeth of modern science, exclude from them, as the Greeks did, all sources for the supply of fresh, and the expulsion of foul air! Hence it is evident that in three thousand years, this great Caucasian race have remained stagnant and stupid, in excluding one of the simplest and most necessary means of promoting health, in the construction of their domicils [sic]."[422]

The column went on to deal with a trip Smith and Bell had made to Baliere's Bookstore in search of knowledge and describes Smith's effort to get information by peering between the uncut pages of newly published volumes. And why did he not buy the book? "Well, I'll tell you; if it be a bit of a family secret." Mrs. Communipaw, we are told, had been wanting new chairs for the sitting room for ten years, "and during all these years the dear, patient woman has exclaimed at least twice, perhaps four times a year, "good bye chairs," as I would march into the house in a perfect ecstasy of delight with some costly book under my arm!—Well, sir, I heard her last month for the first time say this out loud, and—I have bought the chairs this month. It was a plain case of chairs, and smiles vs. Egyptology and the Moon's Revolution—and chairs had it."

Concerning the Election

If James McCune Smith saw little to care about in the election of 1856, he had good reason. The choice of leaders in a democratic system may depend as much or more on charm as on wisdom, but neither was much available in 1856. James Buchanan, the Democratic Party's candidate, had been a member of Congress, senator, and secretary of state, and had served most recently as ambassador to Great Britain. He has been called "one of the best trained men who has ever occupied the presidency."[423] Well trained, yes, but ineffective in a crisis. He was a competent bureaucrat who had never excited any large band of followers. John C. Fremont, candidate of the new Republican Party, was charming enough but inexperienced. He was known for various adventures in California but had never held an administrative or governmental position other than a very brief term in the Senate. A third candidate, Millard Fillmore, was the nominee of the American or Know-Nothing Party, a party concerned mostly with opposition to immigration. Fillmore had served as president from 1850 to 1853 after President Zachary Taylor died in office, but the Whig Party refused to nominate him to run for reelection in 1852, the only time in American history (until 2024) that his own party has not renominated an incumbent president.

In summary, the candidates chosen to contest the election of 1856 were not leaders likely to inspire anyone to reach for a gun. James Buchanan, out of his vast governmental experience, hoped to be a great president, ending sectional strife and uniting the nation, but it was not to be. Smith called him "sober and timid" and felt that "the oiliness, the caution, and the firm prudence of his character . . . leaves nothing to hope for . . . from his government."[424]

Abolitionists in general misread the temper of the country. James McCune Smith wrote an essay for *Frederick Douglass' Paper*, published just two days after Buchanan's inauguration, that said "there is no denying the fact that the Slave Question is now at rest, more surrounded with positive inertia than at any time since the formation of the Federal Government." It seemed to Smith that the "wet blanket of Republicanism" had put out the abolitionist fire by centering attention on keeping slavery out of the Western territories where it did not exist and accepting slavery in the South where it did exist. "There is," Smith told his readers, "a HUSH, almost perfect, IN THE SLAVERY AGITATION." Why not, he asked, accept that nothing can be done in the existing situation and set a new, long-term goal? Why not look forward nineteen years to the hundredth anniversary of the Declaration of Independence as a time when Americans could celebrate a new birth of freedom by bringing an end at last to slavery. "What a throb for the public heart! Bring it fairly before the people and they must be carried along by its generous impulse."[425]

The Dred Scott Decision

But what neither Smith nor Buchanan knew (though Chief Justice Taney may have whispered it to Buchanan on the inaugural platform) was that two days later, on the same day Smith's essay was published, the Supreme Court would hand down a decision in the case of the fugitive slave Dred Scott that would anger almost everyone concerned to end slavery and drown out any hush that might have existed in a torrent of anger. The question at the center of the case was of minor importance and could have been dealt with quietly, but the Supreme Court took the opportunity to stir up a storm.

Dred Scott had been taken into a free state and territory by his owner and then brought back into a slave state. The question before the court was simple: since slavery did not exist in Wisconsin, did Scott's residence there make him free? The court ruled that it did not, but few slaves, except fugitives, traveled enough to be affected by that decision one way or another. The court, however, took the opportunity to lay down broad new principals, saying, for example, not only that a slave was not a citizen, but that neither a slave nor the descendant of a slave could ever become a citizen. The court also overturned the Founding Fathers by ruling that Congress could not prohibit slavery in the territories.[426] In case everyone was comfortable with that, the court went on to remind people how it had always been:

> [Black Africans imported as slaves] had for more than a century before been regarded as beings of an inferior

order, and altogether unfit to associate with the white race, either in social or political relations; and so far inferior, that they had no rights which the white man was bound to respect; and that the negro might justly and lawfully be reduced to slavery for his benefit. He was bought and sold, and treated as an ordinary article of merchandise and traffic, whenever a profit could be made by it. This opinion was at that time fixed and universal in the civilized portion of the white race. It was regarded as an axiom in morals as well as in politics, which no one thought of disputing.[427]

"Why," the court seemed to wonder, "can't we all just get along the way we used to?" But the times had changed, as they often do, and whatever "hush" Smith had detected was quickly ended in the angry response to the court's statement. One year later, the Lincoln-Douglas debates brought the issues of slavery and civil rights once again to the center of attention. One year after that, in 1859, John Brown mounted his attack on Harpers Ferry. A year and a half later still, Lincoln was inaugurated and southern cannon bombarded Fort Sumter. What Smith thought was a "hush" was the start of a rapid descent into the nation's bloodiest war and the death of slavery.

Yet, James McCune Smith was right in terms of the abolition movement as he had known it. William Lloyd Garrison and his followers had, in effect, removed themselves from the national debate by agreeing with slaveholders that the Constitution permitted slavery and that the North could separate itself from slavery only by separating itself from the South and writing a new constitution prohibiting slavery in the North. They offered no program for dealing with slavery where it existed. That left Frederick Douglass, James McCune Smith, and their colleagues to pursue a path that offered no hope of results for the foreseeable future. They had made the best case they could in Albany, for example, to remove restrictions on voting and had been defeated again and again. Smith was far from the only concerned American who was prepared to take the long view and hope against hope that things might be different in twenty years. Lincoln had imagined that slavery might last another century.[428] The expectations of practical men and the actual course of events have seldom been so far apart.

Finding a Way to Deal with Apathy

When August 1 came around with its annual celebration of West Indian freedom, Smith was in no mood to celebrate. West Indian freedom had been *given* by the British government but "[s]uch freedom," Smith wrote, "is not worth having. It is freedom struggled for and won, that fit the mind and the body to enjoy, defend and improve by it." Smith suggested searching the calendar for the dates when Denmark Vesey had headed an insurrection in Charleston or "when Nat Turner turned all Virginia pale with fright." "Our white brethren," he continued, "cannot understand us unless we speak to them in their own language ... That holy love of human brotherhood which fills our hearts and fires our imagination, cannot get through the—in this respect—thick skulls of the Caucasians, unless beaten into them."[429]

It was hardly surprising, then, that Smith would return to that theme two years later from a somewhat different angle and write of the "apathy" with which he now viewed events. Perhaps the "hush" was a lack of voices that spoke to him and to Black Americans. "Is it apathy or what is it," he asked in a column for the *Frederick Douglass' Paper*, "that causes me to take up the morning paper and lay it down, without caring a straw, never looking to see" which side "triumphed or fell yesterday in the House." He thought back to the early days of the abolition movement when William Lloyd Garrison was gaining attention and "no part of the people were so excited, so hopeful as we; our deep craving for the acknowledgment of our brotherhood, welled up in holy expectation, in beatific joy" but that craving was now "crushed, withered and disappointed" and "sinks down in hopeless apathy." Turning, as he continued to do so often to the English poets, Smith quoted Samuel Taylor Coleridge's *The Rime of the Ancient Mariner* to summarize his feeling of being "Alone, alone, all alone."[430]

Fighting On

But Smith was not ready to admit defeat in the battle against slavery. On the contrary, he saw it as a challenge to Black Americans to take leadership in what was, after all, their battle. If "the graven images we have worshipped, the Websters, the Adamses, the Chases, the Sewards, the Garrisons . . . have crumbled away," the question to be faced was what Black Americans could do for themselves. "While we despair that others will do this work, will overthrow this slave power," Smith wrote, "how do we feel about our own will and ability to cope and overcome it?" Smith's summary answer to his own question was, "We have work to do, and we must do it."[431]

Whatever feeling McCune Smith had of being "alone, all alone" must have been sharpened to the highest pitch when he looked at the *New-York Daily Tribune* of August 12, 1857, and saw that his good friend Gerrit Smith had written in general agreement with Horace Greeley's statement that "the mass of the blacks are ignorant and thriftless, &ct." "I think you are sometimes too harsh," Gerrit Smith had written to Greeley, "but I agree with you in the main." It was eight months before James McCune Smith could write calmly and forgivingly to the only white man he considered a friend, but when he did, the following April, he saluted him as usual as "Dear friend" and began with an apology for his long silence. He had been anxious, he said, about the health of his wife and had paid little attention to anything except "the call of business." But that concern had been "for the last two months," and Gerrit Smith's letter had been published eight months earlier. McCune Smith allowed himself adequate time to ponder a reply, and when at last he was able to write, he left no doubt how he felt.

Greeley had written, McCune Smith reminded his friend, that "there are more blacks in this city who seek to make a living by harlotry, rum-selling and other modes of pandering to others than by downright honest labor." "You will at once perceive," McCune Smith wrote, "that by 'agreeing in the main'—you endorsed this foulest charge against us that could have been uttered." It was also, he wrote, "very false." McCune Smith had studied the census numbers and written about them; he had the facts at his fingertips. He knew that in both New York and Philadelphia there were fewer Black paupers than white, and if a "somewhat larger proportion" of the Black population were in prison for petty crimes, it was "more than accounted for by political disparity." "It seemed to me last August," McCune Smith told his friend, "and seems to me still, that the heaviest blow we blacks could possibly receive came from your hand; you surely owed it to your own fame, to say nothing of us, to have ascertained by the widest examination of the facts that your statement was true before you ventured to make it.... I have always been of the belief," McCune Smith went on, "that you had a heart—a belief which this reckless statement has greatly staggered."

But McCune Smith thought differently of his upstate friend than of Oliver Johnson of the *National Anti-Slavery Standard*, who also claimed to be a friend of Black people and had never made such a charge as those Greeley had made and that Gerrit Smith had endorsed. Oliver Johnson called himself a friend of Black people but seemed to have no Black friends. Gerrit Smith, on the other hand, as McCune Smith knew from his own experience, made friends without regard for color and, if he erred, he could be corrected. With Gerrit Smith, McCune Smith could even inject a note of humor in his rebuke: "I must really come up to Peterboro," he wrote, "and auscultate your chest in order to reassure my faith."

It should be noticed that McCune Smith was offering with that statement to make use of the very latest medical technology to examine the state of his friend's heart. The familiar stethoscope, now the identifying badge of a doctor, had just been invented in 1851 in Great Britain and its use to diagnosis cardiac problems and other internal issues could not yet have been common.[432] If McCune Smith used one on his friend, he expected that he would hear a sympathetic heartbeat or at least one that could be corrected if it missed a beat or two. Time had passed and the bitter disappointment that must have come with the reading of Gerrit Smith's letter to the *Tribune* had been softened by its passage. With that passage of time, McCune Smith had returned to his earlier sense of Gerrit Smith as someone who did, at the deepest level and in spite of a careless lapse into the pervasive bigotry of his time, respect him and other Black Americans as "a man and a brother" whose friendship had value.[433]

An Alternative Life

Douglass was not the only abolitionist considering new directions; Smith, too, was looking in new directions in 1859. James McCune Smith had chosen a medical career as a teenager and he had built a successful career as a doctor. There were, however, rumors that he had been offered the opportunity to build an academic career in Scotland, and it may not be insignificant that, when he returned to the United States, he announced himself as a lecturer before he had established himself as a doctor. Only once, however, do we know that he sat down and made a serious decision as to the direction his life should take, and that was toward the end, not the beginning.

Over the years of his active life, James McCune Smith spent time and energy pursuing not only the dream of an industrial college, but supporting an existing college at McGrawville, New York. Located in one of the most remote and least populated sections of the state,[434] Central College had been heavily supported by Gerrit Smith and had not only accepted Black students, but also hired some Black faculty. At some point late in 1858, Gerrit Smith seems to have offered James McCune Smith an opportunity to join that college's faculty, and McCune Smith had given it serious consideration. In January 1859, however, he wrote his upstate friend to decline the offer. It had not been an easy decision. "I am grateful to you for your proposition in regard to McGrawville," he wrote, "there is no life that would so entirely accord with my tastes and desires of usefulness, as a quiet Professorship in an advancing Institution of learning; yet I have delayed an answer until I could think the matter over carefully."

McCune Smith had talked the matter over with an academic friend, Charles Reason, another boyhood friend in the African School, who had gone on to become a professor of literature and languages at an unnamed college or school in the city.[435] Much of the conversation had dealt with the financial implications not only for Smith but for the college. Smith had to be practical. He had a young family and needed to be sure the college could pay him enough to support them. That, the college apparently could not do. The question, therefore, came back to Gerrit Smith and his willingness to endow the college. McCune Smith was very specific: "The sum of fifty thousand dollars at six per cent is as small as we think it would be safe to begin with." That would pay for lecturers in the college and an assistant in a preparatory school. Tuition fees would still be required to build up a library and provide the equipment needed for the science departments. Given such an endowment, Smith wrote that he would "gladly undertake the labor of building up Central College, and Professor Reason, I feel almost sure, would gladly join in the work."

Smith was being careful and thorough. His letter to Gerrit Smith also provides valuable information about his financial situation. His income, he reported, was about $1,600 a year, the equivalent of over $50,000 in 2020. Reason was earning $2,000, or $60,000. Both of them had investments that would yield about $400 a year if they were to leave the city. But both of them had families and therefore "it would be necessary for us to have some certainty to rely on." He was not, however, simply turning to Gerrit Smith and asking for money. He would do his part to build up the endowment. He suggested that he would do his best to raise another $10,000. He also pointed out that it would be reasonable to rename the college. "Why not a Gerrit Smith College? It is a short, strong name, and tells its own story. I would rejoice to see you woven into the coming years" and "would rather see you found and foster it during your life time in the world."[436]

Gerrit Smith, however, was not ready to make himself famous. Lacking correspondence from him, there is no way to understand his thinking, but clearly, he was not prepared to create a substantial endowment for the college and, without the security such an endowment would have brought the college, McCune Smith was not prepared to risk his own security. Less than six weeks after the initial letter, McCune Smith wrote Gerrit Smith to say, "After a careful review of the matter, I cannot see my way clear in regard to McGrawville, unless the college be endowed."[437]

It should also be noticed that in his first letter, McCune Smith wrote to Gerrit Smith that "should you think well of these views . . . I will try and drag myself from this vortex long enough to talk the matter over in Peterboro. I sometimes wonder how I should feel after one week of quiet in the country."[438] Was it, one wonders, simply pressure of work that Smith referred to, or was his health an issue as well? The opening paragraph of his June 24, 1859, column in *Frederick Douglass' Paper* would seem to indicate that Smith's health problems were increasing. He wrote of his "convalescence from a severe and prolonged attack of 'Spring Fever'" and the "comfort" *Douglass' Paper* had been to him during his illness. Spring fever, however, is a mental condition characterized by various mood changes. One website calls it "a fuzzy medical category."[439] The language Smith used makes his disability sound like something more serious.

New Papers, New Possibilities

James McCune Smith had always enjoyed writing. John Stauffer speaks of the "playfulness, allusiveness, rich use of irony, and utter lack of sentimentalism that . . . set him apart from his peers."[440] The journal he kept on his trip to Scotland and his frequent quotation of poetry is evidence of someone who loved to work with words. For ten years, his column in *Frederick Douglass' Paper* gave him the opportunity to develop his skills and make writing a major part of his life.

In 1859–1860, realignments in the publishing world opened new possibilities for writers. Frederick Douglass had been publishing his newspaper for ten years and was feeling a need for a change. Early in 1859, he decided to go on a long speaking tour in the West and persuaded James McCune Smith to occupy the editorial chair, simply writing the editorials, for the five or six weeks he would be away.[441] Douglass had always relied on Julia Griffiths and other staff to do the practical work of putting the paper together while he wrote and set policy, so Smith had no need to go to Rochester or concern himself with any of the mechanical aspects of editing a paper, and he realized again how much he enjoyed the simple act of writing.

Back from his tour, Douglass decided to move in new directions. Shortly after his return, the first number of the twelfth and last volume of *Frederick Douglass' Paper* was published as well as the first number of the *Douglass' Monthly*. Almost simultaneously, good friends of Smith's, Thomas and Robert Hamilton, launched two new publications. *The Weekly Anglo-African* began publication on July 23, 1859, and a monthly, *The Anglo-African Magazine*, appeared at the same time.[442] "This magazine," an editorial in the first issue said,

> will have the aim to uphold and encourage the now depressed hopes of thinking black men in the United States—the men who, for twenty years and more have been active in conventions, in public meetings, in societies, in the pulpit, and through the press cheering and laboring on to promote emancipation, affranchisement and education, some of them in, and some of them past the prime of life, yet see, as the apparent result of their work and their

sacrifices, only Fugitive Slave laws and Compromise bills, and the denial of citizenship on the part of the Federal and State Governments.[443]

It was a pretty good description of James McCune Smith and his colleagues. The new papers would be published in New York, which made it possible for Smith to move to the new publications and be more directly involved than he could be with Douglass. One way or another, he had to write. In March, he wrote to Douglass to say that he was writing out of necessity,

> for I find that writing "agrees with me;" and I could not tell *why* I felt so dull on this blustery Saturday night, until I remembered that my tenure of the office editorial had ceased last week, and that the ideas which doubtless gathered up in my brain for next week's paper, were lolling and stretching themselves in magnificent indolence on the sofas and lounges of my upper story, obstructing by their inertia the genial flow of thought with which the latter part of the week usually finds me blessed.[444]

One of the ideas that had been "lolling and stretching" itself was apparently an essay on the New York custom of "Maying." It was common practice in those days for New Yorkers to move on the first day of May. Renters, homeowners, and merchants would take the opportunity to find a better price or better location and, with everyone doing it, there were opportunities aplenty. Smith recalled how his young wife had talked him into joining the fray early in their marriage, and he had found himself with a child in each arm, a large basketful of things around his neck in front and another basket hanging on his back as they made their move. "It took me some three years to recover my dignity," he wrote, "and we have not moved since." But there was money to be made in the constant fluctuation of property values, and in a world where change was constant, there was hope that social and racial patterns also were not fixed and immutable. Smith's essay on the subject in the *Anglo-African Magazine* found its way also into the April 29 issue of the *Frederick Douglass' Paper*.[445]

In late October, Smith used his familiar role as "Our New York Correspondent" for the *Douglass' Paper* to respond to John Brown's raid on Harpers Ferry. Smith had been present at the Radical Abolition Convention just four years earlier when Brown appealed for support, and money was raised to support his violent anti-slavery campaign in Kansas. Smith may have contributed to Brown's campaign, but he lacked the financial resources to give Brown significant help and was certainly not in physical condition to join him in Kansas or at Harpers Ferry. Gerrit Smith, on the other hand, had been a substantial contributor and his name was found in documents among Brown's papers at Harpers Ferry. Fear of consequences led to a mental collapse in the aftermath of the event and Gerrit Smith was hospitalized in the Utica Lunatic Asylum. Frederick Douglass was involved enough to flee into temporary exile in England. James W. C. Pennington had met with John Brown and turned him away, yet went into his pulpit to tell his congregation to "pray for John Brown."[446] James McCune Smith was left to provide an analysis of the ambivalence felt by so many abolitionists: "And yet there are deep cords within us which thrill and yearn towards the old hero! So brave and yet so gentle! Such iron nerves surrounding such tender heart! . . . But I am rising up to hero-worship; let me slide back into hero dread."[447]

CHAPTER NINETEEN

The Last Chapter 1861–1865

Anglo-African Essays

James McCune Smith loved to write, but the outlets available to him were fragile. The monthly *Anglo-African Magazine* lasted only a year. *The Weekly Anglo-African* was sold in March 1861 but resurrected in July and published until 1865. Both papers provided an outlet for Smith's need to write and Smith helped make sure those outlets would be available to him by providing financial backing for both papers. As long as they lasted, the papers would provide Smith a way to have his say in events that he could no longer participate in physically.[448] In February 1865 he wrote that he was "cut off from active life" by his illness, and yet, in the same letter, he said, "In regard to the Anglo African, I must plead guilty to scribbling the leading editorial of almost every number. Remnants of thought, fragments of old ideas, and shreds of old activities appear to filter down to some portion of my brain and must be let out once a week else I would grow irritable."

So long as it lasted, *The Anglo-African Magazine* gave Smith opportunity to publish several essays longer than any he could have sent to the *Frederick Douglass' Paper*. He dropped his old pen name with the new publications, but William J. Wilson, who also came to the new publications, continued to write as Ethiop.[449]

Surprisingly, in view of the strong personalities involved, there seems to have been no anger or friction in the new alignment. Frederick Douglass, in his new monthly, greeted *The Anglo-African Magazine* as a "gratifying and encouraging" development. He listed the articles in the first issue and noted especially James McCune Smith's lead essay on "Civilization" as "an original and masterly production."[450] He republished it in his own monthly's second number.

The essay on "Civilization" was, in fact, an expansion of a lecture Smith had given by that same title several years earlier. Like Arnold Toynbee a century later, Smith argued that climate and geographical position, not "the innate superiority of any portion of the human race," were critical to social development. The effort necessary to maintain the body's temperature at ninety-eight degrees being greater in arctic or tropical climates, the populations so located will have less energy to develop an advanced civilization. Not only that, but populations moved to more temperate climates will develop as a result: "[T]he dark races of the tropics gain in physical development when transported to a temperate climate. . . . This Afric-American race are not only far superior, in physical symmetry and development, to pure Africans now found on the coast, but actually equals in these respects the white race of the Old Dominion, who have never lived in any but a temperate clime."[451]

The new publications seemed to Smith an opportunity to reuse and develop further other material he had explored in earlier essays or lectures. Entirely new, on the other hand, was the oddly titled essay, "On the Fourteenth Query of Thomas Jefferson's Notes on Virginia." Jefferson's only book-length manuscript, *Notes on the State of Virginia*, had been written as a reply to an imaginary foreigner seeking information about the state. Jefferson methodically laid out answers to questions such an individual might ask: what are the state's boundaries, what mountains does it have, what cascades and caverns are there, what is its wildlife, and so on. Query 14 had to do with the establishment of a revised legal code, but it included a long digression on the nature and consequences of racial differences. Jefferson argued that there seems to be a natural inferiority of Black to white:

> I advance it therefore as a suspicion only, that the blacks, whether originally a distinct race, or made distinct by time and circumstances, are inferior to the whites in the endowments both of body and mind.... This unfortunate difference of colour, and perhaps of faculty, is a powerful obstacle to the emancipation of these people.

Therefore, Jefferson, who was arguing that slavery must come to an end and exploring the legal consequences, asked, "What further is to be done with them?" He answered his own question, "When freed, he is to be removed beyond the reach of mixture."[452] Smith's equally lengthy response went to the heart of the problem on the first of thirteen pages when he asked,

> [W]ho is more elevated—the master, learned, acute, ingenious . . . the framer of laws, the successful financier, the acute philosopher—the one master of all this, with a slave-whip in his hand—or, the poor Christian slave, his breast heaving, his eyes raining down tears, his flesh rooted up, quivering beneath the lash, whilst he prays to God to soften the heart of the accomplished torturer—who is the more elevated?

Smith argued that there was no reason in the institutions of the country or the nature of the people to prevent Black and white from living together. To deal with Jefferson, however, Smith found it necessary to use most of the essay to present what he rightly called "this tedious array of facts" about facial angles and the difference between woolly and straight hair and all the pseudoscientific arguments used by Jefferson and others to defend the slave owner's position. If Jefferson were acquainted with the philosophy of human progress and if he "possessed the insight and sagacity for which he is so celebrated," Smith wrote, he would not be asking, "How shall we get rid of them?" but "[H]ow can we welcome their presence as one of the positive elements of natural progress."[453]

In a much lighter mood—and Smith's sense of humor always emerged sooner or later—Smith wrote an essay titled "A Word for the 'Smith family.'" "If your name be not Smith, dear reader," Smith begins, you don't need to read this article; it's "a family matter." But for those in the family, who have to endure the fact that their family name is so common, Smith hoped to provide some comfort. "Take down your Homer," Smith said to his readers, and look at those early lines in which is written: "Kluthi meu Argurotax . . . Smintheu." This, Smith told his readers, might be "freely translated . . . 'Hear me, Bearer of the silver bow . . . O Smith.'"

This was not, he freely admitted, "the accepted reading of this passage," but Smith suggested that it was not impossible to find evidence there of the "antiquity of the 'Smith family'" and the "glorious fact that *our ancestors were at the siege of Troy holding rank with the gods themselves.*" So "Take up the New York Directory for 1859–60, O Smith, descendant of Apollo!" and rejoice in the fact that there are twenty-one columns listing "10,000 householders or some 50,000 Smiths, men, women, and children, on the island of Manhattan." After all, Smith suggested, those who take less space in the directory are obviously representatives of a weaker clan that is dying out. Smith turned to the recent publication by Charles Darwin of his book, *On the Origin of Species*, to find evidence that the proliferation of Smiths is proof of the "natural selection" of "favored races." Why are there so many Smiths? Why, because nature itself selects those best adapted to survive! And among the Smiths, it is the "John Smiths" who are best adapted of all. Six double-columned pages were used to present this argument. One wonders how many letters to the editor came from irate citizens named "Brown" or "Jones."[454]

Smith's old colleague/competitor William J. Wilson, or Ethiop, contributed a more serious essay with a light touch titled "What Shall We Do with the White People?" Recognizing all that white people had accomplished,

Wilson thought it important to note also that, although "[e]verything that nature could bestow and art devise has been placed at their hands, yet the blight of discord disruption and disunion, has ... settled down upon these people. What then shall we Anglo-Africans do with these white people?" Ethiop rejected the various solutions white people had suggested for Black people: deportation, enslavement, etc. but proposed that if they cannot find a way to live peacefully with others, they should withdraw. "Who knows," Ethiop wrote in ending, "but that some day, when, after they shall have fulfilled their mission, carried arts and sciences to their highest point, they will make way for a milder and more genial race, or become so blended in it, as to lose their own peculiar and objectionable characteristics?" But until then, the question remained, "What for the best of all shall we do with the White people."[455] That "some day" would be echoed a century later by Martin Luther King Jr., saying, "I have a dream that one day ... the glory of the Lord shall be revealed ... I have a dream this afternoon that the brotherhood of man will become a reality in this day."[456] Perhaps Wilson/Ethiop had glimpsed it first.

The Irrepressible Conflict
On March 4, 1861, Abraham Lincoln was inaugurated as president of the no longer United States, pleading in his inaugural address that: "We must not be enemies. Though passion may have strained it must not break our bonds of affection. The mystic chords of memory, stretching from every battlefield and patriot grave to every living heart and hearthstone all over this broad land, will yet swell the chorus of the Union, when again touched, as surely they will be, by the better angels of our nature." But five weeks later, Confederate batteries fired on Fort Sumter and the Civil War began.

On July 21, the first pitched battle between North and South was fought at Bull Run and the Confederate forces won a decisive victory, throwing some northern leaders into a panic. Gerrit Smith had barely had time to recover from his severe depression and hospitalization after Harpers Ferry when the first disastrous battle of the Civil War was fought. He reacted with an attack on northern leadership that led James McCune Smith to write to Gerrit Smith and tell him in no uncertain terms that he was "unequal to the exigency of the hour." Gerrit Smith had written that, unlike Lincoln, "the other President [Davis] is cheered and strengthened by the entire devotion to his cause of all around him."

"Is this true?" McCune Smith asked; "Is it not ignoring one half of those around Jeff Davis (I mean his slaves)? ... A sort of Bull's Run phrenzy seems to have seized on you inasmuch as you are fleeing from a half won field." Gerrit Smith was looking only at the fortunes of the white armies. McCune Smith understood that the Union defeat would set forward the need for Black troops and force the president to think more seriously of the need for an emancipation decree.

"Let me tell you," the Black man wrote to the white man, "how I see this situation and what I expect from you." First of all, McCune Smith wanted Gerrit Smith to understand that "the only salvation of this nation is *Immediate Emancipation.*" "You are the man," McCune Smith wrote to his friend, "to convince the people of this great truth by shouting it in their ears throughout the land by voice and pen." Gerrit Smith had failed again and again, of course, as McCune Smith knew perfectly well, to convince the nation of his ideas, but he still had resources that no Black American had and perhaps he would be heard in a day when the conventional wisdom had been routed. McCune Smith told Gerrit Smith that he must write this "in your own strong style" and tell people that "Slavery [is] the sole cause" and "Emancipation the sole remedy for the rebellion." "Let this pamphlet be showered in millions of copies in every household in the Nation and wherever it can reach in the South. . . . In addition, let the tables of the coming Congress groan with the weight of petitions urging Immediate Emancipation."

Meanwhile, James McCune Smith was intently focused on the war. He had been vice president of the Anglo-African Institute, an organization created to encourage the arts and industry with a monthlong exhibition in New York, but he wrote to the president of the organization to resign on the grounds that the country was "overwhelmed with the horrors of a bloody and disastrous war" and he could no longer "uphold an exhibition which typifies the calm of prosperous peace."[457]

Smith was not only impatiently calling for Black troops, but also writing and speaking again about a vision of America's destiny. On the verge of freedom, he chose to publish again two passages from his lecture on "The Destiny of the People of Color," first given twenty years earlier, and selected the brief paragraphs on patriotism and on the virtue of returning good for evil. Under the heading, "No Retaliation," Smith said again, "[W]e pray not for vengeance, but for mercy on our oppressors—and we throw open the doors that *all*, even those who exclude us, *all* who thirst may come in and drink . . . in a word, in our every act, and all our relations, we are already rendering *Good* for *Evil*, and what can be more glorious in the destiny of any people."[458]

In April 1862, Congress moved to outlaw slavery in the District of Columbia by a vote of more than two to one. James McCune Smith took part in a public celebration in the great hall of the Cooper Institute with a speech that even *The Liberator* called "able and eloquent." "One prop after another had been knocked away," Smith said, "from the support of slavery."[459]

It was not, however, Union defeat that convinced Lincoln of the need for Black troops, but Union victory that persuaded Lincoln and Secretary of State Seward that they could not only proclaim emancipation but also enforce it. Victory at Antietam in September 1862 provided that crucial ingredient and the Emancipation Proclamation was issued on January 1, 1863. New York diarist George Templeton Strong noted that "the nation has washed its hands of slavery. Only the damnedest of "damned abolitionists" dreamed of such a thing a year ago. . . . John Brown's 'soul's a-marching on,' with the people after it."[460]

Black Troops

The failures of the Union troops, as James McCune Smith had clearly seen, would make it necessary to enlist Black troops and that would have enormous long-term consequences for the relationship between Black and white in American society. Others also saw those potential consequences and, therefore, opposed the creation of Black units in the army. When Black New Yorkers raised and equipped three regiments in July of 1861, Governor E. D. Morgan, who had just called for 25,000 volunteers, refused to accept them. There was also Black opposition but for very different reasons. The *Anglo-African Magazine* printed a letter to the editor from R. H. Vashon that pointed out how much Black Americans already contributed to the government and how little they received in return. "What becomes our duty," he asked, when the government we have supported "at the expense of our blood, toil, and degradation" is threatened? "Let your own heart answer this question," he wrote, "and no regiments of black troops will leave their bodies to rot upon the battle-field beneath a Southern sun."[461]

Frederick Douglass was also opposed at first and went to the hall at Cooper Union in New York to say that Black troops would be willing to fight "if"—and insisted that there should be equal pay and equal conditions. Other Black leaders, Smith included, said in effect, "Let's worry about that later; for now, just let us get into it." When Massachusetts governor John Andrew finally got permission from the War Department to raise Black regiments and commissioned James McCune Smith to enlist volunteers from New York in a Massachusetts regiment, Douglass also no longer held back but assured his readers that no one would do more than he to increase the number of Black enlistments.[462] Douglass and Smith immediately set to work as recruiting agents for the 54th Massachusetts Volunteer Infantry Regiment, challenging Black troops to fight in the heroic tradition of Nat Turner. Two of Douglass's own sons quickly enlisted.[463]

In October of 1863, the war came home to Frederick Douglass and James McCune Smith in the most immediate way possible when Douglass's son, Lewis, was sent home from the battlefield suffering from diarrhea and gangrene. Douglass called for Smith and hovered by his bedside in the city for two weeks, but Lewis never recovered his health and was discharged from the army in May of 1864.[464]

The Orphan Asylum and the Draft Riot

No northern city was as badly torn by the Civil War as New York and no New York institution suffered more than the Colored Orphan Asylum. The tension in the city had two primary sources, and the first was economic. New York was a city built by international trade, and cotton was America's leading export. New York merchants depended on slave labor as much as the southern plantation owners. When the Civil War broke out, the mayor of New York, Fernando Wood, suggested to the city council that they declare New York a free city so that they could continue their profitable cotton trade with the Confederacy.

The second source of tension was the immigrant population. One million people had died during the Irish Potato Famine between 1845 and 1852, and another million had emigrated out of a population of eight million. Over six hundred thousand had come to New York. The new Irish immigrants, less skilled even than New York's Black population, saw that Black population as their primary competition for jobs and believed that the Civil War was being fought to free additional Black laborers to compete with them. Archbishop Hughes wrote a letter to Secretary of War Simon Cameron saying:

> The [Roman] Catholics, so far as I know, whether of native or foreign birth, are willing to fight to the death for the support of the Constitution, the government, and the laws of the country. But if it should be understood that, with or without knowing it, they are to fight for the abolition of slavery, then, indeed, they will turn away in disgust from the discharge of what would otherwise be a patriotic duty.[465]

The Democratic Party had warned German and Irish laborers repeatedly that the election of Lincoln would lead to emancipation and the release of thousands of freed slaves to compete for their jobs. A new draft law in 1863 brought that tension to the boiling point.

In July of 1863, a law was enacted that required white male New Yorkers to register for the draft or pay three hundred dollars to be excused. Chauncey Burr, a well-known author, gave a speech in the city on the Thursday before the Saturday on which registration was to begin that *The New York Herald* said was "calculated to stir up a moblike spirit . . . [and] raise a storm that will terminate in insurrection, and bloody scenes in this city." Burr told his audience:

> This act is very simple: It is merely a highwayman's call on every American citizens for "$300 or your life." (Laughter and applause.) For one, I have no $300, but I have a life, and, if it goes, it shall go in defence of the kind of liberty that my fathers established. (Cheers.) Why, it is by your clemency that Abe Lincoln and all his satraps were not upon the gallows eighteen months ago.[466]

Registration began quietly enough on Saturday, but when the time came to return to work on Monday, the city exploded in the most violent insurrection in American history. For five days the mobs controlled the streets, burning, looting, and killing until army units arrived from the recently won battlefield at Gettysburg and restored order.

The Colored Orphan Asylum seems to have been a particular focus of the mob's anger. Here were 233 small Black children being rescued from poverty, well housed and clothed and fed, while white children of immigrants had no such advantages. *The New York World* printed a dramatic account of what happened when the mob reached the Orphan Asylum:

The Last Chapter 1861–1865

Our reporter, who was upon the ground, describes the consternation of the inmates as passing description, the children fainted with terror and were taken out, many of them perfectly helpless. One is reported as having been trampled to death. The teachers were powerless to help them, being utterly terrified at the approach of the mob, not knowing what might be their fate. Their shrieks and supplications for help, when the axes of the invaders sounded at the doors, were most horrible.[467]

Eventually, troops came and restored order. But it was a near thing. Had Gettysburg lasted a few more days or ended differently, New York might have been lost as well—and the war itself.

James McCune Smith was safe at home in a district that the mob ignored, and probably was not well enough to venture out. He might not have survived had he tried to reach the children. Black men caught by the mob were beaten to death and hung from lampposts. Over a hundred Black citizens were killed before the mob was brought under control.[468] Meanwhile, for three days and nights, the orphanage children were sheltered in the 35th Street police station and then, escorted by forty policemen and fifty soldiers with bayonets, they were removed to Blackwell's Island in the East River where they could be accommodated in hospital buildings until a new residence could be provided.

It was three years before a new orphanage could be erected between Amsterdam Avenue and Broadway and between 143rd and 144th Streets.[469]

Smith's Move to Brooklyn and His Death
After the Draft Riots of July 1863, many of the Black survivors abandoned Manhattan. The rioters had spared Smith's neighborhood, but they had destroyed a pharmacy he once owned.[470] It was natural to fear that he and his family might not be so lucky the next time, so the decision was made

early in 1864 to leave the tension and turmoil of Manhattan for the quieter streets of Williamsburg on the far side of the East River.[471] Williamsburg, once a separate village, had been incorporated into Brooklyn in 1855. The Brooklyn Bridge was still twenty years in the future, but ferry service to Manhattan was easy to use if there was a need to be in touch with those on that side of the river. Correspondence by mail was also quick and convenient in those days, so Smith was able to keep in touch easily with the people and causes he cared about. A letter to Gerrit Smith in January of 1864 thanked him for a donation to the "Freedman's Friend Society" and enclosed a receipt from the treasurer. In April a similar letter thanked Gerrit Smith for a gift to the Colored Orphan Asylum and, again, enclosed a receipt.

Smith's health, however, was growing steadily worse. The *Medical Register* said in an obituary that "his health commenced failing eight years ago, but did not materially interfere with the duties of his profession until December 1863, when he saw his last out-door case, and began with reluctance to regard himself in the light of a confirmed invalid."[472]

Final Essays

But Smith could still write. In February 1865, Henry Highland Garnet, who had recently moved to the Fifteenth Street Presbyterian Church in Washington, was invited by the chaplain of the House of Representatives to preach a sermon in the House to celebrate the recent passage of the Thirteenth Amendment to the Constitution, the amendment which abolished slavery. The House was not formally in session, but no Black American had ever before spoken in that building, so it was a significant moment. When the sermon was published, James McCune Smith was invited to write an introduction and responded with a biographical essay almost four times the length of the sermon itself. Smith had known Garnet when both were students at the New York African Free School. Smith, therefore, could provide anecdotes of Garnet's early years and even tell the story of the capture and enslavement of Garnet's African grandfather. He told how Garnet's father was given permission to take his family, including the nine-year-old Henry and several others, to a funeral from which they never returned. He told how they managed instead to reach Quakers in Delaware who passed the party on to New York where Henry found his way to the African Free School and became a friend of James McCune Smith who was almost three years older.

Garnet traveled a more erratic path than Smith and there were times when they were on opposite sides of an issue. Garnet, for example, organized an African Civilization Society at one point and promoted emigration to Haiti at another. Smith remembered especially an evening some twenty years earlier when Garnet had appeared at a meeting in New York where he was neither expected nor welcome. Nevertheless, Smith recalled how Garnet presented "a masterly argument, interspersed with . . . wit, ridicule and sarcasm, and winding up with an appeal to the audience which carried them away with shouts and cheers. The protesters, dreadfully voted down, could not get the hang of things, the why and the wherefore for some time afterwards." Smith had been on the losing side that evening, but many years later, he could tell the story in generous tribute to an erratic but brilliant man with whom he had often been at odds.[473]

Less easy to reconcile was the long-term division between Black New Yorkers and the American Anti-Slavery Society—even when that society decided to dissolve itself. When May meeting time came in 1865, the Civil War was over, slaves in the southern states had been freed, and the constitutional amendment abolishing slavery was well along in the adoption process. Some thought that was enough. When the American Anti-Slavery Society convened in New York, William Lloyd Garrison told the members that their work was over and it was time to go out of business. He, therefore, resigned as president and moved to dissolve the society. James McCune Smith knew well that the battle for a truly inclusive society had barely begun and said so in the columns of the *Anglo-African Magazine*:

> We do not quarrel with their giving up. They are the best judges of their ability to do good in the cause of freedom. If they feel that their power in such a direction is exhausted, we rather admire the frankness which owns up and retires from the field. . . . All that we now find fault with is the reason they give when they assume that labor to be accomplished when it is only half done.

That might have gone unnoticed, but Smith went on to say, "We trust we may be forgiven for adding that it is an unfortunate coincidence that they have made the discovery that their work is done at the very moment that they find that it no longer pays." Garrison, of course, was not at all willing to forgive, and took the exchange to a personal level, responding with the same violence he had once used to excoriate slaveholders. The argument continued in the next issue of *The Liberator* when an article told of a meeting of Black New Yorkers at the Shiloh Church that "took occasion to resolve that the American Anti-Slavery Society cannot in good faith . . . at present dissolve." Garrison's plan to end the work of the Anti-Slavery Society was, in fact, voted down overwhelmingly at its annual meeting and the society died a lingering death instead over the next five years.

Too late to be useful, the possibility of an academic life for Smith surfaced again during the winter of 1864–65 with the call to a position at Wilberforce College in Xenia, Ohio. Founded in 1856 by Black Americans, it is the nation's oldest "historically Black" college, and Smith accepted the call to a chair "*in case my health should permit*. But I am afraid," he wrote, "that such strength is beyond possibility. While I do not grow much worse, owing to a singular tenacity of constitution, neither do I get any better."[474]

Death of an Abolitionist

Perhaps it was his own medical experience that led Smith to understand many years earlier that he would not have a long life. In April 1846, when he was just thirty-three years old, he wrote to Gerrit Smith that "my ailment (dropsy) renders me very sleepy indeed. I have been confined to the house some three months, and the symptoms only now show symptoms of abatement."[475]

The Medical Register of the City of New York called Smith's disease "hypertrophy of the heart, complicated with annoying dropsical symptoms."[476] The more usual term for dropsy today is "edema." The disease causes fluid retention in certain areas of the body leading to shortness of breath and the swelling of certain tissues. Hypertrophy, a thickening of the cells of the heart chambers, produces similar symptoms: chest pain, shortness of breath, and general fatigue. Smith's medical training would have enabled him to diagnose the problem but not to cure it or even to alleviate it to any significant extent. He died on November 17, 1865, but he had lived to see the dream of abolition become a reality and to celebrate the defeat of the slave power.

The *New-York Daily Tribune* posted a small obituary notice headed "Death of a Distinguished Colored Man. Dr. James McCune Smith." The article continued:

> [O]ne of the best known colored men in this vicinity, died in Williamsburgh yesterday morning of a pulmonary affliction, from which he has been suffering for nearly twenty months in the 52d year of his age. He was born in New York, was educated and graduated at Glasgow, Scotland, and had been a practicing physician for a quarter of a century. He had always felt a deep interest in the cause of his race, and had labored zealously and constantly to ameliorate and elevate the condition of the colored race in this country, both bond and free, who have lost in him one of their best friends and most able advocates. [477]

The funeral took place at Smith's home at No. 162 South 3rd Street in Williamsburg at ten o'clock on Monday morning, November 20th.[478] The *Medical Register* said of him, "His character was that of the meek, hopeful Christian—honest, unselfish in his motives, and scrupulous in the performance of every duty." *The Weekly Anglo-African* said, "He will be greatly missed, not only in the line of his profession, and by his immediate family connection, but as a public man; and his death is as well lamented by them as by his family and relatives. A large circle of friends, with weeping hearts, attended his funeral, among whom were ten clergymen of different denominations, most of whom followed him to his quiet resting place" in Cypress Hills Cemetery in Brooklyn."[479]

When Frederick Douglass, looking back over his own life many years later, wrote an appreciation of all those who had helped him along the way, he gave first place to James McCune Smith. He noted that

> on all occasions, in season and out of season, there were brave and intelligent men of color all over the United States who gave me their cordial sympathy and support. Among these, and foremost, I place the name of Doctor James McCune Smith; educated in Scotland, and breathing the free air of that country, he came back to his native land with ideas of liberty which placed him in advance of most of his fellow citizens of African descent. He was not only a learned and skillful physician, but an effective speaker, and a keen and polished writer. In my newspaper enterprise, I found in him an earnest and effective helper. The cause of his people lost when he died. He was never among the timid who thought me too aggressive and wished me to tone down my testimony to suit the times. A brave man himself, he knew how to esteem courage in others.[480]

Smith's lifelong friend, Philip Bell, living by that time in California and editing a newspaper there, wrote: "[A]way over lake and river, through woods and dessert, across prairies and mountains, my heart goes to the quiet resting place in Cypress Hills, where he lies buried.

"Companion of my childhood's early days, associate of my youth, advisor of my manhood's riper years, friend of my life—*farewell!*"

James McCune Smith had once compared his work to that of the insects that build up a coral reef and "work beneath the tide in a superstructure that someday when the laborer is long dead and forgotten, may rear itself above the waves and afford rest and habitation for the creatures of the Good, Good Father of all."[481] The building or "coral reef" that Smith worked on throughout his life was, as he once described it, a nation in which

> our chains shall be broken, our fetters fall, and the American people swelling beyond the links in which Pride and Prejudice have bound them shall become the free and equal participants of one government, one destiny.[482]

The "coral reef" of that vision would grow beneath the surface for another century and is not yet solidly above the waves. By the time it is, perhaps Smith and Pennington and Douglass will indeed be "dead and forgotten," but if some then look back, they will learn that few Americans spoke so eloquently or worked so tirelessly for that destiny as did James McCune Smith.

APPENDIX A

The Family of
James McCune Smith	**Born**	**Died**
James McCune Smith	April 18, 1813	November 17, 1865
Malvina Barnet Smith	1825	?
Amy	December 30, 1843	December 24, 1849
James W	1845	?
Henry M	1847	1853
Anna Gertrude	March 7, 1850	September 19, 1854
Peter Williams	April, 1852	August 27, 1854
Frederick Douglass	February, 1818	February 20, 1895
Mary/Maude*	September (?) 1855	?
Leonard/Donald*	1858	?
John	1860	?
Guy Beaumont	1862	?

*Census takers were not careful and often misrecorded and misdated names. "Mary" (sometimes listed as Maude) is listed as four years old in the 1860 census, but was probably born in 1855 since Smith refers to "a renewed blessing in our house in the shape of a little girl" in a letter to Gerrit Smith dated October 6, 1855. "Leonard" in 1860 is apparently listed as "Donald" in 1870. It would seem that the earlier listings are incorrect.

Sources:
United States Census of 1850, 1860, 1870; New York State Census of 1855; *Frederick Douglass' Paper* October 6, 1854, and June 10, 1853.

BIBLIOGRAPHY

Abbreviations Used

BAP, The Black Abolitionist Papers

CA, The Colored American

FDP, Frederick Douglass' Paper

GSP, Gerrit Smith Papers, Special Collections, Syracuse University Library

NASS, National Anti-Slavery Standard

NS, The North Star

NYT, The New York Times

Journals and Magazines Cited

The Anglo-African Magazine

The Annalist: A Record of Practical Medicine in the City of New York

Anti-Slavery Bugle

Douglass' Monthly

The Glasgow New Liberator

Journal of the Assembly of the State of New York

Journal of Convention of the Diocese of New York, 1838

Journal of the National Medical Association, vol. 95, no. 7, July 2003

The Liberator

The Medical Register of the City of New York, for the Year Commencing June 1, 1866

New-York Daily Tribune

Niles' National Register

The New York World
The Northern Star and Colored Farmer
The Norwich Mercury
Gazette of the United-States
Weekly Register and Catholic Diary

Archival Sources

Archive Services, University of Glasgow

Gerrit Smith Papers, Special Collections, Syracuse University Library

University of Glasgow, Archives and Special Collections, University Prize and Degree List 1833–1863, GB248 R7/1/2, 7.

Articles in Magazines and Journals

Anti-Slavery Pamphlet, Black Abolitionist Archives, Boston Public Library, doc. no. 05354. *The Emancipator.*

Christian, Nichole M. "North Elba Journal; Recalling Timbuctoo, a Slice of Black History." *The New York Times*, February 19, 2002.

Du Bois, W. E. B. "Strivings of the Negro People." Atlantic Magazine, August 1897.

Hewitt, John H. "The Sacking of St. Philip's Church, New York." *Historical Magazine of the Episcopal Church*, vol. 49, no. 1, March 1980.

Journal of the Assembly of the State of New York, January 5, 1841: 15–1147. https://babel.hathitrust.org/cgi/pt?id=uc1.b2998850&seq=6

Lovejoy, Bess. "The Gory New York City Riot that Shaped American Medicine." *Smithsonian Magazine*, June 17, 2014. http://www.smithsonianmag.com/history/gory-new-york-city-riot-shaped-american-medicine-180951766/.

Morgan, Thomas. "The Education and Medical Practice of Dr. James McCune Smith (1813–1865), First Black American to Hold a Medical Degree." *Journal of the National Medical Association*, vol. 95, no. 7, (2003): 603–614.

Murphy, Terence D. "Medical Knowledge and Statistical Methods in Early Nineteenth-Century France." *Medical History*, vol. 25, issue 3 (1981): 301–319.

Peterson, Carla L. "Dr. Smith's Back Room." *The New York Times*, January 19, 2011.

Rein, Lisa. "Mystery of Va.'s First Slaves Is Unlocked 400 Years Later." *The Washington Post*, September 2, 2006.

Smith, James McCune. "Freedom and Slavery for African-Americans." *The New-York Daily Tribune*, 1844, in *National Anti-Slavery Standard*, February 1, 1844.

Smith, James McCune. "To the Rev. Orville Dewey." *The Liberator*, February 16, 1844.

Smith, James McCune. "Lay Puffery in Homeopathy." *The Annalist: A Record of Practical Medicine in the City of New York*, vol. 2, no. 3, 1847.

Books

Andrews, Charles C. *The History of the New-York African Free-Schools: From Their Establishment in 1787, to the Present Time (1830)*. New York: Mahlon Day, 1830.

Association for the Benefit of Colored Orphans. *From Cherry Street to Green Pastures: A History of the Colored Orphan Asylum in Riverdale-on-Hudson*. New York Historical Society, 1936.

Burrows, Edwin G. and Mike Wallace. *Gotham: A History of New York City to 1898*. New York: Oxford University Press, 1999.

Byron, Lord George. *Childe Harold's Pilgrimage*, canto IV, st. 98.

Byron, Lord George. *The Corsair*, canto 1, st. 3.

Calhoun, John C. *The Works of John C. Calhoun: Volume 5*. Edited by Richard K. Crallé. New York: D. Appleton, 1863–64.

Child, Lydia Maria Francis. *Letters from New York*. Athens: The University of Georgia Press, 1998.

Croswell, Sherman and Richard Sutton. *Debates and Proceedings in the New York State Assembly for the Revision of the Constitution, October 1, 1846*. Printed at the Office of the *Albany Argus*, 1846.

Dann, Norman K. *Practical Dreamer: Gerrit Smith and the Campaign for Social Reform*. New York: Log Cabin Books, 2009.

Dewey, Orville. *Autobiography and Letters of Orville Dewey (1883)*. Edited by Mary E. Dewey. The Project Gutenberg eBook of *Autobiography and Letters of Orville Dewey*, eBook #18956, http://www.gutenberg.org/cache/epub/18956/pg18956.txt.

Dickens, Charles. *American Notes for General Circulation*. New York: John W. Lovell Company, 1883.

Douglass, Frederick. *The Frederick Douglass Papers: Series Three: Correspondence, Volume 2: 1853–1865*. Edited by John R. McKivigan. New Haven: Yale University Press, 2018.

Douglass, Frederick. *The Frederick Douglass Papers: Series Three: Correspondence, Volume 3: 1853–1865*. Edited by John R. McKivigan. New Haven: Yale University Press, 2018.

Douglass, Frederick. *Life and Times of Frederick Douglass*. London: Collier-Macmillan Ltd., 1969.

Douglass, Frederick. *The Life and Writings of Frederick Douglass: Early Years, 1817–1849*. Edited by Philip S. Foner. New York: International Publishers, 1950.

Douglass, Frederick. *My Bondage and My Freedom*. With an introduction by James McCune Smith. New York: Miller, Orton & Mulligan, 1855.

Douglass, Frederick. *The Narrative of the Life of Frederick Douglass, an American Slave, Written by Himself*. Cambridge: Belknap Press, 1960.

Dubois, Laurent. *Avengers of the New World*. Cambridge: Belknap Press, 2004.

Ernst, Robert. *Immigrant Life in New York City: 1825–1863*. Port Washington: Ira J. Friedman, Inc., 1965.

Fifth Annual Report of the American Anti-Slavery Society. New York: William S. Dorr, 1838.

Foner, Eric. *Gateway to Freedom: The Hidden History of the Underground Railroad*. New York: W. W. Norton and Company, 2015.

Freehling, William H. *The Road to Disunion: Secessionists at Bay, 1776–1854: Volume I*. New York: Oxford University Press, 1990.

Frothingham, Octavius Brooks. *Gerrit Smith: A Biography*. New York: G. P. Putnam's Sons, 1878.

Garnet, Henry Highland. *An Address to the Slaves of the United States of America, Buffalo, NY, 1843*. Minutes of the National Convention of Colored Citizens. New York: J. H. Tobitt, 1843.

Garnet, Henry Highland. *A Memorial Discourse: Delivered in the Hall of the House of Representatives, Washington City, D. C., on Sabbath, February 12, 1865*. With an introduction by James McCune Smith, M. D. Philadelphia: Joseph M. Wilson, 1865.

Glasgow Emancipation Society. *First Annual Report of the Glasgow Emancipation Society*. Glasgow, Scotland, 1834.

Harris, Leslie M. *In the Shadow of Slavery: African Americans in New York, 1626–1863*. Chicago: University of Chicago Press, 2003.

Hay, John Barras. *Inaugural Addresses by Lords Rectors of the University of Glasgow: To Which are Prefixed, an Historical Sketch and Account of the Present State of the University.* Glasgow: David Robertson, 1839.

Headley, Joel Tyler. *The Great Riots of New York, 1712 to 1873.* New York: E. B. Treat, 1873. Republished by The Bobbs-Merrill Company, Inc., New York, 1970.

Heinl, Robert Debs and Nancy Gordon Heinl. *Written in Blood: The Story of the Haitian People 1492–1971.* Lanham: University Press of America, 2005.

Holzer, Harold. *Lincoln at Cooper Union: The Speech That Made Abraham Lincoln President.* New York: Simon & Schuster, 2004.

Horton, James Oliver and Lois E. Horton. *In Hope of Liberty: Culture, Community and Protest Among Northern Free Blacks, 1700–1860.* New York: Oxford University Press, 1997.

Jefferson, Thomas. *Notes on the State of Virginia.* Ann Arbor: Text Creation Partnership, 2007.

MacGregor, George. *The History of Glasgow: From the Earliest Period to the Present Time.* Glasgow: Thomas Morrison, 1881.

Mackie, J. D. *The University of Glasgow, 1451–1951: A Short History.* Glasgow: Jackson, Son, and Company, 1954.

Minutes of the Fifth Annual Convention of the Colored Citizens of the State of New York: Held in the City of Schenectady, on the 18th, 19th, and 20th of September, 1844. Troy: J. C. Kneeland and Co., 1844.

Payne, Daniel Alexander. *Recollections of Seventy Years.* Nashville: AMEC Publishing House, Sunday School Union, 1888.

Peterson, Carla L. *Black Gotham: A Family History of African Americans in Nineteenth-Century New York City.* New Haven: Yale University Press, 2011.

Potter, David M. *The Impending Crisis: America Before the Civil War 1848–1861*. New York: Harper and Row Publishers, 1976.

Proceedings of the Colored National Convention, Held in Rochester, July 6th, 7th, and 8th, 1853. Rochester: Printed at the Office of *Frederick Douglass' Paper*, 1853.

Proceedings of the Convention of Radical Political Abolitionists, Held at Syracuse, N.Y., June 26th, 27th, and 28th, 1855. London: Forgotten Books, 2018.

Proceedings of the National Convention of Colored People and Their Friends, Held in Troy, N.Y., on the 6th, 7th, 8th and 9th October, 1847. Troy: Steam Press of J. C. Kneeland and Co., 1847.

Quarles, Benjamin. *Black Abolitionists*. New York: Oxford University Press, 1969.

Quiller-Couch, Arthur. *The Oxford Book of English Verse: 1250–1918*. Oxford: Clarendon Press, 1901.

Ripley, C. Peter. *The Black Abolitionist Papers: Volume 2, Canada 1830–1865*. Chapel Hill: The University of North Carolina Press, 1987.

Rosenberg, Charles E. *The Cholera Years: The United States in 1832, 1849, and 1866*. Chicago: University of Chicago Press, 1987.

Scherzer, Kenneth. *The Unbounded Community: Neighborhood Life and Social Structure in New York City, 1830–1875*. Durham: Duke University Press, 1992.

Seraile, William. *Angels of Mercy: White Women and the History of New York's Colored Orphan Asylum*. New York: Fordham University Press, 2011.

Smith, Adam. *The Wealth of Nations*. In the Glasgow Edition of the Works and Correspondence of Adam Smith Volume 2b. Edited by R. H. Campbell and A. S. Skinner. Oxford: Oxford University Press, 1976.

Slaughter, Thomas P. *Bloody Dawn: The Christiana Riot and Racial Violence in the Antebellum North*. New York: Oxford University Press, 1991.

Smith, James McCune. *The Works of James McCune Smith: Black Intellectual and Abolitionist*. Edited by John Stauffer. New York: Oxford University Press, 2006.

Stauffer, John. *The Black Hearts of Men: Radical Abolitionists and the Transformation of Race*. Cambridge: Harvard University Press, 2001.

Strong, Douglas M. *Perfectionist Politics: Abolitionism and the Religious Tensions of American Democracy*. Syracuse: Syracuse University Press, 1999.

Strong, George Templeton. *The Diary of George Templeton Strong, Volume II: The Turbulent Fifties 1850–1859*. Edited by Allan Nevins and Milton Halsey Thomas. New York: Macmillan Company, 1952.

Townsend, Craig D. *Faith in their Own Color: Black Episcopalians in Antebellum New York City*. New York: Columbia University Press, 2005.

Toynbee, Arnold. *A Study of History*. London: Oxford University Press, 1935–1961.

Van Deusen, Glyndon G. *William Henry Seward: Lincoln's Secretary of State, the Negotiator of the Alaska Purchase*. New York: Oxford University Press, 1967.

Webber, Christopher L. *American to the Backbone: The Life of W. C. Pennington, the Fugitive Slave Who Became One of the First Black Abolitionists*. New York: Pegasus Books, 2011.

Webber, Christopher L. *Give Me Liberty: Speakers and Speeches That Have Shaped America*. New York: Pegasus Books, 2014.

White, Shane. *Prince of Darkness: The Untold Story of Jeremiah G. Hamilton, Wall Street's First Black Millionaire*. New York: St. Martin's Press, 2015.

ENDNOTES

1 James McCune Smith, "Heads of the Colored People, No. 3: The Washerwoman," *FDP*, June 17, 1852. We assume that "the washerwoman" is, in fact, Lavinia Smith since everything said about the washerwoman fits with what we know of Lavinia Smith.

2 Thomas Morgan, "The Education and Medical Practice of Dr. James McCune Smith (1813–1865), First Black American to Hold a Medical Degree," *Journal of the National Medical Association*, vol. 95, no. 7 (July 2003), 606.

3 James McCune Smith to Horace Greeley, September 1, 1851, *BAP*.

4 James McCune Smith, "Heads of the Colored People, No. 3: The Washerwoman," *FDP*, June 17, 1852.

5 Kenneth Scherzer, *The Unbounded Community: Neighborhood Life and Social Structure in New York City, 1830–1875* (Durham and London: Duke University Press, 1992), 145.

6 Charles Dickens, *American Notes for General Circulation* (New York: John W. Lovell Company, 1883), 669.

7 Lydia Maria Francis Child, *Letters from New York* (Athens: The University of Georgia Press, 1998), 17.

8 Carla L. Peterson, *Black Gotham: A Family History of African Americans in Nineteenth-Century New York City* (New Haven: Yale University Press, 2011), 79.

9 *Weekly Anglo-African*, January 19, 1861.

10 James McCune Smith, "Dr. Smith's Journal," *CA*, June 30, 1838.

11 James McCune Smith, *The Works of James McCune Smith: Black Intellectual and Abolitionist*, ed. John Stauffer (Oxford: Oxford University Press, 2007), 109.

12 Leslie M. Harris, *In the Shadow of Slavery: African Americans in New York City, 1626–1863* (Chicago: University of Chicago Press, 2003), 61.

13 Eric Foner, *Gateway to Freedom: The Hidden History of the Underground Railroad* (New York: W. W. Norton and Company, 2015), 42.

14 Henry Highland Garnet, *A Memorial Discourse: Delivered in the Hall of the House of Representatives, Washington City, D. C. on Sabbath, February 12, 1865.* With an introduction by James McCune Smith, M. D. (Philadelphia: Joseph M. Wilson, 1805), 28.

15 Harris, *In the Shadow of Slavery*, 65.

16 Harris, *In the Shadow of Slavery*, 131–132.

17 Harris, *In the Shadow of Slavery*, 103.

18 Charles C. Andrews, *The History of the New York African Free Schools: From Their Establishment in 1787, to the Present Time (1830)* (New York: Mahlon Day, 1830), 23–24.

19 Peterson, *Black Gotham*, 81.

20 Sailors were accustomed to dealing with coworkers of every race and ethnicity (cf. *Moby Dick*) and black sailors, away from the prejudices in life on land, often did well.

21 Garnet, *A Memorial Discourse*, 22–23.

22 Peterson, *Black Gotham*, 84.

23 Andrews, *The History of the New York African Free Schools*, p. 148.

24 Garnet, *A Memorial Discourse*, 132.

25 Andrews, *The History of the New York African Free Schools*, 132.

26 Andrews, *The History of the New York African Free Schools*, 39.

27 Benjamin Quarles, *Black Abolitionists* (New York: Oxford University Press, 1969), 12.

28 Harris, *In the Shadow of Slavery*, 134–135.

29 Andrews, *The History of the New York African Free Schools*, 32.

30 James McCune Smith, "Letter from Communipaw," *FDP*, January 12, 1859.

31 The State Census of 1820 showed 1,300,000 "free white" and 29,000 "free black" residents.

32 Harris, *In the Shadow of Slavery*, 126.

33 William Wordsworth, "Liberty", cited in Garnet, *A Memorial Discourse*, 24–25.

34 Edwin G. Burrows and Mike Wallace, *Gotham: A History of New York City to 1898* (New York: Oxford University Press, 1999), 546.

35 *CA*, January 20, 1838.

36 Smith's good friend, Philip Bell, said that Smith and another young Black man, Isaiah DeGrasse, who would later be ordained in the Episcopal Church, were able to continue their studies for two more years at the "Episcopal Seminary" where the headmaster, Samuel Sewall, took a special interest in his two Black students, but the Episcopal seminary in New York is the General Theological Seminary and has a dean, not a headmaster. DeGrasse attended classes there for a few weeks before being forced to withdraw to placate southern students. Smith would not have gone there since he had no interest in ministry. There is no record of a Samuel Sewall in the Diocese of New York or at Trinity School, the only other Episcopal academic institution in the city. An obituary for Smith in the *Medical Register* (June 1, 1866) says that Smith continued his studies under the guidance of "Mr. Curtis, a tutor in Trinity School" and "Mr. Frederick Schroeder." The archives of Trinity School Manhattan confirm the presence of both individuals. John W. Curtis was an Episcopal priest, a graduate of the General Theological Seminary, and a member of the faculty at Collegiate School, affiliated with Trinity School. J. F. Schroeder was a member of the board of trustees of the New York Protestant Episcopal Public School.

37 Philip Bell, "Death of Dr. Jas. Mccune Smith," *The Elevator*, December 22, 1865.

38 John Stauffer, introduction to *The Works of James McCune Smith*, xxi.

39 Bell, "Death of Dr. Jas. Mccune Smith," December 22, 1865.

40 Bell, "Death of Dr. Jas. Mccune Smith," December 22, 1865.

41 Craig D. Townsend, *Faith in Their Own Color: Black Episcopalians in Antebellum New York City* (New York: Columbia University Press, 2005), 29.

42 Townsend, *Faith in Their Own Color*, 29. For the text of Williams's oration, see Carter G. Woodson, *Negro Orators and Their Orations* (Washington, D.C.: Associated Publishers, 1925), 32-41.

43 James McCune Smith, "From Our New York Correspondent," *FDP*, March 25, 1859.

44 Some sources suggest that Smith continued his studies at Trinity School or as a private student of a member of the Trinity School faculty, but the position as blacksmith's apprentice would have limited his studies to evenings and weekends.

45 Townsend, *Faith in Their Own Color*, 75.

46 The principal lighthouse on Sandy Hook goes back to the eighteenth century and is still in use, but it had other smaller lights around it at the time of Smith's voyage.

47 James McCune Smith, "Journal of James McCune Smith, August 16, 1832," *CA*, November 11, 1837.

48 Smith, "Journal," November 11, 1837.

49 George Gordon Byron, *Childe Harold's Pilgrimage*, canto IV, st. 98.

50 *The Norwich Mercury*, March 24, 1832, Immigrant Ships Transcribers Guide, accessed September 12, 2024, http://immigrantships.net/newsarticles/1830_newsarticles.html.

51 "Steerage," Wikipedia, last modified August 24, 2024, https://en.wikipedia.org/wiki/Steerage_(deck).

52 Charles E. Rosenberg, *The Cholera Years: The United States in 1832, 1849, and 1866* (Chicago: The University of Chicago Press, 1987), 30–32.

53 Smith, "Journal," November 11, 1837.

54 CA, November 11, 1837

55 George Gordon Byron, *The Corsair*, canto 1, st. 3.

56 Smith, "Journal," December 2, 1837.

57 Smith, "Journal," December 16, 1837.

58 Smith, "Journal," February 3, 1838.

59 Smith, "Journal," February 3, 1838.

60 Smith's "Journal", as published in *The Colored American*, provides only initials for most of the names of people he met in Glasgow. Thomas Morgan in "The Education and Medical Practice of Dr. James McCune Smith" (see Bibliography) provides some of the names but cites no other authority. Those names are marked with an asterisk.

61 Presumably, Smith is referring to Philip Bell.

62 Smith, "Journal" February 3, 1838.

63 The image was created at the Josiah Wedgwood Pottery in 1787 and was familiar to abolitionists on both sides of the Atlantic.

64 Smith, "Journal," February 3, 1838.

65 This was the Royal Amphitheatre, a recently constructed venue for circuses, plays, operas, and concerts, which is still in use as the Royal Court Theatre on Roe Street.

66 In the monitorial system used in the African Free School there was no real breakdown of classes, and students with similar interests and abilities, like Philip Bell, Aldridge, and Smith, would have thought of themselves as "schoolmates" though of quite different ages.

67 Smith, "Journal," March 16, 1839.

68 Smith, "Journal," March 16, 1839.

69 George MacGregor, *The History of Glasgow: From the Earliest Period to the Present Time* (Glasgow: Thomas Morrison, 1881), 416–417.

70 J. D. Mackie, *The University of Glasgow 1451–1951: A Short History* (Glasgow: Jackson, Son, and Company, 1954), 249.

71 Mackie, *The University of Glasgow*, 250.

72 A similar problem in New York City produced resurrectionists there as well and led to a "Doctors' Riot" in 1788. The burial ground for black New Yorkers in the Five Points area was especially prone to be used for corpses. Bess Lovejoy, "The Gory New York City Riot that Shaped American Medicine," *Smithsonian Magazine* (June 17, 2014): http://www.smithsonianmag.com/history/gory-new-york-city-riot-shaped-american-medicine-180951766/.

73 MacGregor, *The History of Glasgow*, 396–397.

74 John Barras Hay, *Inaugural Addresses by Lords Rectors of the University of Glasgow: To Which Are Prefixed, an Historical Sketch and Account of the Present State of the University* (Glasgow, David Robertson, 1839), xxxiii–lxxvii.

75 A rough equivalent of $400 in the early twenty-first century.

76 Hay, *Inaugural Addresses*, lxxii.

77 University Calendar 1833–1834, University of Glasgow Archives & Special Collections, GB248 SEN10/3, 47.

78 For the Logic prize listing: University Prize and Degree List 1833–1863, University of Glasgow, Archives and Special Collections, GB248 R7/1/2, 7. Cf. also Peter Williams to Gerrit Smith, September 4, 1834, *GSP*.

79 Adam Smith, *The Wealth of Nations*, in The Glasgow Edition of the Works and Correspondence of Adam Smith, Volume 2b, eds. R. H. Campbell and A. S. Skinner (New York: Oxford University Press, 1976), 678.

80 Glasgow Emancipation Society, *First Annual Report of the Glasgow Emancipation Society*, Glasgow, Scotland, 1834.

81 Joel Tyler Headley, *The Great Riots of New York, 1712 to 1873* (New York: E. B. Treat, 1873). Republished by Bobbs-Merrill Company, Inc., New York, 1970, 83–95.

82 The *Courier and Enquirer*, July 3, 1834.

83 Peterson, *Black Gotham*, 102.

84 Headley, *The Great Riots of New York*, 83–95.

85 The story of the 1834 riot is based on accounts given in: John H. Hewitt, "The Sacking of St. Philip's Church, New York," *Historical Magazine of the Protestant Episcopal Church*, vol. xliv, March 1981; Townsend, *Faith*, [pg]; Headley, *The Great Riots of New York*, 83–95; and Bruce Chadwick, *Law & Disorder: The Chaotic Birth of the NYPD* (New York: St. Martin's Press, 2017), 1–4.

86 *NYT*, August 8, 1834.

87 *New-York Weekly Register and Catholic Diary*, July 29, 1834.

88 *NYT*, July 11, 1834.

89 Peter Williams to Gerrit Smith, July 26, 1834, *GSP*.

90 Mackie, *The University of Glasgow*, 258.

91 Archive Services, University of Glasgow.

92 *The Colored American* of August 4, 1838, tells us that Smith, being unable to board the *Canonicus*, returned to New York "on a foreign vessel."

93 *The Glasgow New Liberator*, May 20, 1837, reprinted in *CA*, February 17, 1838.

94 *The Glasgow New Liberator*, May 20, 1837, reprinted in *CA*, February 17, 1838.

95 See, for example, the undocumented statement: "Upon graduation, Smith ventured to Paris for additional clinical exposure before returning home to New York." Morgan, "The Education and Medical Practice of Dr. James McCune Smith," 608.

96 Alfred-Armand-Louis-Marie Velpeau (May 18, 1795–August 24, 1867; Bell misspells the name) was still early in his career having earned his M.D. in 1823. His special skills were as a surgeon, but he wrote over 340 titles on surgery, embryology, anatomy, and obstetrics.

97 Bell, "Death of Dr. Jas. Mccune Smith," December 22, 1865.

98 Terence D. Murphy, "Medical Knowledge and Statistical Methods in Early Nineteenth-Century France," *Medical History*, vol. 25, issue 3 (July 1981), 301–319.

99 *Freedom's Journal*, November 2, 1827.

100 Townsend, *Faith in Their Own Color*, 44.

101 *CA*, November 4, 1837.

102 Norman K. Dann, *Practical Dreamer: Gerrit Smith and the Campaign for Social Reform* (New York: Log Cabin Books, 2009), 422.

103 Stauffer, introduction to *The Works of James McCune Smith*, xiii.

104 Frederick Douglass, *The Narrative of the Life of Frederick Douglass: An American Slave, Written by Himself* (Cambridge: Belknap Press, 1960), 143–144.

105 "Great Fire of New York," Wikipedia, last modified October 31, 2023, https://en.wikipedia.org/wiki/Great_Fire_of_New_York.

106 Peterson, *Black Gotham*, 93.

107 "Dr. Smith," reprinted in The Colored American, September 23, 1837, from the Commercial Advertiser (undated).

108 "Dr. Smith," reprinted in The Colored American, September 23, 1837, from the Commercial Advertiser (undated).

109 Bell's newspaper began publication in January 1837 as the *Weekly Advocate* but changed its name to *The Colored American* in March.

110 "A Classical Scholar," *The United States Gazette*, December 16, 1837.

111 Carla L. Peterson, "Dr. Smith's Back Room," *NYT*, January 19, 2011.

112 Until Smith began running ads in *The Colored American*, it had frequently carried ads for another supplier of "Drugs and Medicines" at another location. After Smith began advertising, ads for the other supplier no longer appeared.

113 Reade Street, Greenwich Street, and West Broadway are all in what is now called the Tribeca area of Manhattan, south of the better-known Greenwich Village but also a very upscale neighborhood. It was a comfortable neighborhood in Smith's day but not upscale.

114 *CA*, July 13, 1839.

115 Peterson, *Black Gotham*, 144.

116 Peterson, *Black Gotham*, 128.

117 *CA*, October 28, 1837.

118 Daniel Alexander Payne, *Recollections of Seventy Years* (Nashville: AMEC Publishing House, 1888), 27–28.

119 *CA*, October 30, 1837.

120 *CA*, January 20, 1838.

121 *CA*, May 3, 1838.

122 *Fifth Annual Report of the American Anti-Slavery Society* (New York: William S. Dorr, 1838), 24–30.

123 *CA*, June 2, 1838.

124 "Public Meeting," CA, June 16, 1838.

125 *CA*, June 16, 1838.

126 *Emancipator*, December 20, 1838.

127 *CA*, January 19, 1839.

128 *CA*, February 9, 1839.

129 *CA*, May 18, 1839.

130 *CA*, May 9, 1839.

131 Dann, *Practical Dreamer*, 438.

132 *CA*, May 23, 1840.

133 *CA*, August 8, 1840.

134 *NASS*, August 20, 1840.

135 James McCune Smith to James G. Birney, February 8, 1841, *BAP*.

136 *CA*, August 22, 1840.

137 Morgan, "The Education and Medical Practice of Dr. James McCune Smith," 610.

138 *CA*, October 24, 1840.

139 Williams was ordained to the diaconate on October 20, 1820, and ordained as a priest on July 10, 1826. He was the second black priest ordained in the Episcopal Church.

140 *CA*, November 7, 1840.

141 Horace Bushnell, the distinguished pastor of a Congregational Church in Hartford, Connecticut, in a Thanksgiving Day (!) sermon in 1860. "Emancipation brings no hopeful promise to the colored race. I know of no example in human history where an inferior ... stock has been able ... to hold its ground." Christopher L. Webber, *American to the Backbone* (Berkeley: Pegasus Books, 2011), 133.

142 *Anti-Slavery Pamphlet*, Boston Public Library, Black Abolitionist Archives, doc. no. 05354.

143 Smith, *The Works of James McCune Smith*, 48.

144 *CA*, February 23, 1839.

145 Robert Debs Heinl and Nancy Gordon Heinl, *Written in Blood: The Story of the Haitian People, 1492–1971* (Lanham: University Press of America, 2005), 90.

146 The death rate among slaves in Haiti was such that the supply of black laborers had to be constantly replenished.

147 Smith, "Lecture on the Haytien Revolutions," *The Works of James McCune Smith*, 36.

148 Laurent Dubois, *Avengers of the New World* (Cambridge: Belknap Press, 2004), 30.

149 Smith, "Lecture on the Haytien Revolutions," *The Works of James McCune Smith*, 39.

150 *CA*, June 5, 1841.

151 James McCune Smith to James G. Birney, February 8, 1841, *BAP.*

152 *Journal of the Assembly of the State of New York*, January 5, 1841, 15–1147, https://hdl.handle.net/2027/chi.12547669.

153 *CA*, May 22, 1841.

154 William H. Freehling, *The Road to Disunion: Secessionists at Bay, 1776–1854: Volume I* (New York: Oxford University Press, 1990), 204.

155 Freehling, *Road to Disunion*, 206.

156 Freehling, *Road to Disunion*, 206.

157 *Niles' National Register*, June 28, 1841, 227.

158 *CA*, June 26, 1841.

159 *CA*, June 26, 1841.

160 *CA*, August 14, 1841.

161 Henry Highland Garnet, *An Address to the Slaves of the United States of America, Buffalo, N.Y., 1843*. Minutes of the National Convention of Colored Citizens (New York: J. H. Tobitt, 1843).

162 "Public Meeting," *CA*, September 25, 1841.

163 "The Proceedings of the New York County Convention," *CA*, October 30, 1841.

164 *CA*, October 30, 1841.

165 *CA*, December 4, 1841.

166 State of New York in Assembly, no. 155, March 29, 1842. Report of the Committee on Privileges and Elections on the petition for an amendment of the Constitution, extending the elective franchise to the colored population. [This is not an accurate title since the issue was removing a restrictive requirement for colored voters.]

167 *The Liberator*, May 27, 1842.

168 James McCune Smith, Ulysses B. Vidal, and Timothy Seaman to William H. Seward, New York City, December 26, 1842, *GSP*.

169 Glyndon G. Van Deusen, *William Henry Seward: Lincoln's Secretary of State, the Negotiator of the Alaska Purchase* (New York: Oxford University Press, 1967), 4.

170 Van Deusen, *William Henry Seward*, 94.

171 *BAP*, December 26, 1842.

172 "Caste Schools," December 28, 1842, *BAP*.

173 Van Deusen, *William Henry Seward*, 70.

174 Morgan, "The Education and Medical Practice of Dr. James McCune Smith," 610.

175 In keeping with contemporary practice, Smith notes that two of the five women are "(colored)."

176 Morgan, "The Education and Medical Practice of Dr. James McCune Smith," 603–614.

177 Orville Dewey, *Autobiography and Letters of Orville Dewey (1883)*, ed. Mary Dewey. The Project Gutenberg eBook of the *Autobiography and Letters of Orville Dewey*, eBook #18956, http://www.gutenberg.org/cache/epub/18956/pg18956.txt.

178 James McCune Smith, "Freedom and Slavery for African-Americans," *The New-York Daily Tribune*, 1844, in *NASS*, February 1, 1844.

179 James McCune Smith, "To the Rev. Orville Dewey," *The Liberator*, February 16, 1844.

180 Smith notes that "the keen and practised eyes of southern men can instantly detect the most remote admixture of African blood.... But here at the North, the boundary line is less distinct: the colored white has merely to change his place of abode, cut his old associates, and courtesy will do the rest—he is a white.... Of one hundred boys who attended with me the New-York African free school in 1826-7, I could name six now living—all white." Smith's own descendants would follow that path within a generation of his death and become ignorant of their ancestry until it was rediscovered with pride by the latest generation. Cf. *The Works of James McCune Smith*, xvi-xix.

181 James McCune Smith, "Freedom and Slavery for Afric-Americans," *The New-York Daily Tribune*, January 29, 1844, and *NASS*, February 8, 1844.

182 Morgan, "The Education and Medical Practice of Dr. James McCune Smith," 611.

183 Smith, "Freedom and Slavery for Afric-Americans," 1844.

184 Smith, "Freedom and Slavery for Afric-Americans," 1844.

185 Tyler became President when William Henry Harrison died after just thirty-one days in office.

186 John C. Calhoun, *The Works of John C. Calhoun: Volume 5*, ed. Richard K. Crallé (New York: D. Appleton, 1863–64), 333–347.

187 Calhoun, *The Works of John C. Calhoun*, 333–347.

188 Some pen names were used a few years earlier in *The Colored American*. James W. C. Pennington, for example, often signed himself "Long Island Scribe."

189 "The Great Meeting," *The Liberator*, May 10, 1844.

190 Smith, "Freedom and Slavery for Afric-Americans," 1844.

191 Smith's committee provided an amusing breakdown, state by state: "Maine: towns where there are no colored persons reported: Insane—27; Blind—1; Deaf and Dumb—2." etc.

192 "Sen. John C. Calhoun and the Free Colored People," *The New-York Daily Tribune*, published in *The Liberator*, May 31, [year].

193 "The American Anti-Slavery Society held its meeting at the Apollo," *New York Courier and Enquirer*, published in *The Liberator*, May 24, 1844.

194 "Letter from Wm. Henry Brisbane," *Boston Morning Chronicle*, in *The Liberator*, May 24, 1844.

195 "To the Friends of Freedom in the U. States," *The Liberator*, May 24, 1844.

196 James McCune Smith, Ulysses B. Vidal et. al., "Report of the New York Delegates," September 18, 1844, *BAP*.

197 *Minutes of the Fifth Annual Convention of the Colored Citizens of the State of New York: Held in the City of Schenectady, on the 18th, 19th, and 20th of September, 1844* (Troy: J. C. Kneeland and Co., 1844), 15–17.

198 Garnet, *A Memorial Discourse*, 43–44.

199 Peterson, *Black Gotham*, 122.

200 "From the Northern Star," *The Liberator*, June 28, 1844. Published also in the *Anti-Slavery Standard*, October 11, 1844.

201 Octavius Brooks Frothingham, *Gerrit Smith: A Biography* (New York: G. P. Putnam's Sons, 1878), 102–103.

202 John Stauffer, *The Black Hearts of Men: Radical Abolitionists and the Transformation of Race* (Cambridge: Harvard University Press, 2001), 136–137.

203 "A Man's a Man for A' That" is a 1795 Scots song by Robert Burns, famous for its expression of egalitarian ideas of society, which may be seen as expressing the ideas of liberalism that arose in the eighteenth century. Note that the same song was quoted by Ransom P. Wake in welcoming Smith back from Scotland.

204 Gerrit Smith to T. S. Wright, C. B. Ray, and J. McCune Smith, November 14, 1846, *GSP*.

205 James McCune Smith to Gerrit Smith, December 17, 1846, *GSP*.

206 Frothingham, *Gerrit Smith*, 9.

207 Arnold Toynbee, *A Study of History* (London: Oxford University Press, 1935–1961).

208 James McCune Smith to Gerrit Smith, December 19, 1846, *GSP*.

209 James McCune Smith to Gerrit Smith, December 28, 1846, *GSP*.

210 James McCune Smith to Gerrit Smith, July 7, 1848, *GSP*.

211 James McCune Smith to Gerrit Smith, May 12, 1848, *GSP*.

212 Statement of Elijah B. Jones, *The Northern Star and Colored Farmer*, Essex County, Town of Keane, January 8, 1849.

213 Gerrit Smith to Elder Charles B. Ray, November 16, 1848, *GSP*.

214 James McCune Smith to Gerrit Smith, February 6, 1850, *GSP*.

215 James Oliver Horton and Lois E. Horton, *In Hope of Liberty: Culture, Community and Protest Among Northern Free Blacks, 1700–1860* (New York: Oxford University Press, 1997), 243.

216 Nichole M. Christian, "North Elba Journal; Recalling Timbuctoo, a Slice of Black History," *The New York Times*, February 19, 2002.

217 Harris, *In the Shadow of Slavery*, 277.

218 After Harpers Ferry and his execution, Brown's body was brought back to his farm and buried there. The John Brown Farm and gravesite is now a National Historic Landmark.

219 "To Gerrit Smith Grantees," October 4, 1854, *GSP*.

220 James McCune Smith to Gerrit Smith, February 6, 1850, *GSP*.

221 James McCune Smith to Gerrit Smith, September 20, 1859, *GSP*.

222 Christian, "North Elba Journal," *NYT*, February 19, 2002.

223 Gerrit Smith to Rev. T. S. Wright, Rev. C. B. Ray, Dr. J. McCune Smith, November 14, 1846, *GSP*.

224 Gerrit Smith to Elder Charles B. Ray, November 16, 1848, *GSP*.

225 James McCune Smith to Gerrit Smith, May 12, 1848, *GSP*.

226 A state license was not required and the church records have not been preserved.

227 James McCune Smith to Gerrit Smith, December 19, 1846, *GSP*.

228 Anti-Masonry was a significant political movement in the 1830s and an Anti-Masonry Party was the first political party to hold a national nominating convention in 1832.

229 *Journal of Convention of the Diocese of New York, 1838*, 84.

230 A third slave, a woman and the personal servant of the captain and his wife, let it be known that she wanted to go back to Brazil.

231 W. E. B. Du Bois, "Strivings of the Negro People," *Atlantic Magazine*, August 1897.

232 Townsend, *Faith in Their Own Color*, 148.

233 "The Brazilian Slaves," *NASS*, September 16, 1847.

234 Townsend, *Faith in Their Own Color*, 190.

235 Cf. Chapter 7.

236 Townsend, *Faith in Their Own Color*, 103–107.

237 Townsend, *Faith in Their Own Color*, 130.

238 Townsend, *Faith in Their Own Color*, 131.

239 Townsend, *Faith in Their Own Color*, 132.

240 Townsend, *Faith in Their Own Color*, 139.

241 James McCune Smith to Gerrit Smith, December 28, 1846, *GSP*.

242 Townsend, *Faith in Their Own Color*, 174–178.

243 Townsend, *Faith in Their Own Color*, 173.

244 Townsend, *Faith in Their Own Color*, 182.

245 Townsend, *Faith in Their Own Color*, 183.

246 James McCune Smith to John Jay, September 18, 1853, *BAP*.

247 George Templeton Strong, *The Diary of George Templeton Strong, Volume II: The Turbulent Fifties 1850–1859*, eds. Allan Nevins and Milton Halsey Thomas (New York: Macmillan Company, 1952), 131.

248 Strong was not without a conscience. When he heard of the factory fire in Lawrence, Massachusetts, in 1860 in which over a hundred workers were killed, he wrote: "Somebody has murdered about two hundred people, many of them with hideous torture, in order to save money, but society has no gibbet for the respectable murderer and homicide. . . . It becomes us to talk about the horrors of slavery! What southern capitalist trifles with the lives of his operatives as do our philanthropes of the North?"

249 Association for the Benefit of Colored Orphans, *From Cherry Street to Green Pastures: A History of the Colored Orphan Asylum in Riverdale-on-Hudson*, New York Historical Society, 3.

250 An alternative tradition says that a white woman had found the two children in jail and turned them over to the Quaker ladies.

251 Association for the Benefit of Colored Orphans, *From Cherry Street*, 6–7.

252 "Colored Orphan Asylum," *CA*, October 28, 1837.

253 Association for the Benefit of Colored Orphans, *From Cherry Street*, 11.

254 Association for the Benefit of Colored Orphans, *From Cherry Street*, 8.

255 "Colored Orphans," *CA*, April 29, 1837.

256 "First Annual Report of the Association for the benefit of Colored Orphans," *CA*, December 30, 1837.

257 "News of the Day," *CA*, October 27, 1838.

258 https://en.wikipedia.org/wiki/Datura_stramonium.

259 "Pathy" is McCune Smith's way of sneering at homeopathy.

260 James McCune Smith to Gerrit Smith, December 19, 1846, *GSP*.

261 Harris, *In the Shadow of Slavery*, 158.

262 "Association for Colored Orphans," *CA*, December 29, 1838.

263 "Asylum for Colored Orphans," *CA*, December 15, 1838.

264 "Dr. Macdonald's Report," *CA*, December 28, 1838.

265 "Colored Orphan's Asylum. Physician's Report," *CA*, January 26, 1839.

266 Association for the Benefit of Colored Orphans, *From Cherry Street*, 15–16.

267 Harris, *In the Shadow of Slavery*, 157. Peterson, *Black Gotham*, 158.

268 Morgan, "The Education and Medical Practice of Dr. James McCune Smith," 609.

269 Morgan, "The Education and Medical Practice of Dr. James McCune Smith," 609.

270 Harris, *In the Shadow of Slavery*, 157.

271 William Seraile, *Angels of Mercy: White Women and the History of New York's Colored Orphan Asylum* (New York: Fordham University Press, 2011), 27.

272 Association for the Benefit of Colored Orphans, *From Cherry Street*, 15–16.

273 On one occasion, James Pennington was unable to get to the orphanage in time to conduct a funeral because no streetcar would take him and a private carriage was beyond his means. (Seraile, *Angels of Mercy*, 28.)

274 Webber, *American to the Backbone*, 392.

275 "Eastern Correspondence," *The National Era*, September 9, 1847.

276 Harris, *In the Shadow of Slavery*, 167–168.

277 "Annual Meeting of the Colored Orphan Asylum," *NASS*, February 22, 1849.

278 Seraile, *Angels of Mercy*, 16–17.

279 "The New York Colored Orphan Asylum," *NS*, May 4, 1849.

280 Seraile, *Angels of Mercy*, 37.

281 James McCune Smith to Gerrit Smith, December 19, 1846, *GSP*.

282 Rosenberg, *The Cholera Years*, 114.

283 James McCune Smith and Ulysses B. Vidal to Gerrit Smith, July 30, 1865, *GSP*.

284 A 63rd County was created in 1914 with the separation of the Bronx from Westchester County.

285 "An Appeal for Rights," *NASS*, January 29, 1846.

286 The full statement will be found in Appendix A.

287 Sherman Croswell and Richard Sutton, *Debates and Proceedings in the New York State Assembly for the Revision of the Constitution, October 1, 1846* (Printed at the Office of the *Albany Argus*), 777.

288 Croswell, *Debates and Proceedings*, 785, 788.

289 James McCune Smith to Stephen Myers, September 21, 1860, *GSP*.

290 James McCune Smith, "Lay Puffery in Homeopathy," in *The Annalist: A Record of Practical Medicine, in the City of New York*, vol. 2, no. 3 (November 1, 1847), 348–351.

291 Smith, "Lay Puffery of Homeopathy," 348–351.

292 The term "quack" may be derived from the German word *quecksilber* for "quicksilver" or mercury, which was widely used in medicine from the Middle Ages through the nineteenth century but might also be derived from the Dutch term *kwakzalver*, a "hawker of salve."

293 James McCune Smith to Gerrit Smith, July 28, 1848, *GSP*.

294 James McCune Smith to Gerrit Smith, December 14, 1846, *GSP*.

295 James McCune Smith to Gerrit Smith, May 12, 1848, *GSP*.

296 James McCune Smith to Gerrit Smith, May 12, 1848, *GSP*.

297 James McCune Smith to Gerrit Smith, May 12, 1848, *GSP*.

298 Douglas M. Strong, *Perfectionist Politics: Abolitionism and the Religious Tensions of American Democracy* (Syracuse: Syracuse University Press, 1999), 9.

299 Strong, *Perfectionist Politics*, 66.

300 Smith made his home at 151 Reade Street until 1842 and then at 29 Leonard Street until 1849. The 1849 street directory shows him living at 15 N. Moore Street, a house apparently built for him and his family. These dates are approximate and based on New York City street directories issued for two-year periods, as, for example, "1849/50."

301 It might also be noticed that the census takers of 1850, 1855, and 1860, given the choice of listing individuals as "White, Mulatto, or Black," listed all members of the household as "Mulatto" with two exceptions: In 1855, Mary Herman, listed as "servant," was recorded as being "Black," while the census taker ignored the classifications provided to list John, age nine, as "Light Brown." After James McCune Smith's death, the family was living in Williamsburg on Long Island when the 1870 census listed all members of the household as "White."

302 James McCune Smith to Gerrit Smith, February 6, 1850, *GSP*.

303 "From Our New York Correspondent," *FDP*, December 15, 1854.

304 James McCune Smith to Gerrit Smith, March 1, 1855, *GSP*.

305 See Appendix A.

306 "The Colored Convention," *NS*, December 3, 1847.

307 Frederick Douglass, *The Life and Writings of Frederick Douglass: Early Years, 1817-1849*, ed. Philip D. Foner (New York: International Publishers, 1950), 77.

308 *Proceedings of the National Convention of Colored People and Their Friends, Held in Troy, N.Y., on the 6th, 7th, 8th, and 9th October, 1847* (Troy: Steam Press of J. C. Kneeland and Co., 1847), 217.

309 Frederick Douglass, *Life and Times of Frederick Douglass* (London: Collier-Macmillan Ltd., 1969), 260.

310 "List of Agents," *NS*, December 3, 1847.

311 "Gleanings by the Wayside," *NS*, February 11, 1848.

312 "The Object of the North Star," *NS*, January 5, 1849.

313 "Great Anti-Colonization Mass Meeting," *NASS*, May 3, 1849.

314 "Editorial Correspondence," *NS*, April 27, 1849; "Letter from the Editor," *NS*, May 4, 1848.

315 James McCune Smith to Gerrit Smith, July 28, 1848, *GSP*.

316 James McCune Smith, introduction to *My Bondage and My Freedom* by Frederick Douglass (New York: Miller, Orton & Mulligan, 1855), xlv.

317 Frederick Douglass, *My Bondage and My Freedom* (New York: Modern Library, 2003), xlvi.

318 "Meeting in New York," *NS*, May 4, 1849.

319 Douglass, *The Life and Writings of Frederick Douglass*, 100.

320 James McCune Smith to Gerrit Smith, July 28, 1848, *GSP*.

321 Senator Webster's dark complexion led to the common nickname of "Black Dan."

322 "To the People of the State of New York," *NASS*, October 31, 1850.

323 "To the People of the State of New York," *NASS*, October 31, 1850.

324 Horton, *In Hope of Liberty*, 253.

325 "Change of Opinion Announced," *NS*, May 15, 1851.

326 *Tribune*, March 20, 1851, cited by Robert Ernst, *Immigrant Life in New York City: 1825–1863* (Port Washington: Ira J. Friedman, Inc., 1965), 104.

327 "Letter from Dr. James McCune Smith," *FDP*, October 16, 1851.

328 "Meeting to Sympathize with and aid the Christiana Patriots," *FDP*, November 13, 1851.

329 Quarles, *Black Abolitionists*, 212.

330 Thomas P. Slaughter, *Bloody Dawn: The Christiana Riot and Racial Violence in the Antebellum North* (New York: Oxford University Press, 1991), 47.

331 The reference is to the Gospel According to St. Luke 22:27, in which Jesus says: "For whether *is* greater, he that sitteth at meat, or he that serveth? *is* not he that sitteth at meat? but I am among you as he that serveth."

332 Smith is referring to Psalm 118:22, which says, "The stone which the builders refused is become the head stone of the corner." Jesus also quotes that Psalm in the Gospels (Mark 12:10 et al).

333 "African Colonization ... The Other Side," *NAS*, August 28 and September 11, 1851.

334 *Macbeth*, Act 4, Scene I.

335 Untitled editorial, *FDP*, December 17, 1852.

336 Note that "Wappinumoc" is a reversed version of the name, but it is not Communipaw spelled backward.

337 "Our Brooklyn Correspondent," *FDP*, April 15, 1853.

338 "Letter from Communipaw," *FDP*, March 8, 1852.

339 "Letter from Dr. James McCune Smith," *FDP*, October 16, 1851.

340 "Address to the People of the State of New York," *FDP*, February 5, 1852.

341 "Meeting of the Colored People of New York, Corrected from a Report in the *New York Herald*," January 8, 1852, *BAP*.

342 "Address to the People of the State of New York," *FDP*, February 5, 1852.

343 Letter to the Governor, February 9, 1852, *BAP*.

344 There are references to a New York State Anti-Slavery Society founded in 1833 (cf. Manisha Sinha (757) but little evidence of its continued existence.

345 "Letter from Communipaw," *FDP*, March 18, 1852.

346 Shane White, *Prince of Darkness: The Untold story of Jeremiah G. Hamilton, Wall Street's First Black Millionaire* (New York: St. Martin's Press, 2015), 199.

347 "Letter from Communipaw," *FDP*, March 18, 1852.

348 "Der Hagel," *FDP*, March 25, 1853.

349 "From Our Brooklyn Correspondent," *FDP*, July 30, 1852.

350 Lisa Rein, "Mystery of Va.'s First Slaves Is Unlocked 400 Years Later," *The Washington Post*, September 3, 2006.

351 "Letter from Communipaw," *FDP*, February 12, 1852.

352 "Der Hagel," *FDP*, March 25, 1853.

353 "Heads of the Colored People," *FDP*, March 25, 1852.

354 "Communications—'Heads of the Colored People,' Done with a Whitewash Brush," *FDP*, March 25, 1852.

355 "Heads of the Colored People, -No. 2," *FDP*, April 15, 1852.

356 "The Washerwoman," *FDP*, June 17, 1852.

357 "Communipaw Gives Us Quite a Vivid Picture," *FDP*, June 17, 1852.

358 "Heads of the Colored People, -No. 4," *FDP*, July 16, 1852.

359 In the issue of June 17, 1852, Smith wrote, "We are annoyed, on reading the outside of this week's paper, at the typographical errors in the "Letter of Communipaw." For "incomputability," read "incompatibility," for "American," read "America."

360 "Heads of the Colored People, -No. 7," *FDP*, September 9, 1853.

361 Smith, *The Works of James McCune Smith*, 189.

362 "Heads of the Colored People, -No. 7," *FDP*, September 9, 1853.

363 Cholera reached epidemic proportions in 1854 in New York City and some 2,000 died. https://www.baruch.cuny.edu/nycdata/disasters/cholera-1854.html.

364 A quotation from Alfred, Lord Tennyson's poem, "Mariana."

365 The National Conventions in 1847 in Troy, New York, and 1848 in Cleveland, Ohio, seem not to have discussed the subject.

366 *Proceedings of the Colored National Convention, Held in Rochester, July 6th, 7th, and 8th* (Rochester: Printed at the Office of *Frederick Douglass' Paper*, 1853), 26.

367 A "People's Guide to Rochester" reports that Susan B. Anthony, Ralph Waldo Emerson, Charles Dickens, William H. Seward, and William Lloyd Garrison were among those who spoke in the Corinthian Hall. It was torn down in the year 1928 and "a parking area was erected in its place."https://rocwiki.org/Corinthian_Hall.

368 The June 10 issue of *Frederick Douglass' Paper* says, "We learn with sincere regret," but provides no date. Smith's first child, Amy, had died in December 1849; James, age eight, survived.

369 *Proceedings of the Colored National Convention*, 1–7.

370 *Proceedings of the Colored National Convention*, 8–9.

371 Douglass may not have realized that James McCune Smith had been admitted to a blacksmith's shop to blow the bellows, but only the physical act, not the higher skills, or that James W. C. Pennington had acquired a blacksmith's skills as a slave.

372 "For Frederick Douglass' Paper," *FDP*, March 25, 1853.
373 "National Convention of Colored Men," *NYT*, July 8, 1853.
374 "From our Brooklyn Correspondent," *FDP*, December 3, 1853.
375 *FDP*, July 15, 1853.
376 *FDP*, March 17, 1854.
377 "From Our New York Correspondent," *FDP*, January 2, 1857.
378 "National Convention of Colored People," *FDP*, December 2, 1853.
379 "Plan of the American Industrial School," *FDP*, March 24, 1854.
380 James McCune Smith to Gerrit Smith, October 6, 1855, *GSP*.
381 "A Colored Savan," [sic] *FDP*, May 5, 1854.
382 "From Our New York Correspondent," *FDP*, May 12, 1854.
383 "Outrage Upon Colored Persons," *FDP*, July 28, 1854.
384 From Our New York Correspondent," *FDP*, January 2, 1857.
385 "Wholesome Verdict," *NYT*, February 23, 1855.
386 "From Our New York Correspondent," *FDP*, December 13, 1854.
387 "From Our Brooklyn Correspondent," *FDP*, January 26, 1855.
388 "Reply to Anti-Slavery Standard," *FDP*, January 19, 1855.
389 "Communipaw and the American A.S. Society," *FDP*, May 18, 1855.
390 James McCune Smith to Gerrit Smith, New York, March 1, 1855, *GSP*.
391 *The Liberator*, July 6, 1833.
392 James McCune Smith to Gerrit Smith, February 16, 1855, *GSP*.
393 *American Anti-Slavery Standard*, January 15, 1855.
394 The arrival of the first slaves in Virginia is usually dated to 1619.
395 "From Our New York Correspondent," *FDP*, May 11, 1855.
396 Proverbs 15:23 (New International Version).
397 "Our New York Correspondent," *FDP*, October 5, 1855.
398 "Our New York Correspondent," *FDP*, March 9, 1855.
399 Frederick Douglass, *The Frederick Douglass Papers: Series Three: Correspondence, Volume 3: 1853–1865*, ed. John R. McKivigan (New Haven: Yale University Press, 2018), 74.
400 "To the Members of the National Council," *FDP*, March 30, 1855.

401 "National Council of the Colored People," *Anti-Slavery Bugle*, May 19, 1855, *BAP*.

402 "Wanted," *FDP*, May 25, 1855.

403 "Call for a Convention at Syracuse," *Proceedings of the Convention of Radical Political Abolitionists, Held at Syracuse, N.Y., June 26th, 27th, and 28th, 1855* (London: Forgotten Books, 2018), https://digital.library.cornell.edu/catalog/may818307.

404 "Radical Anti-Slavery Convention," *The Liberator*, July 6, 1855. See also: *Proceedings of the Convention of Radical Political Abolitionists*, www.members.tripod.com/medicolegal/proceedings1855.htm.

405 "Our Leaders," *FDP*, September 21, 1855.

406 Douglass, *The Frederick Douglass Papers*, 131–132.

407 Douglass, *My Bondage and My Freedom*, xvii.

408 Douglass, *My Bondage and My Freedom*, xxxi.

409 Smith named his second son after Frederick Douglass, but the child died after only three months. Presumably, Smith gave the book to his first son, James, who would have been ten years old when the book was published.

410 "Our New York Correspondent," *FDP*, August 3, 1855.

411 "Our New York Correspondent," *FDP*, October 5, 1855.

412 "Letter from Isaiah C. Weare," *FDP*, November 9, 1855.

413 "Letter from Communipaw," *FDP*, January 12, 1859.

414 "Second Election of State Councils," *FDP*, October 26, 1855.

415 "Discussion Declined," *NASS*, July 26, 1856.

416 In fact, many of them have been collected and published by John Stauffer as *The Works of James McCune Smith, Black Intellectual and Abolitionist*, New York: Oxford University Press, 2006.

417 "The Girl of Cadiz," st. 2, line 1. The pronoun has been changed from "she" to "it."

418 "From Our New York Correspondent," *FDP*, September 5, 1856.

419 Cf. Chapter 18, 332.

420 James McCune Smith, "Chess," *The Anglo-African Magazine*, vol. I, no. 9, September 1859.

421 "Obituary," *The Medical Register of the City of New York, for the Year Commencing June 1, 1866*, 203.

422 "From Our New York Correspondent," *FDP*, October 3, 1856.

423 David M. Potter, *The Impending Crisis: America Before the Civil War 1848–1861* (New York: Harper and Row Publishers, 1976), 297.

424 "From Our New York Correspondent," *FDP*, March 6, 1857.

425 "From Our New York Correspondent," *FDP*, March 6, 1857.

426 Lincoln would point out in his Cooper Union address in 1860 that the Founding Fathers had voted to prohibit slavery in the Northwest Territory in the first Congress and to prohibit the importation of slaves in other territories. Cf. *Lincoln at Cooper Union* by Harold Holzer (New York: Simon & Schuster, 2004), 51.

427 Potter, *The Impending Crisis*, 275–277.

428 Quoted in Potter, *The Impending Crisis*, 344.

429 "From Our New York Correspondent," *FDP*, August 8, 1856.

430 "From Our New York Correspondent," *FDP*, March 6, 1857.

431 "For Frederick Douglass' Paper," *FDP*, April 16, 1858.

432 The verb "to auscultate" itself was new in the nineteenth century, dated from 1881 by the *Shorter Oxford English Dictionary (1959)* but to 1831 by the online *Merriam-Webster Dictionary*, /www.merriam-webster.com/dictionary/auscultate.

433 James McCune Smith to Gerrit Smith, April 9, 1858, *GSP*.

434 The author of this book can attest to the remoteness, having grown up not far away in the underappreciated village of Cuba. The current population of the county is only slightly greater than it was in 1860.

435 Stauffer, *The Black Hearts of Men*, 88.

436 James McCune Smith to Gerrit Smith, January 29, 1859, *GSP*.

437 James McCune Smith to Gerrit Smith, March 9, 1859, *GSP*.

438 James McCune Smith to Gerrit Smith, January 29, 1859, *GSP*.

439 Christie Nicholson, Fact or Fiction?: "Spring Fever" Is a Real Phenomenon, Scientific American, https://www.scientificamerican.com/article/fact-or-fiction-spring-fever-is-a-real-phenomenon/.

440 Stauffer, introduction to *The Works of James McCune Smith*, xxix.

441 "Dr. James McCune Smith," *FDP*, January 28, 1859.

442 C. Peter Ripley, *The Black Abolitionist Papers: Volume 2, Canada 1830–1865* (Chapel Hill: The University of North Carolina Press, 1966), 455.

443 Editorial, *The Anglo-African Magazine*, vol. 1, no. 1, January 1859.

444 "From Our New York Correspondent," *FDP*, March 25, 1859.

445 "From Our New York Correspondent," *FDP*, April 29, 1859.

446 Webber, *American to the Backbone*, 401–404.

447 "From Our New York Correspondent," *FDP*, October 28, 1859.

448 Frederick Douglass to Robert Hamilton, July 27, 1863, in *The Frederick Douglass Papers*, p. 410, footnote 1; also p. 369, footnote 16.

449 James McCune Smith to Gerrit Smith, June 21, 1860, GSP.

450 "*The Anglo-African Magazine*," *Douglass' Monthly*, February 1859.

451 James McCune Smith, "Civilization," *The Anglo-African Magazine*, February 1859.

452 Thomas Jefferson, *Notes on the State of Virginia* (Ann Arbor: Text Creation Partnership, 2007), 209.

453 James McCune Smith, "On the Fourteenth Query of Thomas Jefferson's Notes on Virginia," *The Anglo-African Magazine*, vol. 1, no. 8 (August 1859), 225–238.

454 James McCune Smith, "A Word for the Smith family," *The Anglo-African Magazine*, vol. 2, no. 3, 77–83.

455 Ethiop, *The Anglo-African Magazine*, vol. 2, no. 2 (February 1, 1860), 41–45.

456 Christopher L. Webber, *Give Me Liberty: Speakers and Speeches That Have Shaped America* (New York: Pegasus Books, 2014), 369–370.

457 James McCune Smith to Edward M. Thomas, "A Resignation Tendered," *Pacific Appeal*, October 18, 1862.

458 "Ubi Patria, Ibi Libertas," *The Weekly Anglo-African*, March 29, 1862. "No Retaliation," *The Weekly Anglo-African*, March 8, 1862.

459 "Emancipation Jubilee," *The Liberator*, May 29, 1862.

460 Strong, *The Diary of George Templeton Strong*, 216.

461 R. H. Vashon to *The Weekly Anglo-African*, September 28, 1861. Debra Jackson, "A Cultural Stronghold: The 'Anglo-African' Newspaper and the Black Community of New York," *New York History*, vol. 85, iss. 4 (Fall 2004), 350.

462 "Frederick Douglass at the Cooper Institute," *Douglass' Monthly*, March 1863.

463 Robert S. Levine, *The Lives of Frederick Douglass* (Cambridge: Harvard University Press, 2016), 201.

464 Douglass, *The Frederick Douglass Papers*, 427–8.

465 John R. G. Hassard, *Life of the Most Reverend John Hughes, D. D. first archbishop of New York. With extracts from his private correspondence* (New York: D. Appleton and Co., 1866), 437.

466 *New York Herald*, July 25, 1863.

467 *New York World*, July 12, 1863.

468 Manisha Sinha, *The Slave's Cause: A History of Abolition* (New Haven: Yale University Press, 2016), 363.

469 Association for the Benefit of Colored Orphans, *From Cherry Street*, 19–23.

470 Bob Davern, "Surgeon and Abolitionist James McCune Smith: An African American Pioneer," Readex Blog, April 17, 2012, www.readex.com/blog/surgeon-and-abolitionist-james-mccune-smith-african-american-pioneer.

471 "Obituary," *The Medical Register*, 201–204.

472 "Obituary," *The Medical Register*, 201–204.

473 Garnet, *A Memorial Discourse*, 44.

474 James McCune Smith to Gerrit Smith, February 17, 1865, *GSP*.

475 James McCune Smith to Gerrit Smith, April 26, 1846, *GSP*.

476 Webber, *Give Me Liberty*, 204.

477 "Death of a Distinguished Colored Man," *The Liberator*, November 24, 1865 (from the *Tribune*, November 19, 1865).

478 "SMITH," *NYT*, November 18, 1855.

479 Peterson, *Black Gotham*, 273. *The Weekly Anglo-African*, November 25, 1865.

480 Douglass, *Life and Times of Frederick Douglass*, 467–468.

481 James McCune Smith to Gerrit Smith, May 12, 1848, *GSP*.

482 James McCune Smith, "Ubi Patria, Ibi Libertas," *The Weekly Anglo-African*, March 29, 1862.

ACKNOWLEDGEMENTS

Writing a book is sometimes a lonely occupation but no book comes to the bookstore without a community effort. The story of James McCune Smith is a story that needs to be told and it wouldn't be much of an exaggeration to say, "It took a village." I never knew the names of many of the librarians who helped me find books or tapes or deal with recalcitrant microfilm viewers, but I am grateful to all of them, especially those in the libraries of UC Berkeley and the San Francisco Public Library. I discovered James McCune Smith while working on my biography of James W.C. Pennington, whom I discovered by accident while working on another project. Once I knew the name, I learned an enormous amount through the work of John Stauffer, who told Smith's story in "The Black Hearts of Men" and edited his writing in "The Works of James McCune Smith." More especially I'm grateful to Peter Riva for believing in this book and finding the right publisher. It's been a pleasure getting to know Jared Kuritz, Marvel Harrison and the good people at Mimbres Press. And most especially I'm grateful to my daughter, Caroline Grant, for help in the final proofreading process. She and her husband, Tony Grant, have been a constant support. Thank you to all!

ABOUT THE AUTHOR

CHRISTOPHER L. WEBBER is a priest of the Episcopal Church who has served parishes in Brooklyn and Long Island, Tokyo, Japan, and Bronxville, New York. In retirement he served parishes in the northwest corner of Connecticut. He grew up in Cuba, New York, a small town in the western part of the state, and graduated from Princeton University before earning two theological degrees and an honorary degree from the General Theological Seminary in New York.

Webber's writing career began late in his ministerial life when he was asked to write *A Vestry Handbook*, which is still in print forty years later; his subsequent books are wideranging, from hymnals, church guidebooks, and collections of prayers, to *The Beowulf Trilogy* and *American to the Backbone*, a biography of James W.C. Pennington, a fugitive slave who became a leading figure in the pre-Civil War abolition movement.

His wife, Margaret Rose, died just short of their 60th anniversary. Webber has four children and four grandchildren and lives in San Francisco.

www.ingramcontent.com/pod-product-compliance
Lightning Source LLC
LaVergne TN
LVHW090452141224
798932LV00004B/7